10+

MUSIC
AND
BALLET
1973 – 1983

B. H. HAGGIN

MUSIC

AND

BALLET

1973–1983

HORIZON PRESS   NEW YORK

Library of Congress Cataloging in Publication Data

Haggin, B. H. (Bernard H.), 1900-
  Music & ballet, 1973-1983.

  Includes index.
  1. Music—Addresses, essays, lectures. 2. Ballet—Addresses, essays, lectures.
I. Title. II. Title: Music and ballet, 1973-1983.
ML60. H159   1984   780   84-15739
ISBN 0-8180-1226-9

Manufactured in the United States of America

Contents

Foreword

This collection offers the occasional published comment, in the years 1973 to 1983, on what I continued to hear, see and read—to which I have added accounts of happenings in this period that I did not write about when they occurred. And to the chronicle of music and ballet in New York I have added a published article about a period in the history of the Vienna Philharmonic that was made interesting by the men who conducted it.

"Ballet is not my field," I began in my first published statement, in 1935, on a subject of which I had no professional technical knowledge; but a few years later Balanchine validated my writing about it with his comment "You look; you see; you write what you see; and that's good." And I came to realize that the writing about what *was* my field—the music I did have professional technical knowledge of—was similarly validated: I listened; I heard; I reported what I heard; and this was found "good" not only by authoritative critical opinion—of Stark Young, Randall Jarrell and others—but by readers who wrote to tell me of their profit from it. They still write this to me; and so I still write for them.

—B.H.H.

Contemporary Gimmickry

Contemporary music began, for me, in 1916 with Stravinsky's *Firebird* and *Petrushka*, which I heard when the Diaghilev company performed the Fokine ballets in New York. They presented no difficulty for my ears; nor, in the early 20s, did Stravinsky's *Les Noces* when Stokowski performed it at a League of Composers concert, and *Le Sacre du Printemps* when Monteux performed it with the Boston Symphony. But Stravinsky's *Symphonies of Wind Instruments*, which Stokowski performed with his Philadelphia Orchestra, communicated no expressive sense or mere internal coherence in the sounds my ear found ugly; and this was true of works of other composers that I heard at that time: Schönberg's *Die glückliche Hand* and Varèse's *Hyperprism* among them. Concerning these, I accepted the contention that they would be expressive and attractive only after the repeated hearing required by their new musical language. But Stravinsky's *Symphonies of Wind Instruments*, after the additional hearings of the past 50 years, is as meaningless and ugly for me today as when I first heard it; so are a number of other pieces of his—the Violin Concerto, Duo Concertant, *Movements*—after my repeated hearings of them with Balanchine's choreographies; and so are the Webern pieces I have heard many times with Balanchine's *Episodes*.

In addition to listening I read explanations of this new music in the hope that they would enable me to enjoy it; but what, for example, Gerald Abraham, in his book *This Modern Music*, described in words and pointed out to the eye as the principle of organization in a passage of Schönberg's Five Piano Pieces proved not to be a principle of coherent musical sense in the progression of sounds when I listened to it. And so when Leonard Bernstein, in an *Omnibus* television talk on modern music,

9

discussed and played Schönberg's *Verklärte Nacht* and one of his string quartets, and then asked his audience, "Can you see that this [quartet] had to be the next step after *Verklärte Nacht?*" my own answer was not only "No, I cannot see that the atonal sounds of the quartet had to be the next step after the tonal ones of *Verklärte Nacht*," but "For me the justification and value of that quartet are not to be found in any relation to any other piece of music, but are solely in what it communicates as an object experienced by and for itself." I had, that is, by this time reached the conclusion, for my operation as a listener writing for other listeners, that when I wrote about a work of Schönberg's I must report what my ears heard in that work, which I could not and did not claim was *the* truth about it, but had to accept as the truth about it for me.

Writing in *The New Republic* in 1957 about several records of the Fromm Music Foundation's 20th-Century Composers' Series, I referred to a statement by Edmund Wilson about a novelist—that what she wanted other people to know she imparted to them by creating an object, the self-developing organism of a work of prose. And I went on to say:

> What a composer wants other people to know he too imparts by creating an object, the self-developing organism of a work of musical sound. And the pieces by Kirchner and the others [on the records] demonstrate these composers' ability to put sounds together into objects of size and elaborate organization; but to my ears the pieces are in their various ways unattractive or ugly merely as objects, and do not communicate any understandable musical meaning. Mr. Fromm and the people like him are right in believing in the primary importance of the composer and therefore in . . . commissioning works and sponsoring their performance, publication and recording. But as intelligent people they undoubtedly know . . . that of the hundreds of composers who were encouraged to write in the 18th century by the aristocratic patronage of that period only a bare handful produced music which the world continued and continues to value. And so they probably are not surprised or discouraged by the results of their enlightened support thus far.

Writing today, after the one-week Celebration of Contemporary Music put on in March by the Fromm Foundation, the Juilliard School and the New York Philharmonic, with a grant from the National Endowment for the Arts, I cannot report the agreeable surprise of hearing at last music of quality that justified and rewarded the long support of Fromm and the others. In the objects presented to my ears at the concerts I attended—objects as variously and elaborately contrived as Roger Sessions's Symphony No. 3, Jacob Druckman's *Lamia*, Bruno

Maderna's *Quadrivium*, Barbara Kolb's *Trobar Clus*, Elliott Carter's String Quartet No. 3, Charles Wuorinen's *Arabia Felix*, Gunther Schuller's *Gala Music*, Easley Blackwood's Piano Concerto Op. 24 and Peter Maxwell Davies's *Stone Litany: Runes from a House of the Dead* (among others)—I heard extremes of eccentricity and gimmickry, but not a single succession of sounds that to my mind was a statement of understandable musical sense. And I now realize that the people who put on the Celebration were not undiscouraged by their awareness of the lack of value in the music, but instead were fortified by their delusion that they were celebrating what was worthy of celebration. (*New Republic*, 24 July 1976)

Fools' Approval

"When we read the criticism of any past age," Randall Jarrell wrote once, "we see immediately that the main thing wrong with it is an astonishing amount of what Eliot calls 'fools' approval': most of the . . . poets were bad, most of the critics were bad, and they loved each other. Our age is no different."

And it is no different with music. The musicologists concerned with the music of the past, reasoning in a world of concept miles removed from the world of fact they supposedly deal with, have produced a neat schematization in which each period of the past had *its* music, produced by *its* creative energies, and satisfying *its* esthetic interests; the creative energies of each period that produced great painting and architecture produced equally great music; and since human creative energies have been constant the music they produced in, say, the 14th or 15th century was as great as the music of Bach, Haydn and Mozart, or Beethoven and Schubert, in the 18th or 19th. "The music in this album," Curt Sachs wrote in his notes for some recorded keyboard pieces dating from 1350 to 1700, "is not 'ancient music,' stale, dusty, and at best a curio for historically minded snobs. It is no more 'ancient' than Rembrandt's painting or Gothic cathedrals." And his colleague Paul Henry Lang talked about the shelves filled with the masterpieces of past centuries that remained unperformed and unheard. But the actual works of art in the world of fact have been produced by the creative energies not of periods but of individual creators; and those energies have not been equal in the individual creators either in a single period or in successive periods. It may have been Jarrell whom I heard say there had been no great poetry in England from the death of Chaucer in 1400 to the publication of Wyatt's poems in 1557, and only minor poets between Pope and Blake; and I recall no painting of any consequence in the 18th and 19th-century Germany and Austria of Bach, Haydn, Mozart, Beethoven and Schubert. The early keyboard pieces Sachs wrote about—insignificant in musical ideas, structure and mere size—were not of the artistic magnitude either of Rembrandt's painting and Gothic cathedrals or of the keyboard works of Bach, Haydn, Mozart, Beethoven and Schubert; nor did the many contemporaries of these great composers produce music comparable in magnitude with theirs. And though there are valuable works of Haydn, Mozart and Schubert that are insufficiently performed, it is the uninteresting and negligible works of their contemporaries for the most part that fill the shelves Lang referred to.

The musicologists' schematization concerning the music of the past has been applied by composers and commentators to the controversial music of the present century—of Bartók, Schönberg, Alban Berg, Webern, Boulez, Stockhausen. What most listeners have heard as meaningless ugliness Aaron Copland has urged them to hear as the "enriched musical language" and "new spirit of objectivity attuned to our own times" that make it "our music," as meaningful and moving to us as listeners 100 or 200 years ago found *their* music. And Leonard Bernstein, in one of his *Omnibus* television programs years ago, tried to persuade the enormous audience for which he performed Schönberg's String Quartet Op. 30 No. 3 and *Pierrot Lunaire* and Berg's *Lyric Suite* that this "modern music is your music." Some performers and listeners have been talked into believing this; but many more have rejected it and have dealt with this century's music as they did with the music of previous centuries—by listening to the individual works and deciding which made impressive musical sense and which did not, and discovering in this way that Virgil Thomson's *The Mother of Us All* and Aaron Copland's *The Tender Land*, Roy Harris's *Ode to Truth* and William Schuman's *Prayer in Time of War*, were all music of their period, but the Harris and Schuman works were not, like the Copland and Thomson, music worth listening to. (*New Republic*, 11 June 1977)

Composers' Second Thoughts

The director of an opera company planning to produce *Boris Godunov* will, if he has musical understanding, know that he must produce Musorgsky's own work, not Rimsky-Korsakov's recomposition of it. And faced then with the fact that Musorgsky's own work exists in two versions—the one completed in 1869 and the revision of it completed in 1872—our director will make a distinction between the changes in the 1872 version which Musorgsky made to satisfy the imperial opera administration that had rejected the 1869 version, and the changes that represented his own second thoughts. It was to satisfy the opera administration that he added the two Polish scenes, with a female character, Marina, for the false Dmitri to be romantically involved with; it was his own second thoughts that impelled him to rewrite much of the act in Boris's Kremlin apartment, to compose the new scene in the forest of Kromy as the opera's new conclusion, and—making room for the additional scene—to omit the scene before the cathedral of St. Basil, transferring its episode of the Simpleton tormented by the boys to the Kromy Scene. Recognizing that Marina is a fifth wheel in the essential dramatic action, and recognizing also the musical inferiority of the Polish scenes, our director will feel free to omit them. But for the rest of the 1872 version he will accept the principle enunciated by the conductor Giulini—that when a composer has had second thoughts about a work of his one must defer to them—which doesn't rule out a concert performance of the 1869 version of the act in Boris's apartment to satisfy interest in what Musorgsky produced originally. Moreover, recognizing the musical quality and dramatic importance of the St. Basil Scene, our director will restore it, and with it—transferred back from the Kromy Scene—the episode of the Simpleton tormented by the boys.

14

As against Giulini's good sense there is the mindless musicological attitude exhibited in the statement in Paul Henry Lang's *Music in Western Civilization* that a young reader quoted to me some years ago. He had listened with friends to a tape of a performance of Beethoven's first (1805) version of *Fidelio*, which had left them glad Beethoven had had the second thoughts about it that resulted in the final (1814) version. And they had therefore been amazed by Lang's statement:

> In its first version *Fidelio* shows the guiding hand of the same great classicist who admired so much the disposition of tonalities in *The Magic Flute*, who like his revered model, Cherubini, used the leitmotif with discretion. . . . Despite the great advantages gained by rewriting of the opera, the difference in time caused stylistic inequalities. . . . The opera should be returned to its original form.

As it happened, a concert performance of the 1805 version of *Fidelio* conducted by Erich Leinsdorf at Tanglewood a year later provided an opportunity to hear its diffuse, conventional and derivative writing, and enabled me, when I listened afterward to the 1814 version, to appreciate how unerringly Beethoven had operated at every point in the revision that produced this version's powerful concentration and conciseness of utterance and form. I heard in it no "stylistic inequalities" but only the great work of art that was the one to perform; whereas Lang exhibited the musicologist's failure to recognize the primacy of esthetic value as against historical interest, in his insistence that the version of *Fidelio* to perform was not the one that offered the experience of a great work of art but the one that "shows the guiding hand of the same great classicist who admired so much the disposition of tonalities in *The Magic Flute* . . ."

Recently there has been need for an assertion of Giulini's good sense on behalf of Verdi's revised versions of certain of his works. Of the revised *Macbeth* that we hear in the opera house and on records Francis Toye wrote, in his fine book on Verdi, that "one would not willingly lose the admirable music it called forth"; but the first version without this admirable music was one of Sarah Caldwell's early projects for her Opera Company of Boston, and was one of the several Verdi first versions which Andrew Porter suggested that Philips record in its series of unfamiliar works of Verdi. I cannot recall whether Caldwell actually produced the first version of *Macbeth*; but she did, in 1973, produce the first version of *Don Carlo*, with French text, that Verdi wrote for the Paris Opera. And since the Metropolitan Opera is reported to be planning to use this version in a new production of *Don Carlo* instead of the revised version with Italian text that we know, something should be said about the differences between them.

In his review of the Caldwell production Porter wrote that even before the Paris première in 1867 Verdi had to shorten his enormously long five-act "grand opera": "Three whole numbers . . . and three substantial mid-scene episodes" were not merely omitted in the performances, but cut from the manuscript and not published, so that they were unknown until 1969. And in 1882-83 Verdi made the additional changes of the abridged and revised version, with Italian text, that we know—changes that included omission of the entire original first act (which has been retained, however, in the recorded performances) and some new writing. Caldwell did not present only the five-act version that had been performed in Paris in 1867, but was able to restore the material Verdi had cut from the manuscript and not published, which had been found in 1969. The musicologist David Rosen had found one piece of it folded down in the 1867 performance score; which had led Porter to examine the 1867 performance parts, where he had found the rest. It had been an exciting experience for him to assemble what he copied from the parts into page after page of the "lost" music; and "it was exciting, in Boston, to hear this music in the theater." But in addition, hearing it convinced Porter that no artistic consideration but only the necessity of shortening the work had impelled Verdi to eliminate it. And while he conceded that perhaps we should agree with Verdi's judgment that the 1883 four-act version was "more practicable and . . . maybe also better from an artistic point of view," Porter contended that the uncut original five-act *Don Carlo* performed in Boston was "a masterpiece of its kind . . . well worth performing from time to time".

But he didn't leave it at that. Balancing gains and losses in the two versions, he contended that the restored duet of Elisabeth and Eboli before *"O don fatale"* and duet of Philip and Carlo after Posa's death "deepen the character drawing of the two women and of the king;" that although Verdi, when he recomposed the second-act duet of Philip and Posa, made it even more powerful, "the original version is in its own right very strong and very beautiful;" that the later style of the recomposed passages in the 1883 version created stylistic inconsistency between old and new in the work; and lastly that the Italian translation of the 1883 version blunts "fine musical points and fine dramatic points", and "there is no good reason, outside Italy, for ever using it again."

When, therefore, I listened to a tape of the Caldwell performance it was in the expectation of being impressed by what had impressed Porter; and I did agree with him that the original five-act *Don Carlo* was a fine work of its kind, "well worth performing from time to time". But I also found myself agreeing with what I could only surmise Verdi had thought about the numbers he didn't merely omit in the 1867 performances but cut from the manuscript and didn't publish: that they were good, but not of the magnitude of the numbers whose elimination would inflict great loss on the work—not of the magnitude, specifically, of the second-act duet *"Io vengo a domandar"* of Carlo and Elisabeth, of the fourth-act duet of Philip and the Grand Inquisitor, or of the numbers following it in that extraordinary scene. And performance of the 1867 original did entail, I discovered, the loss of a piece of writing of that magnitude. Listening to the long second-act duet of Philip and Posa, and expecting to hear the incandescent writing that begins with Posa's impassioned description of the monstrous peace Philip envisions for Flanders *("Quant' è la pace che voi date al mondo")* and continues with the duet *("Inaspettata aurora")* that ends the act, I was bewildered by writing that was not only different but much less effective, until I realized that I was hearing the original 1867 version of the scene that Verdi had replaced in 1883 with the incandescent version I was familiar with. Porter not only had had a scholar's excitement over the unexciting unearthed 1867 passages, but had been calmly content with the 1867 Philip-Posa duet in place of the 1883 version that he had conceded was more powerful; but to a mere music-lover like myself this great 1883 passage far outweighed all the ones unearthed by Rosen and Porter. Moreover I was not troubled by any stylistic inconsistency between old and new in the 1883 *Don Carlo*, or by any inadequacy of the Italian text.

All this seems to me important in connection with the Metropolitan's reported intention to produce the 1867 original. It is one thing for Caldwell to perform it two or three times in one of her seasons; it is another thing for the Metropolitan to make it what the public will hear in place of Verdi's 1883 revision for years to come. Not only is he entitled to have his second thoughts about his work accepted by the Metropolitan; but music-lovers are entitled to hear them—to hear the great 1883 version of the Philip-Posa duet and not to be compelled to hear the inferior 1867 version. The one important loss in the 1883 *Don Carlo* is the omission of the 1867 first act; and the sensible thing for the Metropolitan is to add that act to the four of 1883, as the recording companies have done. (*New Republic*, 5 November 1977)

Literature in Opera

In his book *Literature as Opera* Gary Schmidgall sees his "discussion of literature made into opera" as "a kind of sequel and counterpart" to Joseph Kerman's *Opera as Drama* (1956), which he says "asserted what ought to have been obvious . . . namely, that opera is 'properly a musical form of drama, with its own individual dignity and force.'" But Kerman sees it differently: "While [Schmidgall's] book has a method it has no theme or thesis. The method is to select operas derived from works of literature—from epic, autobiography, drama, and the novel—and discuss them in conjunction with their sources. It is never clear what sort of insight the juxtaposition is supposed to provide. . . . The general conclusion seems to be that Mozart found much in common with Beaumarchais, Berlioz with Cellini, Berg with Büchner, and so on. None of this is exactly news. . . . He really likes the operas . . . and he could try telling us why and how. This might seem like an unfashionable thing to do, but hardly more so than assembling conscientious literary 'backgrounds' for operas which are not really analyzed in their own terms" (*New York Review of Books*, 9 February 1978)

It is therefore necessary to say that the terms of pejorative implication in which Kerman describes Schmidgall's performance misrepresent it and are not applicable to what he actually does in his book. His love of the operas he discusses, and the reasons for it, do appear in what he writes about them, but only incidentally; for they are not what his book is primarily concerned with. It does have a theme—i.e. a subject: what in each opera is related to the work of literature it is derived from; and Schmidgall does discuss passages of the music in terms of that relation. This is "the sort of insight"—he does make clear in his introductory chapter—that he intends to provide concerning each opera; and those insights are sufficiently interesting and valuable in and for themselves, requiring no larger contextual theme to give them significance and value; exactly as the instances of musical articulation of dramatic continuity that Kerman pointed out in his *Opera as Drama* were valuable in themselves as examples of the nature of opera, and didn't acquire additional significance and value from the context in which he presented them. (The affirmation of the true nature of opera to which those instances contributed was, as Kerman said, necessary and important, but not, as he contended, for its corrective effect on the situation in our opera houses in which "art and *Kitsch* alternate night after night, with the same performers and the same audience, to the same applause, and with the same critical sanction." Twenty years after Kerman's affirmation of the true nature of opera one finds art and *Kitsch* still alternating night after night in our opera houses.)

From the operas of the past three centuries that were derived from works of literature Schmidgall selects a dozen which exemplify various styles of operatic writing. Beginning with Handel's *Orlando, Ariodante*, and *Alcina*, whose librettos are derived from Ariosto's *Orlando Furioso*, he points out that although this was the Age of Reason, "what displeased men of reason . . . perfectly suited the operatic stage;" and one thing that recommended *Orlando Furioso* to Handel was its fictional world of romance and magic, which provided the occasion for the spectacular staging that appealed to opera-lovers. More important, the episodes from Ariosto's epic, no matter how spectacular or exotic, involved characters with human emotions and passions, whose expression in music was Handel's special gift. Ariosto's characters, says Schmidgall, exhibited the "immensity of passion" of great operatic characters—the great operatic characters that Handel made them with his ability to realize their "passionate explosions" in musical terms of "powerful impact".

Such general statements Schmidgall finds sufficient for the relation of the Handel operas to Ariosto's poem, but not for what he wants the reader to hear in *The Marriage of Figaro* that is related to Beaumarchais's play. After describing the artistic revolution Beaumarchais and Mozart achieved with their mingling of "life's levity and sadness" that displaced heroic tragedy on the dramatic stage and *opera seria* in the opera house, and pointing out the changes by Da Ponte and Mozart that left their adaptation for the most part faithful to the play, Schmidgall directs the reader's ear to examples of Mozart's matching of "the wit, drollery, and expressiveness of the play's dialogue in his music", in some instances merely referring to the familiar aria, duet, or ensemble, in others quoting passages in musical notation.

He continues this procedure in the discussions that follow. The chapter on Donizetti's *Maria Stuarda* and *Lucia di Lammermoor* describes the passion, confrontations and crises of the two romantic literary works, Schiller's play *Mary Stuart* and Scott's novel *The Bride of Lammermoor*, that are translated into the "powerful airborne melody" of the *bel canto* operatic genre. In the chapter on Berlioz's *Benvenuto Cellini* Schmidgall discusses the Cellini of the opera as the surrogate for Berlioz in an operatic self-portrait of Berlioz as romantic artist that is a "key to the French Romantic movement". In the chapter on Verdi's *Macbeth* Schmidgall describes Verdi's breaking away from the still prevailing *bel canto* style of ornamental melody to write in accordance with his creative principle that makes "expression of human feeling . . . the supreme artistic goal", and the remarkable dramatic perception and musical powers Verdi exhibits in his translation of Shakespeare's play into a *dramma per musica*. The chapter on Tchaikovsky's *Eugene Onegin* points out how Tchaikovsky's own emotional nature made it impossible for him to give musical expression to Pushkin's actual poem ridiculing its characters, and impelled him instead to give it to his misreading of the poem that took the characters seriously and sympathized with them. In the chapter on Strauss's *Salomé* Schmidgall describes the relation of Wilde's play to the decadent movement in French and English literature, but contends that Strauss, not himself involved with the similar movement in Germany, "simply saw in the play the possibilities for a highly effective . . . opera"—effective, that is, as a musical realization of what was brutal, ugly and repulsive below the play's surface sensuality. The chapter on Alban Berg's *Wozzeck* discusses the characteristics of twentieth-century expressionistic drama that Büchner astonishingly anticipated in the revolutionary play he wrote early in the nineteenth century, and the characteristics of the expressionist music of Berg for which the play had to wait almost a century. In the postscript to that chapter Schmidgall describes the similarities between Wedekind and Berg in personality, ideas, dramatic theme and style that enabled Berg's musical language to work as successfully with Wedekind's play as with Büchner's, and to produce for *Lulu* a musical score that "may well be Berg's masterwork." In the chapter on Britten's *Death in Venice* Schmidgall finds Britten's particular gifts as a composer—his capacity for musical response to verbal expression of human experience and his powers of understatement—to be precisely what Mann's nondramatic novella, cast almost entirely in interior monologue, demands.

These chapters are followed by an afterword on the crisis of modern opera, which introduces a factor Schmidgall has said nothing about in his previous discussions. Writing about Handel's *Orlando* operas, he accepted their musical treatments of texts derived from a poem written by Ariosto two centuries earlier, as he later accepted Verdi's use of a play by Shakespeare. But discussing opera of today he is disturbed by the settings of literary works of the past, and calls for "opera that is truly modernist in [both] musical style and libretto"—this despite his recognition of the characteristics of contemporary drama and music that are anti-operatic, the mistrust that both dramatists and composers have felt of "the grand style, the elevated gesture and resounding utterance" on which he says "opera as genre depends unavoidably" (but which this century's outstanding operatic masterpiece, *Wozzeck*, does in fact avoid). And so he can write that "no one in this century has proved as perspicacious and successful a musical translator of literature as Benjamin Britten," but point out that Britten ignored "modern literary culture in his search for operatic inspiration . . . [and] turned instead to Shakespeare, Crabbe, de Maupassant, Melville, Henry James." And having written that, he can write further, "This is not to imply that genuinely modernist operas would necessarily be better than operas in which contemporary composers set old masters"—only to add, "Still, I believe contemporary opera is failing us when it ignores the literary creations of our own time."

Not only is this confused thinking by Schmidgall, but he doesn't recognize the primary failure of modern and contemporary opera. He cites, among others, Douglas Moore's *The Ballad of Baby Doe* and Jack Beeson's *Lizzie Borden* as American operas that failed us by ignoring the literary creations of our own time; whereas the actual and important way they failed us was with their music that didn't satisfy the first requirement of any musical writing, namely the intrinsic musical interest and value that would make it worth listening to for itself, merely as music, and the additional requirement of operatic writing, namely the expressive force related to the words and action of the drama.

This is also the failure of European modern operas, including some that Schmidgall thinks of as successes. Britten was England's one outstandingly gifted modern composer; but the gift that was most evident was the resourcefulness that often operated in the place of genuine creative power and produced arid writing which merely carried the words and action without any expressive relation to either. A notable example of this was the love duet of Sid and Nancy in *Albert Herring;* but this opera also offered examples of the real and brilliantly successful invention for the words and dramatic situation that Britten produced occasionally—among them Lady Billows's grand announcement to Albert of his election to be king of the May, and the dirge for the supposedly dead Albert. The one work with such successful invention from first to last was *A Midsummer Night's Dream;* and one of those I found unsuccessful from first to last was *Death in Venice.* The characters, situations and action that had been made convincing in Mann's novella by the prose that presented them to my imagination were made unbelievable by what was presented to my eyes and ears by the opera: not only the boy Tadzio embodied in a mature ballet-dancer executing Ashton choreography, but the librettist's words, and Britten's music, in which I heard no expressive relation to the words, and nothing of interest in itself.

So with Berg's *Lulu.* Whereas in his *Wozzeck* one hears discordant vocal writing which heightens the expressive effect of the powerfully moving words of Büchner's play, in a context of discordant orchestral writing which intensifies the nightmarish character of the happenings on the stage, in *Lulu* one hears an extreme of stratospheric screaming which has no expressive relation to the unmoving words, and an extreme of discordant orchestral writing which has no relation to the dramatic situations and action. *Wozzeck* is, then, this century's outstanding achievement in opera; *Lulu*, one of its outstanding failures.

And so with Strauss's *Salomé*, which illustrates the deterioration in the quality of his musical ideas after his masterwork, *Don Quixote*, with no diminution in his prodigious technical virtuosity and inexhaustible facility of invention. These enabled him—though genuine creative power had left him—to go on producing endless pages of expertly contrived writing of enormous complexity with no musical value in itself and no real expressive relation to the words and action they carried, but with the effect on the listener that Ezra Pound once described in a passage on the method of Wagner, "which is not dissimilar from that of the Foire de Neuilly; i.e., you confuse the spectator by smacking as many of his senses as possible at every possible moment; this prevents his noting anything with unusual lucidity, but you may fluster or excite him to the point of making him receptive; i.e., you may slip over an emotion, or you may sell him a rubber doll or a new cake of glassmender during the hurly-burly." The musical hurly-burly in *Salomé* flusters the listener to the point of getting him to think it is conveying what is brutal, ugly and repulsive below the surface sensuality of Wilde's play.

Schmidgall ends his book with a section entitled "Literature in Opera: A Symposium," which quotes a number of statements about opera, some concerned with the point made by Berlioz in the first one—that "it is not possible to transform any sort of play into opera without modifying it, disturbing it, corrupting it more or less." This might well have been quoted at the beginning of the book—in the introductory chapter in which Schmidgall deals with the changes that plays must undergo to be usable in opera—to insure correct understanding of the book's title. The title can be taken to mean a discussion of the setting to music of works of literature as they were originally written by Shakespeare, Beau-marchais or Schiller—as the poem of Goethe is set without change in the song of Schubert; whereas what it actually means is, with two excep-tions, a discussion of the setting to music of librettists' rewriting and refashioning of selected parts of the original works of literature. (The exceptions are *Wozzeck*, with the original play of Büchner, and *Salomé*, with the original play of Wilde, but in a German translation which changes its character.)

Since I have mentioned the Goethe poem in the Schubert song I will point out that although it is used exactly as written it loses, in the combination with the music, everything that makes it a poem and that achieves its specific poetic effect, retaining only its literal sense; and whereas one is supposed to be moved by the poetic effect as heightened by the music, actually one is moved by the expressive effect of the music, which is related to the words in the way the Cézanne still life is related to the apples and pears that were its subject. This is what happens also, on a larger scale, in opera, in which, much of the time, the words don't convey even their verbal sense because they are made even less clearly audible than in the song by the orchestral sound and the distances between the singers and the majority of listeners in the opera house. And in opposition to the view that the expressiveness of the music is com-municated fully only when every word is understood I cite two state-ments which for me are closer to reality.

The first is the English critic E. J. Dent's observation that the only thing which made a character in an opera interesting and convincing was the music he was given to sing. This meant that the drama in an opera is in the music; that one goes to the Metropolitan for the *dramma per musica*, not for the play *Norma* or *Aïda;* and that it is the quality of the music that makes or does not make an opera valuable and worth listening to: good music converts dramatic absurdity into a *Rigoletto* or *Il Trovatore* that one wants to hear; poor music cannot make a good play into anything but a worthless and uninteresting opera.

The other statement was made by Leonard Bernstein in an *Omnibus* talk on opera in which he described how the music in an opera could magnify emotion to the point where words were almost unnecessary. The mere general knowledge of the dramatic action enabled us to apprehend Isolde's exaltation at the end of *Tristan und Isolde:* we didn't have to understand her every word, to know that she is saying,

> *Soll ich schlürfen, untertauchen,*
> *Süss in Duften mich verhauchen.* . . .

And this had an implication which Bernstein didn't develop: if the general knowledge of the dramatic action, not the understanding of every word, was all we needed, then there was no need of hearing *Tristan* or *Macbeth* or *Figaro* sung in English. There was no need, then, to lose what the mere sound of the Italian words of *The Marriage of Figaro* added to the effect of the music written for them: listening with knowledge of the sense of the words obtained from previous reading of the libretto, one could enjoy, in the aria "*Non più andrai*", the effect with the music of Figaro's

> *Per montagne, per valloni,*
> *Con le nevi e i sollioni,*
> *Al concerto di tromboni,*
> *Di bombarde, di cannoni,*
> *Che le palle in tutti i tuoni*
> *All' orecchio fan fischiar.*

Or when Susanna astonished the Count and Countess by emerging from the dressing room, one could enjoy the effect with the music of her

> *Signore!*
> *Cos' è quel stupore?*

So in Verdi's *Falstaff:* one could enjoy the effect of Mistress Quickly's repeated *"Revere-e-e-enza"* to Falstaff, her repeated " *Po-o-o-overa donna!"*—the effect that was lost when, in a performance in English conducted by Beecham, I heard instead "Oh most honored sir" and "Unhappy lady!". These examples demonstrate that it is on comedy— where the greatest gain is claimed for understandable English words— that they inflict the greatest loss. (*Sewanee Review*, Summer 1978)

Conducting on the Genius Level

One can begin with the 20-year-old Bernard Shaw's perception of the "highest faculty of a conductor" as the "establishment of a magnetic influence under which an orchestra becomes as amenable to the baton as a pianoforte to the fingers." Shaw was limiting himself to the conductor as conductor; and there is also the conductor as musician—a matter too important to be left undiscussed; but I want first to elaborate on Shaw's statement.

The "pianoforte" he referred to—which I will assume is a good one—presents built-in tonal capacities to the fingers that produce the sounds the pianist puts together in his performance. But the sounds the conductor puts together are those produced by the capacities and efforts of the hundred or so members of his orchestra; and facing the orchestra at a rehearsal or a concert, with an idea in his mind of the sounds he wants, he can get those hundred musicians to produce them only if the wishes he communicates with the movements of his baton are enforced by the magnetic compulsion Shaw spoke of. The famous conductors of the past—Nikisch, Toscanini, Muck, Mahler, Weingartner, Richard Strauss, Furtwängler, Stokowski, Koussevitzky—exercised that extraordinary magnetic power; and Toscanini's, according to musicians who played under him, was uncanny.

There have been pianists with powers of virtuoso magnitude in the manipulation of their instrument; and the conductors I just mentioned had such virtuoso powers in the obtaining of extraordinary playing from their orchestras. Some of those pianists—Hofmann, Lhevinne, Rosenthal, Horowitz—have misused the music they have played to excite audiences with displays of their virtuosity and with distortions of

27

musical shape that falsified expressive meaning; others—Schnabel, Ashkenazy, Cliburn, Pollini—have used their mastery of the instrument in the service of their shaping of the music with their distinguished insight. And this has been true also of the conductors. Concerning a performance by Furtwängler with his Berlin Philharmonic in London the great English critic W. J. Turner wrote: "These extraordinary pianissimos, these marvellously manipulated accelerandos, ritardandos and crescendos can absolutely get in the way of the music when they are all produced for the sake of effect, as a piece of showmanship. . . . On this occasion [Furtwängler and his orchestra] were quite obviously displaying their virtuosity to the disadvantage of the music." But after a concert of Toscanini with the New York Philharmonic a few months later Turner wrote: "No conductor I have heard has succeeded in achieving such virtuosity and in keeping it always subservient to a purely musical intention."

Concerning this musical intention Turner—after a Beethoven series a few years later in which Toscanini conducted the BBC Symphony—observed that Toscanini's "grasp of the musical structure of the work he is conducting is unique," and that "one of his greatest virtues is his subtle variation of tempo, but always in the service of shape, and the shape is derived from the rightful expression of the music." To this I would add something else that was unique: the seeming control of the operation of Toscanini's powers by a mental governor that held them to the achievement of the unfailing rightness of shape and expression from the first phrase of a work to the last. This was something I experienced only with him, and expected not to experience when he was gone; and so it was astounding, in January 1949, to hear a similar unfailing rightness, similarly achieved by powers as extraordinary as Toscanini's, in the performances of young Guido Cantelli, whom Toscanini—after hearing him for the first time in Milan the preceding summer—had immediately invited to conduct the NBC Symphony. In Cantelli Toscanini found a continuation of his own musical self: at Cantelli's rehearsals in Studio 8H he sat nodding his head in approval and smiling in pleasure at what he heard; and in conversation he exclaimed delightedly, "I love this young conductor! I think is like me when I was young!" (Years later the NBC Symphony cellist Alan Shulman recalled Toscanini at those rehearsals, "beaming like a proud father. If he had had a son who was musically endowed, this was what he would have wanted him to be." This was something Toscanini's actual and musically ungifted son Walter also had observed at the rehearsals; and his resentment had caused him to assert falsely, in a broadcast after Toscanini's and Cantelli's deaths, that it was Cantelli's dedication, not his musical gifts, that his father had admired.)

The perception of Cantelli embodied in Toscanini's statement differed from that of the musical journalists, for whom Cantelli's youth and Toscanini's sponsoring of him provided an opportunity to use the immaturity ploy that is so plausible and profitable. The general idea was that Cantelli's performances were those of a gifted but not yet fully matured young disciple of Toscanini; a memorable particular example was the pronouncement designed to impress a reader with the awesomely long experience that enabled Irving Kolodin to discern that "that degree of musical culture and experience which can settle, almost instinctively, on proper tempi and sonorous values for such works as the . . . Mozart are not yet his." But Toscanini, who could distinguish between youthful maturity and immaturity, heard in this young conductor's performances fully developed powers in an assured operation as conductor and musician that was similar to his own—and this not only in the sure instinct it revealed for right tempo and sonority. Cantelli, like Toscanini, brought a passionate commitment of all his powers to the task of producing in sound the shape of a work prescribed by the composer's directions about tempo and dynamics in the score; the shaped progression, like Toscanini's, had unfailing continuity, cohesive tension and coherent structural proportion, and extraordinary clarity of outline and texture; and like Toscanini's it was produced by orchestral playing that was breathtaking in its perfection of execution and tonal beauty. For Toscanini, moreover, this similarity in operation did not preclude the differences in tempo, inflection of melodic phrase, and shape of larger structure that he recognized as manifestations of the differences in musical taste that were exhibited even by exceptionally gifted musicians. Nor did it preclude the striking difference between the powerful intensity and tensions of Toscanini's performance of Beethoven's Fifth or Schubert's Ninth and the relaxed grace and lyricism of Cantelli's, its seeming to assume its emerging shape in sound without human effort, in its own world of quiet and serenity. It was, as Toscanini said, a performance like his own when he was young—completely and marvelously achieved, and overwhelming in impact.

The continuation of his musical self that Toscanini heard in Cantelli's performances ended shortly before Toscanini's death (in January 1957) when Cantelli, in November 1956, was killed in a plane crash. The loss to the musical world was what it would have been if Toscanini had been killed in 1903 in a train wreck; and one's grief was increased by the fact that Cantelli died on the journey to an engagement with the New York Philharmonic from which he had, the previous spring, tried unsuccessfully to get the Philharmonic management to release him because of the orchestra's misbehavior to him.*

It was not until the spring of 1965 that I encountered again an operation on what I regarded as the genius level of Toscanini and Cantelli, as against what I heard achieved by conductors as gifted and dedicated as Colin Davis and Giulini. Impelled by what Stravinsky had written about Boulez, I attended a concert of his with the BBC Symphony; and though I had expected to be impressed by a conductor who impressed Stravinsky, I was unprepared for what I heard: the marvelous sounds of strings and winds in marvelously clear textures and perfectly shaped progressions, the extraordinary precision of ensemble execution, the absolutely exact rightness of statement, that revealed Boulez's possession of an ear for orchestral balance, a sense for continuity and proportion in shape, a power of magnetic compulsion exercised over the orchestra, and a mental governor exercising control over all these.

With this momentous and exciting fact of Boulez's singular powers as conductor and musician the concert revealed another fact of importance to the musical public: that he chose to devote these powers to the performance of a special limited repertory of the 20th-century music that interested him as a composer—a composer, as it happened, of some of the century's recent far-out music. The program of this concert ranged from Debussy's *Images* to excerpts from Alban Berg's *Wozzeck*, Webern's Six Pieces Op. 6, and Boulez's own *Doubles;* and though the programs of

*A young member of the orchestra described to me one of the incidents at rehearsals, in which Cantelli asked the first oboe to repeat a phrase and received the insolent refusal: "It'll be okay at the concert." And someone else told me of seeing Cantelli in his hotel room, in the spring of 1956, immediately after a rehearsal of a Beethoven piano concerto with Backhaus; of hearing Cantelli's anguished account of a morning of vain effort to overcome the indifference the orchestra had revealed in the shocking playing it wasn't ashamed to do in Backhaus's presence; of listening as Cantelli telephoned the Philharmonic's manager and requested a release from his contract. It was refused; and unfortunately Cantelli, after his return to Milan, did not decide to cancel the contract and remain in Europe, out of reach of a legal action by the Philharmonic.

his guest engagements the next few years with the Cleveland Orchestra and his two guest engagements in 1969 and 1971 with the New York Philharmonic did include a few works of earlier centuries that I will speak of in a moment, they continued to offer chiefly music by Debussy, Stravinsky, Ravel, Schönberg, Berg, Webern, Bartók, Ives, Varèse, Messiaen. Moreover, while this music included a few of what the general musical public regards as the century's great classics—the climactic masterpieces of Debussy's fully developed orchestral writing, *La Mer*, *Rondes de Printemps*, *Ibéria;* the young Stravinsky's astoundingly original *Petrushka* and *Le Sacre du Printemps*, his delightful *Pulcinella*—it included the much larger number of works by the other composers that I think most of this public finds as meaninglessly ugly as I do (except for Berg's *Wozzeck*, whose distorted vocal writing and discordant orchestral context do make the expressive sense of the nightmarish drama). And to the great examples of Debussy's late orchestral writing Boulez added *Jeux*, a boring succession of the mere mannerisms of that writing; to the young Stravinsky's masterpieces Boulez added, on the one hand, his ugly and uninteresting *Symphonies of Wind Instruments*, and on the other hand the old Stravinsky's *Requiem Canticles*, one of the pieces that resulted from his involvement with Schönberg and Webern, which are as ugly and mean-ingless as those of Schönberg and Webern. As for the few works of earlier centuries, broadcasts enabled me to hear Boulez's superb perfor-mances of Mozart's *Posthorn* Sérenade and Piano Concertos K. 453 and 467, Beethoven's Symphony No. 2, Schubert's Symphony No. 5, Ber-lioz's *Romeo and Juliet* and *Symphonie Fantastique* with the Cleveland Orchestra; his Philharmonic programs in 1969 included a group of Purcell's string fantasias and Haydn's Symphonies Nos. 89 and 91; the ones in 1971 offered excerpts from Gabrieli's *Symphoniae Sacrae*, Schu-bert's Symphony No. 6, excerpts from Berlioz's *Beatrice and Benedict*, and Mahler's *Lieder eines fahrenden Gesellen*. And it was interesting to note in these choices the avoidance of the major symphonies of Mozart, the dramatic and grand symphonies of Beethoven and Schubert, the sym-phonies of Brahms, the various orchestral works—symphonies, suites, ballets—of Tchaikovsky, the engaging earlier Symphonies Nos. 1 and 4 of Mahler.

I have gone into these details of programs because a conductor's value to music-lovers is not only in how he conducts but in what he conducts—which is to say, what he makes it possible for them to hear. Art-lovers can see the great art of the past whenever they like at the Frick Collection or the Chicago Art Institute or the National Gallery in Washington; but music-lovers can hear the great music of the past only when it is performed by the Boston Symphony or New York Philharmonic or some other orchestra. And in the years when subscribers heard programs that ranged from the classics of the 18th century to those of the 20th, with an occasional new work of a contemporary composer as a novelty, these orchestras performed what could be regarded as their proper museum function. The Frick Collection was not browbeaten into replacing its old masters with canvasfuls of Campbell soup cans and the other recent types of pseudo-art; but the New York Philharmonic did yield to the pressures of the music-of-our-own-time polemicists in its programs; and Boulez, one of the most vocal of these polemicists, was allowed programs for his guest engagements that reversed the old formula—programs predominantly of 20th-century music, most of it the music of the radical innovationists which the general musical public finds ugly and meaningless, with the occasional work of Haydn or Schubert as the novelty.

A Philharmonic subscriber could accept one such program of a remarkable conductor if the other programs of the series satisfied his one simple requirement—that they make it possible for him to hear the music, old and new, that he was interested in hearing, as the museum made it possible for him to see the paintings he was interested in seeing. But it turned out—when Boulez was made Musical Director of the Philharmonic in 1971 and had the task of planning the programs not just of his own concerts but of all the concerts of the next three seasons—that the subscriber's one simple idea was not among the numerous ideas about the Philharmonic's programs that Boulez disclosed at his first press conference in January 1971 and in an interview with the English critic Peter Heyworth a few months later. One major idea he revealed at the end of his Heyworth interview: he had, he said, accepted the Philharmonic post, and the similar post with the BBC Symphony, in order "to create models of concert life . . . in London and New York," by which he meant "conditions in which the music of our own time is once again an integral part of concert life." This was to be achieved not at the Philharmonic's subscription concerts, but in the two new series of concerts outside of the subscription series: "Prospective Encounters: 7-12," four concerts in a small hall at which programs of contemporary chamber music performed by members of the Philharmonic under Boulez and

other conductors would be preceded and followed by discussion involving performers, composers and listeners; and "Informal Evenings," two
concerts in a small hall at which Boulez would conduct the Philharmonic
in works (in 1971-72 works of Berg) that he would discuss and explain
and answer questions about. These two series—like Boulez's *Domain
Musical* concerts in Paris in the 50s—were set up for the people interested
in "the music of our own time," in accordance with the belief which
Boulez expressed to Heyworth—that just as people in London who
wanted to see Titian could go to the National Gallery and people who
wanted to see Klee could go to the Tate, audiences with different tastes
in music should be given the possibilities of hearing the different programs they wanted to hear, and it was wrong for orchestras to put a
contemporary piece in a program of classical pieces.

This was admirable good sense, which, however, Boulez didn't ad-
here to in his programs for the Philharmonic's subscription series. He
did put pieces by Nono, Ligeti, Maderna, Elliott Carter, Schönberg,
Berg, Bartók, Ives, Varèse, Ruggles and Riegger into programs with
older repertory works. And he damaged the programs further, from the
subscribers' viewpoint, with other ideas of his that represented interests
and attitudes different from theirs. The ordinary listener approaches a
piece of music very much as E. M. Forster—at the Harvard Symposium
on Music Criticism in 1947—said the critic, the professional listener,
should:

> [Criticism] has two aims. The first and the more important is esthetic. It
> considers the object [i.e., the work of art] in itself as an entity, and tells what it
> can about its life.

Boulez, on the other hand, is concerned with what Forster said was the
second and subsidiary aim of criticism:

> the relation of the object to the rest of the world [e.g., other works of art] . . .
> the influences which formed it (criticism adores influences), the influence it
> has exercised on subsequent works. . . .

For the Philharmonic subscriber, who listened to a piece of music in and
for itself to perceive what he could of its life, a good program was one in
which each of the works had such a perceivable life that made it worth
listening to; but for Boulez, who "adored influences," a good program
was one in which the works—even uninteresting works—demonstrated
such relations among them. A good museum, he said to Heyworth,

exhibited not only Rembrandt masterpieces but "other paintings of the same period that form the background to his work and help you to understand more precisely why that particular work [of Rembrandt] is a real masterpiece"; and for the same reason one had to perform Telemann as well as Bach. But actually the greatness of a masterpiece of Bach like his D-minor Clavier Concerto is apprehended directly, and solely, from that concerto, not from anything outside of it—not even from the other clavier concertos of Bach, and certainly not from a boring work of Telemann. Boulez was mistaken, then, in thinking it was necessary for the Philharmonic audience to be bored by Telemann's work in order to be excited by Bach's D-minor Concerto; but he had the power to act on his mistaken idea; and so the Philharmonic subscribers had to listen to the Telemann work and be bored by it.

This lack of interest in the individual quality and effect of the particular work, and concern instead with relations between works, produced Boulez's opening statement in the Heyworth interview, about not wanting to give a series of concerts that were like so many menus of which one remembered particular works or performances, and wanting instead "to give each season a profile" which listeners would remember: "Ah yes, that was the year of so and so." This was one reason for the "retrospectives" of certain composers' work that he planned for the Philharmonic seasons; and at his press conference he had, *The Times* reported, given another reason for them: "Museums . . . always have masterpieces on display, but they also arrange special exhibitions devoted to a big painter, an important period, special phases of art. . . ." The Philharmonic's 1971-72 season would, then, offer a retrospective of the music of Berg, which Boulez had chosen to emphasize as the "most obvious link between the late romantic style and the new language of today"; and another of the music of Liszt, "a great innovator" whose choral and symphonic works, in the words of the Philharmonic's press release, "had great impact and influence on the musical life of their time, but are virtually unknown and unperformed today." And the season of 1972-73 would offer retrospectives of Haydn and Stravinsky—Haydn, Boulez explained to Heyworth, as the example of the famous composer "who wrote a lot of works that are very rarely performed"; Stravinsky, "not just as an act of homage, but to try to get a general view of his music and see what he really means in the music of his time."

Translated into the realities of the actual music to be performed, these impressive words of Boulez meant that because of Liszt's influence on the musical life of his time the Philharmonic subscribers were going to have to listen to works of his that were unperformed and unknown today for the simple reason that in the hundred years since then music-lovers had found them empty and boring in their pretentiousness. ("[Liszt's] devotion to serious composition," Bernard Shaw wrote after performances of *St. Elizabeth* and the *Dante Symphony*, "seems as hopeless a struggle against natural incapacity as Benjamin Haydon's determination to be a great painter.") And the Philharmonic subscribers were going to have to listen to a number of works by Berg—the *Lulu* Suite, the Violin Concerto, the *Lyric Suite*, among others—in a musical language they found ugly and disliked, in order to perceive that these works provided a link to the musical language of today which the subscribers disliked even more.

On the other hand subscribers would have welcomed a Haydn retrospective offering, among rarely heard great works, the incandescent last series of symphonies, Nos. 92 to 104; but of these the actual retrospective Boulez put together offered only Nos. 95 and 96 with the superb No. 86, and in place of the other last masterpieces—in accordance with his belief that a masterpiece could be appreciated as such only in a context of the lesser products of the composer or his period—several earlier Haydn symphonies that were of less consequence and interest in themselves and did not increase the significance and effect of Nos. 86, 95 and 96. And the subscribers would also have welcomed "a general view of Stravinsky's music" provided by a series of major works, including some that were unfamiliar, above all the ballet score *Le Baiser de la Fée*, unique in its beautifully wrought, expressive and dramatically imaginative writing, and in my opinion Stravinsky's greatest work after *Le Sacre*. But Boulez's retrospective offered the derivative and unintegrated and uninteresting Symphony Op. 1, the transitional *Fireworks*, and *Firebird*, the first work in which the Stravinsky powers began to assert themselves impressively, but not the overwhelmingly original achievements of his matured powers, *Petrushka* and *Le Sacre*, that followed; the uninteresting *Rossignol* and ugly *Symphonies of Wind Instruments*, but not such major achievements of the Stravinsky mind working in earlier styles as *Oedipus Rex*, *Apollon Musagète* and *Le Baiser de la Fée*; a number of inconsequential, unattractive or ugly pieces, but not the delightfully witty *Jeu de Cartes* and *Danses Concertantes*, the moving *Orpheus*—all of which provided a "general view of Stravinsky's music" that was highly misleading.

Moreover, whereas a museum keeps most of its collection of master-pieces on view during a special show, Boulez's retrospectives, added to the contemporary works, left little room in the programs for the master-pieces the Philharmonic subscribers attended the concerts to hear.

I had my first encounter with another conductor on the genius level when, in 1971, I heard the Boston Symphony with Michael Tilson Thomas. As it happened he performed the Webern Six Pieces Op. 6 and Debussy *Images* that Boulez had performed at his first New York con-cert; and I was astounded again by what had astounded me in the Boulez performances. I was in fact even more astounded this time, since it was someone so young whose extraordinary gifts produced those marvelous sounds and textures, those perfectly shaped progressions, that abso-lutely exact rightness of statement.

Like Boulez Thomas had innovative ideas about programs. At that first concert of his that I heard he added to the pieces by Webern and Debussy Bach's Brandenburg Concerto No. 3 for strings and Ingolf Dahl's Concerto for Alto Saxophone, in accordance with his idea that the way to make a program interesting was to present works for groups which differed in size and instrumental composition. One could point out that such interest was achievable with the works in which essentially the same orchestra was used in the different ways of Haydn, Mozart, Beethoven, Mendelssohn, Berlioz, Tchaikovsky, Brahms, Strauss, Mahler, Debussy and Stravinsky. And on the other hand the next program I heard Thomas perform with the Boston Symphony demon-strated how boring Bach could be with a small group of strings, winds and drums in his Suite No. 4, how boring Schönberg could be with the entire symphony orchestra in his Five Pieces Op. 16, how boring Stra-vinsky could be with a differently constituted small instrumental and vocal group in *Rénard*, but how interesting Tchaikovsky was with his varied use of the entire orchestra in the different styles of the divertisse-ments in Act 3 of *Swan Lake*.

This act of *Swan Lake*, which I doubt had ever been performed at a symphony concert before, illustrated the wider range of Thomas's musi-cal interests that made his combinations of old and new more satisfying than Boulez's. Thomas's very first program with the Boston Symphony in October 1969 began with Haydn's Symphony No. 98, continued with

Ives's *Three Places in New England* and Stravinsky's Variations, and ended with Debussy's *La Mer*. And similar programs for his subsequent guest appearances included a piece by the 12th-century composer Perotin, part of Monteverdi's Vespers of 1610, Vivaldi's *The Four Seasons*, Bach's Contatas Nos. 4, 51, and 140, Mozart's Symphonies K. 297 and 338 and Serenade K. 388, Haydn's Symphony No. 97, Beethoven's Symphonies Nos. 7 and 8, Brahms's Symphony No. 2, Tchaikovsky's Symphony No. 1, Borodin's Symphony No. 2, Strauss's *Till Eulenspiegel*, Mahler's Symphonies Nos. 5 and 9, Stravinsky's *Firebird* Suite, *Le Sacre du Printemps* and *Pulcinella* Suite, Prokofiev's *Scythian Suite*.

Thomas made it known that he didn't want to be tied to the old format of symphony concerts but wanted to do special things; and also that he liked to hear music he had never heard before. And so after a couple of years he began to do special things in his Spectrum Concerts outside of the regular Boston Symphony series. His two-part Stravinsky retrospective did include *Le Sacre du Printemps* at the end of the first concert, the *Symphony of Psalms* at the end of the second; but these were preceded by some of Stravinsky's most unattractive works—the *Symphonies of Wind Instruments*, Violin Concerto, *Scènes de Ballet*, and *Requiem Canticles*. Enough people wanted to hear his performances of *Le Sacre* and the *Symphony of Psalms* for these two concerts to be sold out; but a Boston friend informed me there wasn't much interest in the other concerts, which offered some of the oddities Thomas had discovered in his exploration of unfamiliar music. Certain of the programs my friend characterized as "awful," referring specifically to "Variations of the Orchestra," with pieces by Mouret ("Music from the court of France c. 1675"), Stamitz, Richter, and Filtz ("Music of Mannheim c. 1770"), Webern's *Sommerwind* ("Music from Vienna c. 1900"), and Berio and Cage ("Music of the world c. 1972"); and to "A Multiples Concert," with a piece for four organs by Reich and Liszt's *Hexameron* for six pianos and orchestra.

"I haven't always been in music," Thomas was quoted as saying. "I have other areas of interest"; to which he added, "I never want to be just a conductor," and "I'd hate to be tied to the old format of conducting symphony concerts." Boulez too began to conduct only quite recently, and with the interests of a composer of today, which may lead him to give up conducting for the direction of the projected research center in Paris in which there will be the collaboration of composers, performers and scientists that he thinks necessary for the renewal of a dying art. All this reveals an important difference between these two supremely gifted conductors of today and those of thirty years ago. Cantelli, like Toscanini, had always been in music, content to be just a conductor and to perform the music it was considered the conductor's duty to perform within the established format of symphony concerts. And the result was that with the occasional uninteresting piece by Martucci on a Toscanini program, or the one by Ghedini on a Cantelli program, music-lovers heard great performances of music which for the most part they were interested in hearing; whereas today they can hear the Boulez performance of the one work they are interested in, or the Thomas performances of the two such works, only by sitting through the two or three unattractive works Boulez and Thomas are impelled to perform by their thinking about new models of concert life. (*Commentary*, January 1968 and November 1973)

Postscript 1983 Thomas's pronouncements about his activity in the concert world, in interviews in 1976, dealt with that world not as it is in reality but as it was transformed in his mind, which perceived it as "fossilized," "designed for dead people," by whom he meant people who want to "hear the same thing over and over again," and whose ears are closed to what is new. It was to remedy all this that he made up programs of old and new music—to open audiences' ears, to "contrast one esthetic with another," to present the old music "in fresh, novel perspectives" provided by the new. But in the real concert world the continuing performance of our heritage of great music of previous centuries at concerts can no more be characterized as "fossilization" than can the continuing exhibition of our heritage of great paintings in museums; and the people who continue to want to hear that music at the concerts are no more "dead" than those who continue to want to see the paintings in the museums. If music-lovers at concerts don't want to hear Schönberg, Varèse and Stockhausen it is not because they have listened with, so to speak, closed ears, but because they have disliked what they heard when they listened with open ears. What Thomas actually wanted of them was not merely that they listen to Schönberg and the rest, but that they like what they hear—which they are entitled not to do. Nor does Schönberg provide fresh perspectives for Mozart or Debussy: these perspectives are provided by exceptional performances like Boulez's of Debussy's *Images*,

Thomas's of Mozart's Symphony K. 338. Thomas related that when he performed Schumann's *Rhenish* Symphony after a work of Stockhausen in Buffalo, people in the audience exclaimed that they had never before realized the Schumann symphony was such a masterpiece; but that was not because of any new insights into the symphony provided by Stockhausen: it was because after the Stockhausen piece anything would sound like a masterpiece—and also, probably, because of Thomas's performance.

This was saddening, and left one wishing that Thomas would come out of the imagined musical world in which he wasted his real gifts and opportunities on the mistaken attempt to bring those he mistakenly regarded as the musically dead back to what he mistakenly regarded as musical life, and that he would be content to do in the real musical world what he was put on earth to do: produce the performances with which he imparts exciting new life to the great works of our musical heritage. And fortunately, not only for him but for the musical world, that is what he did—by the evidence of superb performances I have heard him produce in recent years in broadcasts with the Los Angeles Philharmonic, San Francisco Symphony and Cleveland Orchestras, and in recordings of Tchaikovsky's Suites and *Manfred* Symphony, Debussy's *Nuages* and *Fêtes*, his *La Mer*, Stravinsky's *Petrushka* and Beethoven's symphonies with the Los Angeles Philharmonic, London Symphony, Philharmonia and English Chamber Orchestras.

Toscanini and the
New York Philharmonic

An article by John Rockwell in *The New York Times*, *Why Isn't the Philharmonic Better?*, included an account of Toscanini's operation with the orchestra which should not be left uncorrected. The New York Philharmonic's modern history, said Rockwell, began with its merger in 1928 with the New York Symphony and Toscanini's "assumption of the sole conductorship of the combined orchestra." His "glamorous charisma and fierce authority" achieved "concerts [that] were brilliant"; but he did not reveal the "skills as an orchestra builder" required for a "longer-range effect upon the orchestra." "Star conductors and patient orchestra builders can be combined within one man, as Stokowski and Koussevitzky proved;" but no building process like theirs "took place at the New York Philharmonic in the 1930s, for all of Toscanini's impassioned interpretive genius." And his brilliant concerts were "achieved . . . at a cruel price. The orchestra had been [in the quoted words of another writer] 'whipped into shape' and 'wore the scars of its flagellation' "—scars which were for Rockwell the cause of a "retroactive resentment" and "determination to resist the authority of lesser mortals" that he saw in its mediocre playing under Toscanini's successors.

Actually the Philharmonic's modern history began in 1926 with Toscanini's first guest engagement. On Sunday afternoon January 10 of that year I heard the playing of a highly competent and well disciplined orchestra under Mengelberg; and four days later I heard the astoundingly different playing of a seemingly different orchestra—a virtuoso orchestra as sensitized to Toscanini's direction as the Philadelphia Orchestra was to Stokowski's and the Boston Symphony to Koussevitzky's, which produced the tonal radiance, transparent textures and sharply defined contours of phrase that were as distinctive in Toscanini's performances as tonal sumptuousness and splendor were in Stokowski's, and subtleties and refinements of sonority were in Koussevitzky's. This transformation had not been achieved by years of patient building and drilling: it had been achieved in a few hours by the "magnetic influence" that Bernard Shaw had called "the highest faculty of a conductor", and that Toscanini possessed in exceptional degree. As for the merger in 1928, it was Toscanini who auditioned and selected the members of the combined Philharmonic-Symphony that he conducted in Europe in May 1930 in performances described by George Szell years later as "orchestral performance of a kind new to all of us" in its "clarity of texture, precision of ensemble, rightness of balances, virtuosity of every section, every solo player"—all of which I had heard Toscanini achieve at his very first concert with the Philharmonic in January 1926.

Describing to me in 1966 Toscanini's similar achievement with the Vienna Philharmonic in 1933, Hugo Burghauser—who played bassoon in that orchestra and was its chairman—said that Toscanini's ability "to *project* whatever was in . . . his mind into the orchestra *unmistakably*" with his conducting technique and facial expression was "a sort of miracle" of "telepathic communication" which told one, "without his saying a word, that it meant not *piano* but *pianissimo*, not *forte* but *mezzo-forte;*" and that this "didn't need months or years: it was at the first rehearsal, from the very first hours." "Look at me!" one hears Toscanini exclaiming at rehearsals, meaning "Look at what my stick is telling you to do!"; and William Carboni, who had played viola in the NBC Symphony, explained in 1966 that "a lot of conductors you don't look at: they don't have . . . the magnetism to hold your attention; so you play with your head buried in the music, you see only by peripheral vision [their] beat going up and down;" but Toscanini and Cantelli "you had to look at . . . and when you looked you saw what they wanted and you had to do it." And David Walter, who had played bass in the NBC Symphony, said that "the outbursts of rage have been made too much of [and] have given people a false impression of what went on at rehearsals. The fact is that most of the time Toscanini worked with the orchestra with quiet and superb efficiency."

The Philharmonic's astounding playing at its very first concert with Toscanini in 1926—produced not by flagellation but by the unique magnetic force that implemented his unique musical powers—was what one continued to hear only when the orchestra played under the compulsion of that force—which is to say that one didn't hear it when Furtwängler followed Toscanini in 1926, or when Mengelberg returned the next year, or when Barbirolli succeeded Toscanini in 1936. The orchestra's poor playing under Barbirolli was not caused by the "scars of its flagellation" by Toscanini that required the healing ministrations by a patient orchestra-builder; it was caused by Barbirolli's lack of the "magnetic influence" Shaw and Carboni considered essential, and required only a conductor who had it—as Toscanini demonstrated in April 1942, when he returned to the Philharmonic for a Beethoven cycle. At the first rehearsal he stepped onto the podium and without a single preliminary word began to conduct the orchestra that at once produced the playing it had done with him in 1936; and he conducted long stretches with only an occasional stop for a quickly achieved correction of balance or phrasing. Again in January 1945, returning for a Pension Fund concert with the orchestra in which Rodzinski had changed a number of players, Toscanini devoted the first half-hour of his first rehearsal to working out the complex climactic statement of the Funeral Music from *Die Götterdämmerung* and the balances of the winds at the beginning of the piece, and then simply led the orchestra through it, producing again the performance he had produced in 1936.

Nor were Toscanini's the only such demonstrations. Cantelli, whom the Philharmonic mistreated at rehearsals; Boulez, whom members of the orchestra were quoted in the press as disparaging; and Michael Tilson Thomas, whose re-engagement the orchestra was reported to have voted against, are three conductors whom I heard demonstrate the essential condition for the Philharmonic's playing to be what it is not most of the time—that of a great orchestra. (*Musical America*, November 1984)

Van Cliburn

What I occasionally refer to as Haggin's Law—that you can't keep a bad man down—is depressing; but even more so is the converse—the good man who *is* kept down. A prime beneficiary of the law is Daniel Barenboim; the outstanding victim of the converse is Van Cliburn. Some years ago, when Barenboim's performances of Beethoven sonatas in the concert hall and on records were reported in the press to be those of a gifted artist who at 25 exhibited the maturity of a performer twice his age, I pointed out that maturity in a pianist meant discipline, the rarest of a performer's gifts, and the crucial one whose control of the others produced a coherent conception of a musical work in his mind and achieved an accurate realization of this conception from his instrument. As it happened, one of the Beethoven sonatas recorded by Barenboim, Op. 81a *(Les Adieux)*, had been recorded also by Cliburn—which made it possible to hear the contrast between the disciplined Cliburn operation that produced the progression in which one note led to the next with unfailing cohesive tension, continuity of tempo and volume, and rightness of relation in what emerged as a coherently proportioned shape of sound in time; and on the other hand the lack of discipline evident in Barenboim's preoccupation with the effect of the particular moment without regard for any relation to the moments before and after, which resulted in a progression without continuity, cohesive tension and coherent shape, exhibiting what could be characterized as the immaturity of a performer half his age. But in the press that credited Barenboim with the matured musicianship he clearly lacked, Cliburn was not conceded the matured musicianship he clearly possessed.

This erroneous opinion of Cliburn began with his return from his

43

triumph in the Moscow competition of 1958. He had won in Moscow
with performances not only of works for the display of virtuosity like the
Tchaikovsky Concerto No. 1 and the Rachmaninov No. 3, but of sonatas
of Mozart and Beethoven and Chopin's Fantaisie in his solo recital; and
his greatest moment in Moscow, he told an interviewer, had been his
having to get up four times to acknowledge the applause after his
performance of Mozart's Sonata K. 330. The celebration of his triumph
in New York, however, was limited to a single concert with orchestra at
which he played the Tchaikovsky and Rachmaninov concertos; and his
not adding the solo recital with the pieces by Mozart, Beethoven and
Chopin turned out to be a bad mistake. For its result was the idea which
the reviewers formed of him as a brilliant virtuoso who had yet to acquire
the matured musical understanding needed for the performance of Mozart and Beethoven—which conceivably they might not have thought if
he had played the recital with its Mozart and Beethoven sonatas after the
concert with the Tchaikovsky and Rachmaninov concertos.

For my part, even with only the performances of the concertos to
judge by, I heard the playing of an extraordinary musician, who treated
those display works as Toscanini treated a Sousa march or Liszt Hungarian Rhapsody—as pieces of music in which he employed the same
musical powers as in Mozart and Beethoven. And as it happened the
musical powers that Cliburn employed in the concertos were astonishingly like Toscanini's: a similar plastic sense in the shaping of a
progression that gave it unfailing note-to-note continuity, cohesive tension and coherently proportioned structure. When the performance of the
Rachmaninov concerto was issued on an RCA record I kept playing the
cadenza of the first movement, fascinated by the shaping of the progression, and the build-up of tension in it, through the alternation of gradual
acceleration and deceleration of tempo—most remarkable and overwhelming in the climactic pronouncement of the movement's principal
theme. And I was certain that the musical powers Cliburn exhibited in
this trashy music he would exhibit in the music of Mozart and Beethoven—as in fact he did in the recorded performances that followed, each
of which made me aware of something more that was extraordinary in his
operation as a musician, while the reviewers continued to report his
musical immaturity.

Thus when the performances of a number of pieces by Chopin were
issued on RCA LSC-2576, Irving Kolodin, in *The Saturday Review*,

pronounced them no better than one would hear from any number of students at the Juilliard and Eastman Schools; but I had to report that in all my years of concert-going I had never heard a performance of the Polonaise Op. 53 like Cliburn's on this record. Its distinctive characteristic was its elegance, in the sense in which that word is used of a mathematical demonstration to describe its economy, its reduction to absolute essentials. One heard, that is, instead of the traditional flamboyant modifications of tempo and volume, a disciplined holding of the grace and lilt and plasticity of the piece within the limits of perfectly proportioned shape—a shape, moreover, in which, as in a Toscanini performance, every note, whether of melody or accompaniment, fell into place with absolute accuracy of timing and sonority. This elegance, once I perceived it in the performance of the Polonaise, I continued to hear in all of Cliburn's playing.

From the performance of the Ballade Op. 47 on the record I learned another such characteristic of his playing. Listening to Ashkenazy's recorded performance of the introduction of this piece, one could not imagine it being played more sensitively and beautifully; and so I was astounded, when I listened to Cliburn's playing of it, by his additional subtleties of timing and inflection. And again, what I heard for the first time in this performance—that Cliburn perceived and revealed more in a piece of music than other great musicians did—I found myself hearing in all his playing. Another example of it, in Chopin's Sonata Op. 58 on RCA LSC-3053, was his powerful inflection of the left hand's countermelody in the middle section of the Scherzo, which I could not recall hearing in any other performance. Moreover the style of his playing in the entire work was one I had never heard in another performance. The first movement was usually played as if Chopin's direction were *Allegro appassionato ed agitato;* but Cliburn, like Rubinstein before him, and unlike other pianists, perceived that the direction was *Allegro maestoso;* and this produced not only the grandly declamatory style of the opening of the movement, but the maintaining of this style in the movement's lyrical sections, and in the movements that followed. And once more what I first perceived in this performance I found to be characteristic of all his playing: he enunciated music with a grandeur that was uniquely his; and he did this with whatever music he played.

But the performances that made me increasingly aware of his towering stature as a musician continued to elicit only condescension and denigration in the press. It was true that he was open to criticism—not for the way he played music, but for the music he did not play. One could, that is, expect him to employ his great powers in the great works that required them: the concertos of Mozart, the last sonatas of Beethoven, the late sonatas and smaller pieces of Schubert, the Fantasy, Symphonic Etudes and other major works of Schumann. And he could be criticized for letting the years pass without even a beginning of the fulfillment of this expectation—without his adding a single one of those works to what he had learned as a student and repeated year after year in his recitals. But what was treated with condescension and worse in the press was the great performances of the works of Beethoven and Chopin he did perform (which, a friend has suggested, may have discouraged him from playing the greater works). The performance of Chopin's Concerto No. 1 that demonstrated to Harold Schonberg of *The Times* Cliburn's lack of understanding of how such a work intended to show off the pianist's virtuosity should be played and that demonstrated to Winthrop Sargeant of *The New Yorker* his lack of understanding of the Chopin style, actually was one that impressed me not only with the elegance of its grandly impassioned enunciation of melody but with the scaled down execution of brilliant passage work that demonstrated Cliburn's understanding that one didn't play such passage work in a concerto of Chopin as one did in a concerto of Liszt. And the performance of Beethoven's Concerto No. 3 in which Sargeant heard the *rubato* elasticity in tempo carried to the point of incoherence was one in which I heard every note, in the powerfully sculptured playing, in the place allotted it in the emerging shape by a mind with a complete conceptual grasp of that shape and complete control in its achievement.

I had no interest, last January, in hearing Grieg's Piano Concerto even as it would be played by Cliburn with the New York Philharmonic under Previn, until I read Donal Henahan's report in *The Times* that it had been no more than an "absent-minded run-through . . . by the Cliburn-Previn duo" for its repetition the following night in the first "Live from Lincoln Center" telecast, and that Cliburn in particular had given an "uninterested—and uninteresting—reading" of the piano part. I found it impossible to believe that Cliburn and Previn had regarded a Philharmonic concert as an occasion for anything less than the best they were capable of; and my disbelief was strengthened by my recollection of the excitingly impassioned performance of *Don Carlo* I had heard

Abbado conduct at the Metropolitan, which Henahan had reported the next day as having been "conducted slackly and without passion." Feeling certain that Cliburn and Previn would perform in the telecast as they had performed at the concert, I decided to watch and listen to the telecast. And so I saw Cliburn's intense concentration and heard the grandeur of his playing in the inconsequential work—a moving operation of extraordinary human powers that left me in tears and with my throat too constricted for speech.

Forty years ago the English critic W.J. Turner wrote that without detracting from the merits of great conductors like Nikisch, Weingartner, Strauss, Bruno Walter, Furtwängler and Klemperer he would say Toscanini was a unique phenomenon. And with full recognition of the greatness of Schnabel in the past, and Ashkenazy and Pollini today, I would say Cliburn is another unique phenomenon. (*New Republic*, 11 September 1976)

Glenn Gould

One of the resolutions passed by the musicians of the Chicago Symphony Orchestra in 1905, for the banquet which their conductor, Theodore Thomas, did not live to attend, placed on record their "love for the man who never trifled with his gifts." It was recalled to mind by the death of a man with phenomenal musical gifts who did trifle with them—"trifle" being the apt term for Glenn Gould's misuse of them in his combination of extreme eccentricity, perversity, erroneous ideas, impulse to shock, and addiction to pranks. The tragedy, for me, was not the one described in the obituaries—the death of so gifted a musician at the very moment that his newly recorded performance of Bach's *Goldberg Variations* revealed the impressive maturity of his gifts. It was instead, for me, the life in which, from first to last, Gould had offered an alternation of what excited one with its marvelous execution and musical rightness, and on the other hand what, however impressively it was executed, one could not hear as a valid statement of the music.

Though Gould recorded several of his finest performances in the early years of his career, even the very first of them, the remarkable one of the *Goldberg Variations* in 1955, offered the alternation I have described; and the superb one of Beethoven's Concerto No. 1 in 1958 followed the ones of Beethoven's last three sonatas in 1956, with the eccentricities that included Variation 4 in the finale of Op. 109, for which Beethoven prescribes, in Italian and German, a tempo slower than the *andante* of the theme, but which Gould played in a tempo faster than the *andante*, giving the variation a light-hearted expressive character instead of the profoundly serious and impassioned character it has in Beethoven's tempo. Mozart's Sonata K. 330, which Gould shaped and articulated so effec-

48

tively in 1958, he ripped through in 1972 at speeds that made it meaningless; and even in 1958 one heard a few instances of two idiosyncratic practices that became increasingly damaging in his performances—the overemphasizing of left-hand accompaniment as if it were melody, and the arpeggiating of what Mozart writes as solid left-hand chords. In Mozart's Concerto K. 491 in 1962 Gould carried these practices to an extreme that was made especially deplorable by the extraordinary nature of the performance—the powerful sculpturing of phrase, the energy of fast runs and figurations, the sustained tension and momentum that were unprecedented in the playing of this music and gave the work new and overwhelming magnitude. In 1966 the slow movement of Beethoven's Concerto No. 5 was damaged by Gould's thumping out the figuration that is a mere delicate embellishment of the orchestra's final restatement of the principal melody—this following the perversity of his playing the opening movement in an exaggeratedly and unconvincingly slower tempo than the *allegro* Beethoven prescribes. In 1970 again the first movement of Beethoven's Sonata Op. 57 (*Appassionata*) played *andante sostenuto* instead of the *allegro assai* prescribed by Beethoven, and the middle movement played *adagio* instead of the prescribed *andante con moto*, were impossible to hear as valid statements of the music. And all this continued to the end in 1982. One heard in the last six of Haydn's sonatas the electrifyingly executed inflection of a *cantabile* phrase in a slow movement that gave it continuity of tension and shape, followed by the unsuitable exaggerated staccato treatment of the next *cantabile* phrase; the overemphasized accompaniment figuration that predominated over a melodic statement; the disturbingly obtrusive "brrrrups" of arpeggiated accompaniment chords. And in the final new performance of Bach's *Goldberg Variations* the results of Gould's continued thinking about the initial aria and the thirty variations in the years since the performance in 1955 turned out to be only a different alternation of what was wonderfully effective and what was musically unconvincing.

In both performances of the *Goldberg* one gets this alternation in the first two pieces. In 1955 the aria is made excitingly effective by the extraordinary enlivening inflection in the *andante* tempo that seems exactly right and leaves one unprepared for the excessively fast tempo of the first variation. In 1981 the first variation's slower tempo is not only right itself but related to the tempos of the next three variations, so that the series has a coherence it doesn't have in 1955. But this plus in 1981 is outweighed by the minus of the opening statement of the aria, which astonishes one first with the extreme slowness that Gould, in an interview, ascribed to his feeling "ruminative"; and which astonishes one further not only with its extreme softness but with its extreme elimination of the expressive inflection of tone implied by "ruminative". With many pianists the long progression played this way would lack cohesive tension and fall apart, but with Gould what is astonishing in the end is the continuity he maintains in the strangely perverse progression. It is, then, an extraordinary tour de force, but not, for my ears, a musically convincing statement of the aria. And a few other such changes for the better and worse call for mention. Both the slow opening section and fast concluding section of Variation 16 are made more effective by the slower tempos of 1981, which, again, are related to the tempos of Variations 17 and 18; but Variation 19, effective in its relaxed minuet tempo in 1955, is made stodgy in 1981 by its overdeliberately slower tempo and exaggerated staccato. In the interview Gould stated his conviction that what Bach wanted was not legato but *détaché;* but doubts concerning this view are increased by his inconsistency in applying it: he plays the first part of Variation 15 legato, as it is written, but his repetition of it ranges from *détaché* to exaggerated staccato. (Moreover the performance of this variation in 1955 is made more effective by its more relaxed *andante* flow and the extraordinary way the sensitively inflected voices of the texture are kept distinct and continuous themselves and in continuous relation to each other—which I maintain in the face of Gould's statement to an interviewer in 1981 that in 1955 he had made the variation "sound like a Chopin Nocturne.") And finally, the distentions that create powerful tensions and expressive point in the extremely slow tempo of Variation 25 in 1955 produce a statement of it which, although obtrusively idiosyncratic, is musically impressive; but the 1981 statement flows more naturally in its more animated tempo, and achieves satisfying coherence and expressiveness without the distensions and tensions of 1955.

From the beginning Gould, in addition to playing the piano, talked—first in notes for some of his recorded performannces, then in lectures, radio and television programs, interviews. And the author of *Glenn Gould: Music and Mind,* Geoffrey Payzant, contended that what Gould had written about "the composer-performer-audience relationships, music and morality, music and technology, the mode of existence of a work of musical art", had to be "taken very seriously, for Gould is talking about the salvation of mankind." But actually the mind that produced the eccentricities and perversities in the performances produced also the eccentricities and perversities in the thinking about music and everything else as it existed not in the real world but in the private world of that mind.

To begin, as Gould did, with music: Concerning the eccentricities in performance I have described he said either nothing or what was as eccentric and disputable as what it explained. Thus, his notes for Beethoven's last three sonatas didn't include his musical purpose in playing Variation 4 in the finale of Op. 109 in the faster tempo that changed the expressive character Beethoven intended; and on the other hand, in explanation of the exaggeratedly slow tempo of the first movement of Beethoven's Concerto No. 5, he told an interviewer of his belief that the excuse for making a recording at all was that "one is going to perform that particular work as it has never been performed and heard before;" of his suggestion to Stokowski, therefore, when they were planning the recording of the concerto, "that we do it in one of two rather extreme ways—either very fast . . . or very slow;" and of his delight when Stokowski "opted for the slow version, which was very grandiose." But actually neither of Gould's alternatives was a legitimate way of playing the work, or a necessary way for his objective: the one legitimate way was to produce in Beethoven's prescribed tempos what one felt to be the right flow and articulation of the music; and the resulting performance would inevitably be different from everyone else's. Leon Fleisher and Van Cliburn, that is, both playing the concerto in the generally accepted tempos, had produced performances that were made different by the two musicians' idiosyncratic ways of shaping music with inflection of phrase—as Gould, if he played it in those tempos, would produce a performance similarly different from theirs. And as it happened he did produce it: Four years after recording his eccentric performance of the concerto Gould—a last-minute replacement for another pianist in a televised concert of a Canadian orchestra conducted by Ancerl—played it not only in the generally accepted tempos but without the disturbing eccentricities of the recorded performance—which is to say without, among others, the thumping out of the figuration in the second movement that is a delicate embellishment of the orchestra's statement of the principal melody—and produced in this way not only one of the most overwhelmingly effective performances of his career, but one that had the distinctive impress of his powerful musical mind.

The idea responsible for the excessively slow tempo in Beethoven's concerto presumably accounted also for Gould's excessively slow tempos in Beethoven's Sonata Op. 57, and for his ripping through Mozart's Sonata K. 330 in 1972. But it was, exceptionally, from his notes about Mozart's Concerto K. 491 that one apprehended the equally disputable idea responsible for the practices that damaged his performance of that work. The pianist and his instrument were properly employed, in Gould's view, by polyphonic or contrapuntal writing which required the operation of all ten fingers, exemplified by the "chromatic fugal manner" of Mozart's variation for piano alone in the concerto's finale; and the left-hand chords or single notes accompanying the right-hand melody in Mozart's more usual homophonic writing in the concerto Gould heard as "unrealized continuos"; hence the line of left-hand accompaniment, and even mere accompaniment figuration, that Gould played with the emphasis and expressiveness of melody, and at times made more prominent than the actual melody of the right hand; and hence also his "realizing" of the "unrealized continuos" by arpeggiating what Mozart wrote as solid left-hand chords, and inserting such arpeggiated chords where Mozart wrote single notes. These "very few liberties in this regard" Gould considered, in his notes, "wholly within the spirit and substance of the work"; but when Mozart wanted a polyphonic or contrapuntal texture he wrote it himself, in the variation for piano alone; and the homophonic passages in the concerto were likewise what he wanted, not polyphony with "unrealized continuos" left to be realized by the performer. And for my ears the interpolations of Gould's realizations were obtrusively alien to Mozart's writing.

It was in 1963, a year after the recording of Mozart's Concerto K. 491—when I transmitted to Gould the request of several young instructors of English in Cambridge for his recordings of the other great Mozart concertos—that he astonished me not only with his disclosure that he had no great enthusiasm for Mozart and had recorded K. 491 with many reservations, but with his description of what he found disturbing in the concertos: that they were outrageously padded and either obsequiously saccharine or unguardedly melodramatic, making him reluctant to play them on the piano, an instrument which itself tended toward these excesses. (He had thought of trying to lessen them by doing a couple of the concertos with the harpsichord, treating the solo part as continuo; but this experiment did not materialize.) And in the spring of 1968 he discussed K. 491 again in a CBC television program, concerning which a reader reported to me that "Gould would play something marvelous from K. 491 and say 'Nothing there. Arid. Mechanical clichés like inter-office memos.'" I found and sent to Gould the proofs of an article of mine on the Andantes of Mozart's Concertos K. 453, 467 and 482, asking him to mark on them any passages I referred to that he considered mechanical clichés like inter-office memos. And while I was at it I asked him the reasons for details in his recorded performances of two Mozart sonatas. From the prescribed *adagio* tempo and the slurs over the right hand's notes in the opening measures of the Sonata K. 282 it seemed clear that Mozart had in mind a slow, legato expressive *cantabile* statement; what, then, was Gould's reason for his *andantino* tempo and non-legato touch that made it instead a *scherzando* statement? And in bars 25 to 42 of the slow second movement of the Sonata K. 280 Gould's reason for stressing the left-hand part was clearly its melodic relation to the right-hand part; but the left hand's mere accompaniment figuration in the passage that followed had no melodic significance whatever; what, then, was his reason for giving this figuration emphasis which made it not just as prominent as—but in the final crescendo even more prominent than—the right hand's melody?

In his reply Gould began by conceding that the television program had included a degree of exaggeration which the editing and structuring process made difficult to avoid; however he had meant much of what he had said, and had been careful to limit his unfavorable comments to the concertos and express his relative enthusiasm for the sonatas. Having no score with him [in his home in Toronto!], he went on, he would side-step my questions about the performances of the sonatas until we met; but since they involved the relation of melodic and accompaniment compo-nents of the textures he had to say that the concept of this segregation of attention was one he never had accepted. He had always considered the idea of a melodic element distinguished from the other component elements in a harmonic environment to be anti-structural; and the melodic element seemed to him to require no special emphasis, only the careful delineation of its profile that permitted one to reveal the harmonic texture.

All this had no relation to the realities of the subject, of his performances, and of my questions. Awareness, as one listened, of the melodic character of what the right hand was playing and the unmelodic character of the left hand's Alberti bass did not constitute segregation of attention: one heard both melody and Alberti bass as related components of a musical whole. Listening to a Gould performance I heard, much of the time, the proper balance of these two components that made both clearly audible, with the melody, because of its expressive character, given more prominence through tonal emphasis than the inexpressive Alberti bass. And whereas Gould replied as if I were an advocate of the *im*balance resulting from a special emphasis of the right hand's melody that would obscure the left hand's harmonic component, actually I had asked the reason for the imbalance *he* created at times by giving the left hand's Alberti bass or other inexpressive figuration the special emphasis that made it excessively prominent, and on occasion caused it to obscure the carefully delineated melody. I pointed this out to Gould and rephrased my questions, which he never answered.

In the spring of 1969 he revealed that his enthusiasm for the sonatas was limited to a few early ones. Asked—at the beginning of a interview with a CBC producer—what his aim was in playing an all-Mozart program after his previous derogatory remarks about Mozart—Gould replied that it was "to prove the derogatory remarks." He felt that in his music-making Mozart was an exhibitionist, and "like a child in the sense that first of all he wanted to please," and "had so much facility . . . that he was content to sit back and say, 'Well, I think a scale will do quite handily here, and an arpeggio, that will do to get us to the next main point.'" And having said to his interviewer that with Mozart one could throw onto the turntable "a serenade or a piano sonata or string quartet and get pretty much the same bland tap-water result," Gould mentioned as the single exception "the early works [that] do . . . for me make a very special impact," and above all the Sonata K. 284, which for him was "the best thing that Mozart ever wrote for the piano—infinitely better than anything from his 'mature' phase." To this one has to reply that what Gould described and demonstrated at the piano about K. 284 did establish the impressive quality of this work of Mozart's early twenties, but not its superiority to the K. 533 of his maturity, with its extraordinary Andante. But Gould told an interviewer in 1981 that he found the later sonatas "intolerable, loaded with quasi-theatrical conceit".

In this interview he made a similar statement about Beethoven, expressing admiration of the early piano works—specifically the Sonatas Opp. 26, 27 No. 2 and 28, and the Variations Op. 34—for "Beethoven's senses of structure, fantasy, variety, thematic continuity, harmonic propulsion, and contrapuntal discipline", but finding in the works of his middle period—specifically the Fifth Symphony, *Emperor* Concerto and *Waldstein* Sonata—an almost total absence of "the harmonic and rhythmic variety [and] contrapuntal invention" he expected in great music, and instead "the predominance of those empty, banal, belligerent gestures that serve as themes" in the period he described as offering "the supreme example of a composer on an ego trip". And Gould also revealed his having always felt that "the whole center core of the piano recital repertoire is a *colossal* waste of time;" that "the whole first half of the nineteenth century—excluding Beethoven to some degree—is pretty much of a washout as far as solo instrumental music is concerned;" that the composers of that period—Schubert, Schumann, Chopin—didn't know how to write for the piano, producing only " . . . dramatic effects . . . empty theatrical gestures . . . exhibitionism . . . very little real *composing*", because they "labored under the delusion that the piano is a homophonic instrument." It was, he maintained, a contrapuntal instrument, and interesting only in writing "in which the vertical and harmonic dimensions are mated." But actually the piano was not essentially—by its very nature—either a harmonic or a contrapuntal instrument: it lent itself to the various ways, homophonic as well as contrapuntal, in which it was used with various impressive effect not only by Mozart, Haydn and Beethoven but by Schubert, Schumann and Chopin. It was only in Gould's private world that Chopin's "one-minute Mazurka . . . can be charming and full of interesting, ironic shifts and changes," but his "seven-minute sonata movement . . . will be useless, a disaster, incapable of sustaining itself in an integrated way, of matching form and content."

The reference to the piano-recital repertory related to Gould's withdrawal from the concert hall and his belief that it had been superseded by the recording studio. There are realities in live performance in a hall— the possibility not only of wrong notes but of unsatisfactory details of tempo, dynamics, shaping of phrase—which made it reasonable for Gould to have decided to restrict himself to the studio where, he said, an artist could, by splicing together parts of several recorded takes, not only eliminate inaccuracies but "prepare his conception of a work to the best of his ability" and "create a homogeneous entity." But he offered additional reasons for his decision: that playing in a large hall and having to project to the listener in the top balcony had caused him to do things "that had no part in the structure" of the music and "ultimately destroyed [its] fabric;" and that it had been made a degrading experience by the "case-hardened concertgoers" who treated a recital as a gladiatorial event, waiting with an "almost sadistic lust for blood" for a disastrous accident to happen. And these were not the realities of the Carnegie Hall recital at which not only I but everyone else waited in anticipation not of witnessing a disastrous accident but of marveling at the beautiful performances that were free of the eccentricities and perversities Gould was able to insert into his recorded performances.

Not only did the recording studio's technology make it possible for him to play at close microphone range for listeners who didn't disturb him with their physical presence, but it created the possiblity—described in his article *The Prospects of Recording*—for the listener to create his own ideal performance of a movement of a Beethoven symphony by splicing passages of the performance recorded, say, by Bruno Walter, with passages from the performance recorded, say, by Klemperer. (When, during the preparation of the article, he asked what I thought of this, I said the rights of the owner of a record were limited to his listening to it.) On a later flight of his technology trip he said that "once introduced into the circuitry of art, the technological presence must be encoded and decoded . . . in such a way that its presence is . . . at the service of that spiritual good that ultimately will . . . banish art itself." Also, as a singularly reclusive person who eventually restricted personal communication—with an interviewer, for example—to the telephone, he could believe that technology, in offering the possibility of communication in isolation, "possesses mediative power which can minimize, or even eliminate, the competitive follies which absorb so large a share of human activity." And one of those who shared Payzant's view of Gould as a thinker cited as memorable his statement of how technology might save man from self-destruction:

> Computers can store so much information that the day may come when our national leaders will first read a computer printout before arriving at a decision. Since the printout would contain masses of factual information, the decision-maker might be guided by its message rather than "gut feelings" or advice from "experts." Thus, man would more likely be guided by reason than emotion.

Worth mention, it seems to me, is an exchange in 1964. Gould, in a letter, suggested a lengthy essay in which I would explain the bias against Bach that produced my many statements about works of his being dull; and I replied that those statements represented neither a bias against Bach (since I spoke also of the greatness of some of his works), nor a general theoretic position that I could formulate, but instead my immediate perception of the quality of each work considered individually—the perception that Bach applied his technical powers and procedures now to musical ideas whose quality made the result a great work, and now to ideas whose quality made it a dull one. It seemed to me that Gould's attention was concentrated on the technical operation in a piece of music—which made every work of Bach's fascinating for him; whereas mine was given to the musical substance the technical operation was concerned with in a piece—which made some of Bach's works dull for me. And I added that when I spoke of the quality of musical ideas I meant their expressive communication—which I can't recall Gould ever saying anything about. (*High Fidelity/Musical America*, August 1984)

Notable Writing on Music

In theory the music critic is the professional listener, who has the equipment of perception, judgment and taste which the non-professional listeners who read him do not have, and which he uses to make them aware of what they might miss in a piece of music or a performance. In fact most of the writing about music—in newspapers, magazines, books—is done by people who lack the judgment and taste needed to evaluate correctly what they have heard, and even the perception needed to hear it accurately. Their use of the critic's terminology gives an appearance of such perception and judgment to writing in which in reality the terminology is applied incorrectly. Fortunately there have been occasional exceptions, three of them outstanding: on the one hand Donald Tovey, a professionally trained musician and scholar who wrote with an accuracy of mind and a literary skill not characteristic of musical professionals; and on the other hand two literary professionals with extraordinary sensitivity to music, Bernard Shaw in the 1890s, and W. J. Turner in the 1920s and 30s. And in 1960 I learned of another outstanding exception when readers sent me clippings from *The Spectator* of articles by David Cairns—impressive in their perception and judgment, their liveliness of mind and literary style—about the Covent Garden production of Berlioz's *Les Troyens*. Clippings of Cairns's articles continued to arrive irregularly until a few years ago, when he appeared to have given up journalism for other writing: notes for Colin Davis's recordings of Berlioz; the translation of Berlioz's *Memoirs* that was universally praised as a remarkable equivalent in English of Berlioz's vivid and impassioned French, but that in fact had Berlioz writing in the unimpassioned manner of a well-bred Londoner. (*"Que d'abominables*

Notable Writing on Music

sottises j'ai entendu dire aux uns et aux autres sur ces merveilles de savoir et d'inspiration!" Berlioz exclaimed about the response in Paris to Beethoven's symphonies; "I have heard them airing the most lamentable nonsense about these marvels of beauty and technical mastery," Cairns had him remark.)

But now a collection of Cairns's critical writing, *Responses*, has been published here which includes some—about Beethoven's *Fidelio*, Verdi's *Falstaff*, Mozart's *Idomeneo*, Schubert's large-scale works—that is as good as I have ever read. Its high value derives from the fact that Cairns has managed not to do what other writers usually do when they have occasion to hear the music, which is to listen with minds filled with the generally accepted ideas about it, and therefore to hear what those ideas lead them to expect to hear. He has been able, when listening, to keep everything out of his mind except the music reaching his ears; and he reports what he heard and the conclusions it led him to that contradict the generally accepted ideas. Thus *Idomeneo* was regarded for almost two centuries as "a noble fossil" by those whose minds were too full of their knowledge of what made *opera seria* a lifeless genre to be able to hear the life in Mozart's music; whereas Cairns, having listened to this music, writes: "To know *Idomeneo* is to discover one of the marvels of dramatic music."

> . . . The test with any musical form is what it becomes in the hands of the particular composer. It is above all a test we must not forget when the composer is Mozart. With Mozart, the genre is what he makes of it. . . . In *Idomeneo* we watch Mozart making of it very largely what he wants. No work more strikingly demonstrates his ability to take a convention and put it to his own transcendent purposes. Far from being inhibited by it, he uses it to create music which rarely falters in its dramatic impetus and which is not surpassed in grandeur and intensity by any of the later masterpieces.

And he makes a similar point about *Fidelio*, which is "a flawed work by a composer of genius wrestling with an uncongenial art form" for those who, listening, hear only the mixture of genres which they know from the generally accepted idea of *Fidelio* to be a major flaw in it. But Cairns's listening has provided him with the evidence he presents for his belief that the work is one of "the supreme masterpieces in any medium," and specifically "a dramatic masterpiece" whose mixture of genres represents not Beethoven's inexperience in opera but "the freedom of mastery [that] uses whatever [the work] needs, to say what it has to say. . . . The work is true to its own laws. They are the only ones that matter." Moreover, having listened also to the original version of 1805, Cairns is able to demonstrate—in reply to the *"Urtext*-obsessed" musicologists' demand for a return to that original version—that the stripping away of its "beautiful elaboration and conventional repetition" produces the "devastating directness of the final version we know," and to characterize "the clear-sighted ruthlessness of the musical revisions that produced the final form" as "a feat of artistic discipline with few equals in the history of music."

More important is Cairns's similar dealing with Schubert, since it is concerned with what impels Cairns to ask, "Is there a comparable case of a great composer—one that many would unhesitatingly place among the half-dozen supreme creators . . . whom commentators feel so free to patronize; a master who is so often approached in the expectation of finding weaknesses?" Cairns can see how the surface appearance of ease and abundance gave plausibility to the view of Schubert as a purely instinctive composer who achieved extraordinarily beautiful lyrical utterance by inspiration, not by disciplined thought; and how this view could raise doubts of his capacity for the large-scale construction that required such thought. But these doubts should have been removed by "the towering form of the Great C major Symphony, a work of ferocious mastery on the grandest scale"—and indeed by the other large-scale works. And what critical opinion heard in these works as evidence of Schubert's inability to handle the forms he had taken over from his predecessors, Cairns can hear as evidence rather of his handling them in his own way. Listening with the belief that Schubert, like every artist, was entitled to that own way, and must be judged by what it achieved in each particular work, Cairns presents convincing evidence for his conclusion that

> short though it was, his life was long enough for the naive, instinctive genius to develop into an articulate and single-minded artist, and to achieve, in a dozen richly original masterpieces, a disciplining and organization of his miraculous talent, an assertion of creative self-reliance and pertinacity . . . that was perhaps the most miraculous thing of all.

I have so far been discussing the statements of Cairns that are confirmed by my own experience (the critic writes not what is true, period, but what is true for *him*, and what becomes true for the reader who finds it is verified by what he hears); and I must add that some of the things he says—for example about the greatness of Tippett's opera *A Midsummer Marriage* and Elgar's First Symphony—are contradicted for me by what I heard. Similarly my experience enables me to recognize the faults Cairns describes in the Zeffirelli production of *Don Giovanni* and to share his disapproval if it, but causes me to share Victor Gollanez's disapproval, rather than Cairns's approval, of the manner of staging opera initiated by Wieland Wagner at Bayreuth. It enables me also to appreciate the accurate perception Cairns shows in his pointing out of the flaw in Fischer-Dieskau's otherwise admirable singing of *Lieder*, and in his description of Karajan's unadmirable use of his impressive gifts; but to recall, on the other hand, the actual nervelessness and feebleness of what Cairns cites as the marvels of the old recorded Furtwängler performance of Act I of *Die Walküre*. Moreover, I hear with Cairns the Furtwängler "idiosyncrasies" of tempo that destroy shape in the music; but not the revelations, in place of this outer shape, of "the music's inner life," its inner organic unity. And I find a misstatement of the issue between Furtwängler and Toscanini ("who despised him," Cairns mentions) in the further comment that sets against each other Toscanini's alleged insistence that a performance produce only and exactly the notes in the score, and Furtwängler's search for the life and organic unity beyond and around the notes; Toscanini's alleged insistence that adherence to the score produced the one correct performance of the work, and Furtwängler's belief tht the score was "not a blueprint but an encouragement to re-creation" which might produce a variety of conclusions. (Even his destructive idiosyncrasies of tempo must therefore command respect, according to Cairns, since they show there is no one correct way of performing a work; but how these destructive idiosyncrasies can show the possibility of any correct way of performing a work is something only the Cairns mind can see.)

Actually, Toscanini didn't hold the beliefs Cairns attributes to him. He did insist that the score was what a conductor had to begin with; but his understanding that there was something the conductor had to add to what was in the score was evident in his statement to me once about the need, in performing Mozart, to know what had to be done between the *piano* in the score here and the *forte* eight measures later; in the profusion of subtle inflections marked between the *pianos* and the *fortes* in his score of Mozart's Divertimento K. 287; in the actual profusion of inflection between them that is to be heard in his recorded performance of the piece. And the evidence of his understanding that this way of dealing with the score could result in more than one correct performance was his delight in the performances of Guido Cantelli that adhered as strictly to the score as Toscanini's but were strikingly different from his. On the other hand, listening in Salzburg to the beginning of Furtwängler's performance of Beethoven's Ninth, Toscanini despised the conductor who couldn't get the two horns to play the two notes of their opening fifth precisely together; and continuing to listen as one whose own performances exhibited, in W. J. Turner's words, "subtle variation of tempo . . . always in the service of [a] shape . . . derived from the rightful expression of the music," Toscanini despised the musician whose extravagances in variation of tempo and volume produced distortions of shape and excesses in expression.

It is worth noting that Furtwängler responded by professing disdain for the technical accuracy that he said (to the conductor Hans Schwieger) fitted Toscanini only for the conducting of a military band, and maintaining that "I begin to make music where this man stops." One can understand this being said by a vain man accustomed to triumph after triumph with the public, who could not endure this public's lessened response to him—notably in New York in 1926—after it had heard Toscanini, and could not forgive the man responsible for what he felt as an intolerable humiliation. But it is astounding that it was believed by others who could be expected to hear that Toscanini did not stop with technical accuracy. And the explanation I have arrived at is that they were the dupes of an extraordinarily gifted musical demagogue who was able to get himself thought of as—in Cairns's words—"one of the supreme interpretative musicians of the 20th century." (*Commentary*, January 1974)

"Editors," as Bernard Shaw wrote, "by some law of Nature which still baffles science, are always ignorant of music"; and so "an editor who can tell at a glance whether . . . a leading article . . . or a news report is the work of a skilled hand or not" will accept from a music critic "every conceivable blunder and misdemeanor that a journalist can commit." Nor was Harold Ross an exception: in the years in which he was publishing in *The New Yorker* the work of the remarkable writers he had gathered on his staff, he was content with writing on music that was not worth reading either for what it said about music or for any intellectual or literary distinction. And this continued to be true of *The New Yorker* long after Ross had been succeeded by William Shawn. But in the fall of 1972 a London music critic named Andrew Porter, whom *The New Yorker* brought here as guest reviewer for the season, began to write the reviews and essays that are reprinted in *A Musical Season*. I had first learned of Porter's writing when someone had shown me his reviews of a New York City Ballet season in London, which had delighted me with their accurate perception. And after that readers had occasionally sent me his reviews of opera recordings in *The Gramophone*—almost the only competent reviews in that magazine—which had shown him to be as perceptive about music as about ballet. The 37 weekly round-ups in *A Musical Season* confirm those impressions but also provide puzzling surprises.

Since his eye noted that the Washington Opera Society performance of *L'Incoronazione di Poppea* "moved swiftly, in a striking unit set by Neil Peter Jampolis," I am surprised by a comment on the Metroplitan's *Don Giovanni* in which he speaks of Herbert Graf's production—"firm, traditional, and apt; though old, it remains fresh"—but isn't impelled to say anything about Eugene Berman's scenery, which not only is extraordinarily beautiful and dramatically effective, but is remarkably devised for the swift movement of this particular opera without the usual interruptions between its scenes.* And I am astonished by the statement about the New York City Opera's "very decent repertory *Carmen*" with José Varona's "traditional" sets—this about a first act cluttered with newly devised scenic details which obscure the scene's essentials but make possible the happenings thought up by Tito Capobianco that distract attention from the principals' singing and action. Nor do the words "wonderful, and impressive," which Porter applies to the Schneider-Siemssen scenery for the von Karajan staging of Wagner's *Ring*, seem to me applicable to, among other unmentioned details, the hollowed-out base of an enormous tree that Schneider-Siemssen substitutes for the room in Hunding's hut as the performance area of the first act of *Die Walküre*—one that repeatedly draws attention to its deficiencies and occasional absurdities in relation to the action. And I am amazed by Porter's characterizing Zeffirelli's eccentrically and senselessly innovative production of *Otello* for the Metropolitan as "basically conven-

---

*(1981) He did, a few years later, refer to the Berman scenery as "heavy".

tional", and its innovations—which damage the scenes of the choral homage to Desdemona and Otello's overhearing of Cassio—as "clever solutions to the tricky points of stage disposition (the garden chorus, the overhearing scene)", when in reality the only "tricky points" in the scenes are the ones created by Zeffirelli's "clever solutions".*

Porter is generally accurate about what he has heard—the superb singing of Jon Vickers and Teresa Zylis-Gara in *Otello*, Murray Perahia's beautiful playing in a Mozart piano concerto, Erich Leinsdorf's insensitive conducting of *Die Walküre*, among many examples. But here too there are surprises. He begins a review by illuminating for his readers the art of the *Lieder*-singer:

> The poet's lines must suggest to her the unwritten details of rhythmic phrasing: here a sweet, lingering accent, there a sudden urgent advance. Verbal sense will indicate the vocal hues. Yet vivid declamation is not in itself enough; *Lieder*-singing, like just about every other kind of music-making, needs a command of pure line—line that is beautiful and eloquent in an "absolute" way.

And a passing reference, many pages later, to "Elena Gerhardt, the greatest of *Lieder*-stylists," suggests that he learned from her wonderful recorded performances what he describes so well. Anyone capable of appreciating those performances should be able to hear that some of Elisabeth Schwarzkopf's performances are beautiful examples of the *Lieder*-singer's art, but others are flawed by excessively mannered and affected phrasing and expressive hamming—exaggerated pouting, archness, gasps, whispers—that reveal a lack of Gerhardt's controlling sense of measure and fitness, which is to say her unfailing taste. And having heard all this at Schwarzkopf's recitals and on her records for twenty years, I am dumbfounded when Porter tells his readers that "Elisabeth Schwarzkopf is of all *Lieder*-singers before the public today the most accomplished," and fills two pages with the details of the marvels at her recital, without a word about the occasional flaws in her performances.

On the other hand he begins a review of the New York City Opera production of Monteverdi's *L'Incoronazione di Poppea*—a work outside of the operatic repertory that musicians and the public know—with an enlightening description of the dramatic character and musical style of the work; the problems created for its performance today by the incomplete notation of its musical substance and instrumentation, the un-

*See p. 167.

familiarity with the manner of its performance, the voices it was written for; and what Porter thinks is wrong with the Raymond Leppard performance version—all this to establish the basis for Porter's criticisms of the way this version was used, staged, acted, and sung by the New York City Opera. The review shows Porter to be, like Donald Tovey, an example of the rare combination of authoritative scholar and perceptive critic (and I think it important to understand that the scholar's *knowledge about*, and the critic's *perception of*, a work are different things, and don't necessarily occur together: Bernard Shaw and W. J. Turner, who were not musical scholars, were great critics; Paul Henry Lang demonstrated in the *Herald Tribune*, and David Hamilton has recently demonstrated as Porter's temporary substitute in *The New Yorker*, that a scholar's knowledge doesn't give him the critic's perception and judgment).

The review also is an instance of a scholar's knowledge being useful to performers and listeners—which Porter is mistaken in thinking it always is. He has the scholar's infatuation with scholarly activity seemingly unrestrained by regard for the value of what it is concerned with. Unlike the information about *L'Incoronazione*, the three pages about the sources of the libretto of *The Magic Flute* are uninteresting and not necessary, as Porter says they are, for someone to be stirred by the work or to recognize what has made a performance effective or the opposite. And I can't imagine *New Yorker* readers sharing the interest in "a neglected byway of musical history" that impels Porter to devote several pages to discussion of an opera, Zandonai's *Francesca da Rimini*, which, in the end, he establishes has little musical value or music-dramatic effect; or the interest in anything and everything contemporary that impels Porter to discuss at length a work of "flawless mediocrity," von Einem's *The Visit of the Old Lady*, or even the works of Henze that Porter admires inordinately. Moreover, it is true that someone producing an 18th-century opera needs the information a music historian can provide about the character and range of the voices of the *castrati* who sang some of the roles, in order to decide what voices to use today; it is not true, as Porter contends, that a soprano of today, in order to sing a role in a Haydn opera, needs to know what the historian can tell her about the soprano Haydn wrote the role for. Capobianco reveals lack of historical understanding in having Elizabeth and Leicester roll on the floor in Donizetti's *Maria Stuarda*; but the poignancy of Beverly Sills's singing of the two notes of Mary Stuart's "*Ah! si*" does not demonstrate, as Porter contends, that historical understanding is required for Donizetti's music, and Mozart's, and Mahler's, to "yield its full eloquence." And the 1915 Metropolitan *Il Trovatore* that was talked about for decades thereafter was produced by Toscanini without Martin Chusid's treatises on tonal structure in *Rigoletto* and *La Traviata*, which Porter, reviewing a Metropolitan performance of *Il Trovatore*, thinks "should be mastered by the men . . . directing [the] performers" in Verdi's operas at the Metropolitan.

But one must, in conclusion, apply to Porter what Tovey said of Schubert, and say that his occasional inequalities of performance cannot make him a critic of less than the highest rank. (*Commentary*, October 1974)

Though a music critic is presumed to be a professional listener with the special powers of perception and judgment that enable him to make his non-professional readers aware of what they might not notice by themselves, in practice what he says is found to be true by some readers when they listen and not by others. For a piece of music is a communication of a special kind, representing the operation of the composer's sensitivity to his medium of sound moving in time and—through this sensitivity—his personal resources of mind, emotion and the rest; and what it communicates is affected by the differences in its *recipients'* sensitivity to the medium and *their* personal resources. What a critic reports, then, is not the single possible truth about a piece of music or a performance, but what is true for him and becomes true for the readers who find it confirmed when they listen. And to say that two of the past year's books—the collections of reviews and articles in Robert Craft's *Prejudices in Disguise* and Andrew Porter's *A Musical Season*—were made notable for me by their authors' possession of the critic's essential equipment of perception and judgment, is to say that as a reader I found in the writing a great deal that was confirmed by my experience as a listener—enough to outweigh the statements that my experience contradicted.

Whereas Porter is a professional reviewer whom *The New Yorker* brought from London to provide its readers with the weekly reports and comments on musical events of the season of 1972-73 that are reprinted in his book, Craft is a musician, a conductor whose first concerts in the late '40s revealed gifts that impressed not only outsiders like myself but insiders like Stravinsky; who continued his conducting during the many years of his association with Stravinsky; and whose writing was something he began to do with Stravinsky in their books of conversations and then continued to do on his own. *Prejudices in Disguise* contains the reviews of some events of that 1972-73 season that Craft wrote for *World*, and in addition his occasional articles on other subjects for other publications. And the surprising thing is that although he limited his conducting almost entirely to the works of Stravinsky, Schönberg and Webern, his book contains only one article on Solti's concert performance in Chicago of Schönberg's *Erwartung* and another on his stage performance in Paris of Schönberg's *Moses and Aaron*. For Craft *Moses and Aaron* is "one of the handful of twentieth-century operas with contemporary musical and dramatic power" and "deserves precedence over the Delius and Britten, Henze and Ginastera operas that have been included in the recent repertories"; for me—and I am sure for the majority of the musical public—it communicates, like most of Schönberg's music, no expressive sense or mere internal coherence in the sounds that are unpleasant to the ear; and one is surprised as well as pleased by the large number of articles of Craft on music which that majority of the public is interested in— Bach's contatas, Mozart's piano concertos, the music of Schubert, Chopin, Brahms, Mahler, Berlioz's *Benvenuto Cellini*, Glinka's operas, Wagner's *Ring* music-dramas.

Porter, on the contrary, writes comparatively little about the music that interests most of his *New Yorker* readers, and a great deal about the music of today—by Boulez, Henze, Ginastera, Elliott Carter, George Crumb and dozens of others—which those readers probably find even more eccentric, outlandish, meaningless and unattractive to the ear than Schönberg's. This represents Porter's agreement with Boulez about the necessity of making the music of our own time an integral part of our concert life; but his readers may not want that much of the music of our time in the concert hall and that much writing about it in *The New Yorker*. After a review of Porter's book in which I characterized him as a critic of the highest rank, a musician wrote in reply that even if Porter's perceptions were clear he was boring to read; and it may have been all the writing about the music of our time that bored this musician.

It may also have been something else. One reads on the jacket of the book that Porter's "erudite and beautifully crafted reviews . . . have often been compared with the music commentaries of George Bernard Shaw";

but I see no basis for this comparison. For one thing, Shaw is not erudite; he is a perceptive critic who is not a scholar; and though Porter is one of the rare examples of a scholar who is also a perceptive critic, he is, like most scholars, compulsively erudite and unable to recognize that the pages and pages of historical and musicological minutiae that fascinate him may be found boring, exasperating and unreadable by readers of *The New Yorker*.

As for style of writing, the striking difference between Shaw's and Porter's is precisely the high-spirited spontaneity of Shaw's as against the obvious studied "crafting" of Porter's that becomes tiresome. Moreover it isn't only the words that are crafted but the ideas; so that one gets things like this:

> Ballet began when Terpsichore touched Apollo's finger, as on the Sistine ceiling God touches Adam's, and inspired a *pas de deux* in which movement became form and bodies learned to speak and sing—a *pas de deux* that whenever it is re-enacted holds implicit in its plastic images all dance, past, present, and future. This symbolic moment outside time, when Terpsichore joined her sisters Polyhymnia and Calliope on equal terms, was first shaped in mortal history on June 12, 1928, on the stage of the Théâtre Sarah-Bernhardt in Paris: in cold print it is recorded just before rehearsal-figure 64 of Stravinsky's score *Apollo Musagetes*.

In reality the art of ballet did not begin with Balanchine's *Apollo; Apollo* itself does not begin with the *pas de deux* described by Porter, but is preceded by the wonderful *pas d'action* of Apollo and the three Muses and their solos; and Porter's over-crafted fantasy about the *pas de deux* is one of the regrettable inequalities (to use Tovey's term) in the performance of a critic who, looking at the courtiers' stately sarabande at the beginning of Act 2 of Balanchine's *Don Quixote*, could perceive how in "the cold, precise [dance] . . . aristocratic formality suddenly takes on the accents of menace to suggest the Spain of Philip II." (*New Republic*, 29 November 1975)

More of the New Higher Music Criticism

My first encounter with this writing that professed to describe what I neither could hear when I listened to the music, nor discover in the printed score of the work, was provided by a few articles in *The Nation* years ago by someone new to me named Benjamin Boretz. My comment on it in *The Hudson Review* caused a composer I knew to assure me that Boretz was a good musician. And when I said I had expressed an opinion only of what Boretz had written in *The Nation*, the composer exclaimed plaintively: "Yes, but they're all writing like that! It's the influence of Babbitt at Princeton." He was referring to the writers in the magazine *Perspectives of New Music*, published at Princeton, with Boretz as one of the editors; and my impression at that time was that this magazine was the outgrowth of a seminar on music criticism at Princeton a few years earlier.

I next ecountered this writing associated with Princeton in *The Classical Style*, the book by Charles Rosen, another Princeton graduate (with a PhD degree in French literature). The book's subject had been dealt with at length by the great English scholar and teacher Donald Tovey in his *Essays in Musical Analysis*, which for many years have provided a non-academic musical education for countless musicians and music-lovers; and Rosen's references to Tovey caused one enthusiastic reviewer to perceive "Tovey's catalyzing influence . . . on virtually every page," and to credit Rosen with "fill[ing] out and consolidat[ing] Tovey's view of the classical revolution" in the generalizations he said Tovey had failed to draw from his analyses of particular works of Haydn, Mozart and Beethoven. And he pointed out Rosen's insistence that "the priorities of the ear must be respected," his adherence to Tovey's guiding principle that one "should never set down anything that his ear has not recognized apart from the appearance on the printed page," which made Rosen "a sensitive guide to this music," and his book one "definitely for the intelligent general reader, not for the specialist alone."

But actually Tovey did draw generalizations from his analyses of particular works, such as this statement about Haydn and Mozart:

> [Haydn] is rightly believed to be on a level with Mozart as a master of form; but his form is described as 'regular and symmetrical' . . . [But] Haydn's most nearly regular works are his earlier ones, when he wrote on the lines of J.C. and C.P.E. Bach; whereas his freedom of form becomes manifest just about the time when he came to know Mozart. The mutual influence of Haydn and Mozart is one of the best known wonders of musical history; and the paradox of it is that while its effect on Mozart was to concentrate his style and strengthen his symmetry, the effect on Haydn was to set him free, so that his large movements became as capricious in their extended course of events as his minuets had always been in the cast of their phrases.

Also, Tovey did set down, in the generalizations as well as the analyses of particular works, only what his ear had heard apart from the appearance on the printed page, and what the reader's ear could hear after reading him. And actually Rosen—after proclaiming the priority of the ear in his words—did *not* respect that priority in his practice, setting down about passages of music in his book what, on the contrary, the eye could see on the printed page but the ear could not hear. This was true of the cello's four Fs, in bars 26-9 of the first movement of Haydn's Quartet Op. 50 No. 6, that one was, according to Rosen, to continue to hear— while one followed the activity of the four strings in the next eight bars—as the anticipation, the preparation of the F-major chord in bar 38. I found it hard to believe Rosen's ear had recognized this apart from the printed page; *my* ear couldn't hear it even *with* what I saw on the printed page; and I couldn't imagine the general reader being able to hear it. So with the numerous occurrences of the note E to which Rosen directed the reader's attention in that movement; and with the things he pointed to in the passages from Beethoven's *Hammerklavier* Sonata, Mozart's Piano Concerto K. 488 and other works: they were things the general reader couldn't hear (which consequently provided him with no guidance, and were not ascribable to the ideas and influence of Tovey).

Next, as it happened, there was the article on Tovey by another Princeton graduate, Joseph Kerman, in *The American Scholar*. Kerman respected Tovey in spite of what he thought were limitations based on conceptual errors. Tovey's primary belief, said Kerman, was that "everything of esthetic importance in music lies within the province of his famous 'naive listener' "—the person "with no specific musical training, only a willing ear and a ready sensibility"; and for this listener he wrote as "a 'foreground' analyst . . . an analyst of the rhythmic surface of music." Even when he wrote for professionals "he always assumed that they experienced music on its rhythmic surface. For that is where he considered that its esthetic effects are made, effects that are democratically available to all, irrespective of musical training, and that he assumed to be the central interest of all listeners, whether amateur or professional." But the "modern musical analysis" that is "directed to a strictly professional readership" penetrates below the surface, behind the foreground, to "some sort of background . . . as in Schenker." It was not Schenker whom Kerman quoted for the modern analyst's position as against Tovey's, but Hans Keller (who after the last war began to make the air of the London musical scene hideous with his wide-of-the-mark ponderous ferocities). Tovey's writings, according to Keller,

> are a symptom of a social tragedy, for they are both a function of the stupidity of his audiences, the musical *nouveaux riches*, and too much of a mere reaction against the unmusicality of his academic forbears. . . . "The pianoforte enters," reports Tovey [concerning the beginning of Mozart's Concerto K. 503], "at first with scattered phrases. These quickly settle into a stream of florid melody. . . ." But why are they scattered? How are they scattered? Why are they scattered in the way they are scattered? What, in short, is the compositorial cause of these absolutely unprecedented, utterly "new" triplets?

("What *is* the moon?" Captain Boyle asks himself in *Juno and the Paycock*. "What *is* the stars?") And Kerman's comment was that "rather than looking backward from the music he described to compositorial causes . . . Tovey looked forward from the music to its esthetic effect"—evidently, for Kerman, a regrettable error.

Reading all this one had to translate; and I translated the "rhythmic surface" Kerman said Tovey dealt with as what one could hear happening in the music, and the things Boretz, Rosen, Kerman, Keller and their associates disclosed below that surface as what one could not hear.

At this point I felt I should investigate the seminar on criticism that I thought had been held at Princeton; and it turned out to have been instead The Princeton Seminar in Advanced Musical Studies, published in 1960 as *Problems of Modern Music*, in which I found a paper, *Analysis Today*, by Edward T. Cone of Princeton, who wrote that "true analysis works through and for the ear. The greatest analysts (like Schenker at his best) are those with the keenest ears; their insights reveal how a piece of music should be heard, which in turn implies how it should be played." And Cone demonstrated this in the passage in the second movement of Beethoven's Piano Sonata Op. 109 in which—the middle section having quieted down to a final soft chord—the quiet is broken by the vehement opening phrases of the movement that begin the recapitulation of the first section. To the effect of the abrupt dynamic change from soft to loud without a transitional crescendo Beethoven adds the effect of the abrupt harmonic progression of the (soft) chord on the second step of E minor (designated therefore as II sharp) going *directly* to the (loud) chord on the first step (designated as I) without the prescribed transitional chord on the fifth step (V). Beethoven clearly wants the greatest shock effect, for the ear, of the lack of relation between the end of the middle section and the beginning of the recapitulation. But for Cone it was only "from a narrowly descriptive point of view [that] one could call this [omission of V] an ellipsis. . . . Looking ahead, . . . one will find that the first phrase of the recapitulation ends on V, and its consequent on I. The puzzling II sharp, then, only temporarily and apparently resolved by what immediately follows it, actually points ahead in such a way that the whole passage is bound together in a cadential II-V-I." And then, "I need hardly mention the obvious effects of such an analysis on the performance of this passage. Whatever doubts one had as to the proper placing of the main accent in these phrases when they first appeared can now be resolved; the exposition can be reinterpreted . . . in the new light of the recapitulation."

But I, on the contrary, considered it very necessary for Cone to spell out what I found anything but obvious from those summary statements. I needed to be told what was doubtful about the placing of what accent at what point; for Beethoven's directions seemed to me to leave nothing in doubt. What they made clear to me was that if one obeyed them—if one made the end of the middle section soft and the beginning of the recapitulation loud—one heard not the cadential II-V-I of Cone's analysis but II-I-V-I; and that the only way to make Cone's II-V-I audible to the listener was to reverse Beethoven's directions by emphasizing the final chord of the middle section, subduing the beginning of the first phrase of the recapitulation, and banging out its conclusion—which would produce a monstrous falsification of the music. And if reinterpreting the exposition in the new light of the recapitulation meant falsifying the opening phrase of the exposition in the same way as that of the recapitulation, I needed to be told why this should be done.

The unexpected and astonishing conclusion to all this was provided by a statement of Rosen's to someone who passed it on to me—that "Haggin doesn't know diagrammatic writing. He thinks you have to hear it." (*New Republic*, 7 October 1977)

Violette Verdy

Ballerina, by Victoria Huckenpahler, is made more informative and interesting than other books of its kind by Verdy's unusual candor about living persons (not all living persons—not Jerome Robbins, for example—but some, including Balanchine), and is enlivened by frequent quotations of this perceptive and vivaciously articulate artist's own words. We learn that—born in 1933 in a little town in Brittany—she manifested in infancy a sensitivity to music, and in early childhood an impulse to dance to it, that led to her being taken to Paris at the age of nine for disciplined study of dancing; that Roland Petit gave her a small part in one of his ballets when she was only twelve; that her continuing association with him brought her bigger roles and increased recognition, and at the age of sixteen the leading role in a film, *Ballerina*, in which—when it was shown here a few years ago—one was amazed to see the distinctive Verdy style fully achieved. We learn further that tours with Petit made her known in other European countries and the United States, and brought her engagements with other companies which provided opportunities to dance in excerpts or acts of the classics—*Coppélia, Swan Lake, The Nutcracker, The Sleeping Beauty, Les Sylphides*—and eventually in the Ballet Rambert productions of *Coppélia, Swan Lake* and *Giselle* in their entirety; and that a film of her performance in the *Nutcracker Pas de Deux* seen by Nora Kaye led to an engagement with American Ballet Theatre in 1957.

American Ballet Theatre brought two ballet greats into her career. One was Erik Bruhn, a dancer with dedication like hers—"the same love and comprehension for the true classic dance," she wrote to her mother, "for proper preparation . . . for total realization"—that created complete

74

understanding between them. The other was Balanchine, in whose *Theme and Variations* she encountered "choreography . . . of an exceptional beauty and purity" and "everything that is capable of transporting me." Balanchine—who had seen her in Paris in Petit's *Le Loup* and in Doubrovska's *pointe* class at the School of American Ballet when the Petit company had been in New York—saw her again with American Ballet Theatre; and when it was disbanded temporarily in 1958 he invited her to join the New York City Ballet. We are told that Verdy—offered "this chance of a lifetime"—"accepted the challenge without a moment's hesitancy;" we are not told what she said to an interviewer in 1972—that if she had not accepted she "could have made a career with Bruhn," with whom she felt she "would have achieved perfection in classicism and dramatic roles;" and that she had chosen instead to become "one of the instruments of Balanchine—the eternal creator."

She was impelled to this choice not only by the creative powers, but by the sensitivity to music, that Balanchine revealed in his choreography—as he had been led to invite her into his company not only by the technical perfection and distinctive style, but by the musical sensitivity of her dancing. They met, she said, "on a field of musicality." And for Edward Villella, talking in 1963, her "extraordinary, complete musical understanding, almost like Balanchine's, in the way she can make you *see* the music," had a great deal to do with her amazing ability to understand a new role—whether in a new ballet like *Episodes* in 1959, *The Figure in the Carpet*, *Tchaikovsky Pas de Deux* and *Liebeslieder Walzer* in 1960, the second-act divertissement in *A Midsummer Night's Dream* in 1962, or in a work of the existing repertory—and develop it immediately as she learned the steps. Villella also remarked on how "this French dancer, coming here to another style and another repertory . . . brought out things in roles that were always there . . . but that other dancers just didn't bring out. . . . Everything she did she made her own—she made a real performance of." But it turned out that Balanchine felt differently about the Verdy way of dealing with roles—about what is described in the book as her "tendency to punctuate Balanchine's choreography with personal comment" which was "not always appreciated." ("Don't perform; just do the steps," I was to hear him say to her at a rehearsal of *La Source* in 1968.) We are told that "he was accustomed to dancers . . . who accepted [what he devised for them] unquestioningly, whereas in Violette he was dealing with an intelligence that had to add something of its own . . . to his [choreography.]" And not only with that intelligence but with what she calls her "strong, independent personality," fortified by her years of experience in other companies, which made her "not always as manageable as I should have been."

This she recognized as a major cause of his lessened use of her after the first years; and she recognized as another important cause the injuries necessitating surgery that kept her out of action from May 1964 to April 1966, and again for periods of months in 1973 and 74. To be out of action was to be out of Balanchine's sight; and since it was seeing how dancers moved in class, in rehearsal, in performance, that gave him ideas for use of them, not seeing Verdy for two years while he saw other dancers had the result that when she returned the others had replaced her in his mind. Moreover, she could only rarely take his company class, which was now too strenuous for her. Actually he did—for the "pleasurable novelty" of her musical sensitiveness, her "stage security . . . and sense of total theatre" acquired in previous professional experience—continue his occasional "choreographic venture" with her that was "geared to her particular strengths": in *Jewels* and *Glinkiana* in 1967, *La Source* in 1968, her breathtaking solo in the first performances of *Pulcinella* in 1972. This was not, for her, a sufficient use of her energies; but she accepted it because after her injuries "I am so glad that I can dance at all," and because even the lessened work with Balanchine was an enriching experience not to be given up. Fortunately her morale was sustained by out-of-town appearances in *Giselle*, *La Sylphide* and *Swan Lake* (the complete ballet) with Villella, *The Sleeping Beauty* with Peter Martins, without which, she says, "I might have had to defect."

In the fall of 1975, therefore, in anticipation of what she was to dance in that year—a few performances of *Symphony in C*, *Swan Lake* Act 2, *Donizetti Variations*, *Raymonda Variations*, *Emeralds* and *Sonatine*—she remarked, "I am returning to my retirement;" and at the end of that year one expected to continue to see her in a few works of the company's repertory in the three or four years she thought she could continue to dance. But these expectations were ended by her acceptance of the directorship of the Paris Opera Ballet; and the reasons for this acceptance given in the book don't include what she said privately had been the decisive reason. One would have thought that Balanchine—from a feeling of obligation to his work, to Verdy, to the public—would want *Emeralds* to be performed as effectively as only Verdy could perform it, for as long as she was available for it; but in the seasons of 1975-76—not once but a few times—he had the undistinguished Christine Redpath dance ineffectively in Verdy's place (with the dumbfounding explanation once that Redpath had nothing else to dance that week). The Paris Opera offered Verdy an escape from a situation with which she said she "could no longer cope;" and one must grieve not only over the waste of a great artist's energies in a notoriously hopeless administrative task, but over the loss of those three or four years of unique performances. (*Ballet News*, April 1980)

Peter Martins

We first heard of Peter Martins in the summer of 1967 when—having that year, at the age of 21, been promoted to principal dancer in the Royal Danish Ballet, and in the spring assigned to Balanchine's *Apollo*—he flew to Edinburgh to dance in it with the New York City Ballet in place of Jacques d'Amboise, who had been injured. And a few months later, when he came here for a few weeks of guest performances with the company in *The Nutcracker* and *Apollo*, we saw the distinctive style of his unassertively doing what was at all times extraordinary: the unstraining execution of brilliant technical feats, the partnering that framed with heightening effect the movements of Suzanne Farrell—for whom his height and youthful handsomeness made him the predestined partner—and, in one of the *Nutcracker* performances, Mimi Paul. That style made his performances in *Apollo* also individual and special—i.e. different, not only from the stiff, pompous performances by d'Amboise we had been seeing for years, but from the few beautiful performances we had seen by Edward Villella and Conrad Ludlow. To these performances of *Apollo* with Farrell as Terpischore he added his partnering of her in *Diamonds* and *Liebeslieder Walzer*.

Understandably, after these demonstrations of what he could do, he was invited for longer periods in 1968-69, in which he demonstrated it in additional roles—the first movement of *Symphony in C*, *Swan Lake*, *Ballet Imperial* (now *Tchaikovsky Piano Concerto*), in which he partnered Violette Verdy, and *Divertimento No. 15*, whose taxing solo in the variation movement he executed with the seeming ease, precision and elegance that only Erik Bruhn had exhibited in it previously. And not surprisingly, after this trial year, he was invited to join the company as a

78

full-time member in 1969-70. As such he performed, the first two years, in additional ballets of the Balanchine repertory—most memorably, in the spring of 1971, in the concluding *Theme and Variations* of *Tchaikovsky Suite No. 3*, with his seemingly effortless execution of the solos and his partnering of Gelsey Kirkland, and, in the Andante of *Concerto Barocco*, with the extraordinary enlivened context his partnering created for her movements, in place of the mere efficient supporting, lifting and carrying that others had done in the piece. Roles in new ballets were provided in that period only by Jerome Robbins's *In the Night* and *Goldberg Variations;* and it was not until early in 1972 that Balanchine used him in a new piece of his—the new *Pas Classique Espagnol* for Act 1 of *Don Quixote*, which included a strikingly effective solo by Martins. Having begun, Balanchine went on to contrive with him the more extensive and intricately novel solo passage that was for me the high point of *Duo Concertant*, one of the new ballets Balanchine contributed to the company's Stravinsky Festival in June 1972. And Martins's and Kay Mazzo's were the bodies with which Balanchine contrived the astoundingly novel involvements of the supported adagio of Aria II in *Stravinsky Violin Concerto*—this in addition to the similarly astounding Aria I with Karin von Aroldingen and Jean-Pierre Bonnefous, and the equally novel invention in the animated opening Toccata and final Capriccio, which included excitingly effective passages contrived with Martins.

These new Balanchine roles constituted a major break-through in Martins's career with the company; and another break-through occurred when Farrell returned to the company early in 1975. Her first appearance, in *Symphony in C* with Martins, revealed the breathtaking new beauty of her slimmer body and the grander style of its movements; but the Martins she performed with had changed too in the years of her absence: his earlier slim body had become robust; its movements also were grander, and had more projective force; and he had a new power of mere presence. The two dancers were, in appearance and style, an extraordinarily matched pair, whose operation—in *Symphony in C, Diamonds, Concerto Barocco, Allegro Brillante, Tchaikovsky Piano Concerto, Tchaikovsky Pas de Deux, Chaconne*—was overwhelming. And in the 1975 *Tzigane*, when he appeared at the rear of the stage after her long opening solo, his movements—first in his measured, accented approach to her, then in their duet—were, as executed with his contained intensity and

passion, so compelling as to draw to them the eyes that ordinarily were
fixed on the movements of Farrell.

For someone who had been seeing the results of the association of this
extraordinary dancer with the century's creative genius in ballet it was
dumbfounding to read in interviews in 1975 and 76 Martins's statements
about his difficulties with Balanchine in the early years of that association: that when he had found he couldn't do Balanchine's unusual and
strenuous company classes and was getting injured in them he had begun
to stay away from them and take class elsewhere; that as someone
Balanchine didn't see in class he had been someone Balanchine didn't
use, whose activity in the company had consisted in dancing in a *Serenade*
one week and a *Symphony in C* the next week, not enough to keep him in
good form; and that when he had told Balanchine, on one occasion, that
he was there because he wanted to dance in his ballets, Balanchine had
accused him of merely wanting to use his ballets for his purpose as a star.
All this made it difficult to understand Balanchine's having invited him
to join the company after the trial year of 1968-69, and his having
retained him in the company after that. Nor could it be reconciled with
what I recalled having seen. In the fall of 1968, when I had watched
Balanchine make *La Source* with Verdy and John Prinz, I had, at her
suggestion, several times watched him conduct company class, and had
each time seen Martins doing with no apparent difficulty whatever
Balanchine asked for. Also I had seen Martins dance several times each
week. And knowing that "star" was Balanchine's word for dancers who
used ballets to exhibit their virtuosity and glamorous personality (despite
which he tolerated Eglevsky's gesture and smile of greeting to the
audience at his first entrance in *Swan Lake*), I couldn't understand his
seeing such behavior in Martins's unassertive use of his capacities in the
service of the Balanchine works he danced in.

All this was made even more incomprehensible by the first chapter of
Martins's book, *Far from Denmark*, in which he writes that in his first
years in the Royal Theater's school he was "rowdy, quarrelsome . . .
completely undisciplined," but that his behavior changed when Stanley
Williams, a principal dancer with the company who was also on the
teaching staff, became his teacher—"the one who determined my style . . .
set my goals . . . my standards of movement," and who became "that figure
of authority, that guide and model who gives shape and purpose to a boy's
ambition." In Williams's class he was well behaved and "worked hard,

trying to gain his attention and respect." And in Edinburgh in 1967, where Balanchine changed everything Martins had been doing in *Apollo* ("He was very pleasant about it, and he showed me what he wanted by demonstrating."), Balanchine's "clarity and directness about what he wanted" and the "knowledge and authority [he radiated]" were "the same qualities that had attracted me to Stanley Williams." To these qualities in Balanchine Martins responded as he had done to them in Williams: "What I did was listen, and allow myself to be instructed." Williams, who by then had moved from the Royal Theater to Balanchine's School of American Ballet, and who had been in Edinburgh for Martins's performances in *Apollo*, could report later that Balanchine had been impressed—that he had said, "I changed everything for him, and he remembered everything." And in New York, in the visits of 1967-68 and 1968-69, Martins evidently had continued to listen and allow himself to be instructed by Balanchine in the roles of the Balanchine repertory, and to remember everything he was told.

It is in his second chapter that Martins makes clear what happened after those two years that ended this harmonious and fruitful working relation—revealing, as he does so, the confusion in the thinking and doing in that backstage world apart out of which have come the wonderful appearances of order Balanchine has presented to our eyes on the stage. In 1970, Martins writes, Balanchine noticed his lessened attendance at company class, which Martins characterizes as unconventional in its insufficient warm-up period: he had never been asked to do only a ten-minute barre before a first step in the center that was a *double tour en l'air* to *grand plié*. Because of this Verdy took Balanchine's class only rarely, and Villella didn't take it at all; but whereas Balanchine accepted that from them, it impelled him, in Martins's case, to what was for Martins an additional reason to stay away. Balanchine did not merely correct Martins, as he had done in Edinburgh, but made him the object of his ridicule, with imitations of what Martins did that "humiliated me in front of the whole company." To this incredible treatment Balanchine added what I would call manifestations of his perversity (the perversity exhibited in his statement once deriding the references to Nijinsky's greatness, "Nobody saw him!"; his insistence recently that Stravinsky's *Le Sacre du Printemps*, for which Nijinsky produced the historic ballet that Stravinsky (in a letter to Maximilian Steinberg after the premiere), characterized as "incomparable," and *Les Noces*, for which Nijinsky's sister Bronislawa produced her powerful ballet, cannot be danced to).

That is, when, late in 1970, Balanchine for the first time assigned Martins to the role in a new ballet of his that Martins had been longing for, it was the male role in the opening *Elegy* of *Tchaikovsky Suite No. 3*, in which Martins was asked not to do ballet steps but to rush about barefoot; and after the second rehearsal at which Balanchine ridiculed his "stiffness, formality, lack of expression, and general clumsiness," he told Martins he "was simply no good at all" in that piece. What he could do, possibly, said Balanchine, was the work's final *Theme and Variations;* but after a first rehearsal in that, a few days later, he told Martins that some day, if he practiced, he would be able to do this piece made with Igor Youskevitch, who could do "all these things, *double tour, double pirouette*" that Martins now could not do the way they should be done. This was perverse not only in the light of the virtuoso feats Balanchine had seen Martins execute in the ballets he had danced in, but in the light of his execution of them in *Theme and Variations* only a few months later. And all this represented, in my opinion, the suspicion revealed in the accusation that Martins wanted to use his ballets for his purpose as a star. This accusation, which Martins reported in one of the interviews, he doesn't mention in his book. He writes that when (early in 1972, apparently) he got up his courage and cornered Balanchine to obtain a clarification of the situation in which he felt unappreciated, frustrated, disappointed, angered by what he perceived as the lack of any faith in his capacity to learn and change, he told him that until he had come here he had had no appreciation of Balanchine's achievements and exalted place in ballet; that "I had come to the United States to dance . . . and my ambition now was to dance his ballets. It was all I wanted to do. And I would do anything to make this possible. I was not an unwilling student, and I worked hard." And he wanted to know why Balanchine was avoiding him. "You don't seem to be interested," Balanchine replied. "I never see you anywhere, not in class, maybe in O'Neal's restaurant. When people show interest, I use them. If they don't, I leave them alone. And you don't show interest." But actually Balanchine did see Martins constantly, as he saw Villella—not in class but in performances; he didn't take Villella's absence from company class as signifying lack of interest that made Villella someone to "leave alone," but used him in new ballets; why, then, didn't he use Martins in them? This inconsistency was something Martins may have perceived, but did not point out to Balanchine. He was shocked: "We had been getting the wrong messages." And "if that was what my behavior was suggesting, then I had to change my behavior, which certainly didn't represent my true attitude." Balanchine agreed that the change was necessary: "I had . . . to show him that I was willing to work hard . . . and prove to him my seriousness and determination." But actually, again, this was not what Martins had to begin to demonstrate: he had demonstrated it from the start of his association with Balanchine; and if, as Martins says correctly, this conversation produced the new working relation he describes, it was because *Balanchine's* attitude changed, as a result of what Martins had said, from his suspicion to the trust that enabled him to see in Martins's behavior what suspicion had prevented him from seeing.

It was during the making of *Stravinsky Violin Concerto*, Martins writes, "that Balanchine first worked with me closely." Balanchine demonstrated a passage; Martins not only mastered it, but extended its implications, played with its accents; and "once he saw that he had captured my intensity and interest, that I was devoting my gifts to his work, he gave still more"—which Martins felt was evidence of Balanchine's trust in him. And with increased trust Balanchine became less specific: he might come to rehearsal with the beginning of an idea, and, after watching Martins improvise around it, might say "That's exactly right, that's good"; or something else might occur to him that he would demonstrate. Martins felt himself to be engaged in a collaboration with Balanchine— the collaboration of choreographer and dancer in the use of what the dancer's body can do that is in fact, says Martins, what Balanchine considers the making of a ballet to be. The result of this process is what a dancer wants most: that the choreographer " 'create' him, show him as the unique, special creature he is"; and Martins cites a few outstanding examples of this: Helgi Tomasson's solo in *Divertimento from Le Baiser de la Fée*, Verdy's solo in *Emeralds*, Verdy in *La Source*, Merrill Ashley in *Ballo della Regina*. In Martins's case it was in the making of *Stravinsky Violin Concerto* and *Duo Concertant* that Balanchine's exploration of his dancing extended its range and brought about Martins's discovery of "my own way of moving." This exploration of what dancers were capable of, Martins came to understand, was what Balanchine did also in his company classes, and what he considered them to be for; and Martins accommodated himself to them by warming up with a barre before class (as Verdy did on the rare occasion when she took Balanchine's class).

The exploring collaboration continues, Martins writes, when a role made on one dancer is later taken over by another: for the ballet to remain effective the new dancer must look good in it; and for this Balanchine alters the choreography to bring out the dancer's special qualities. Martins also writes that the company's no-star policy is evident in the repertory that is not star-oriented and is dancer-proof: though major roles may continue for a long time to "belong" to the dancers on whom they were made, other dancers eventually perform them; and the audience doesn't come to see a particular dancer in a ballet. But in this Martins is repeating *idées fixes* of Balanchine's, proclaimed by the company as its guiding principles, that ignore the realities perceived by experienced members of the audience. These people recognize the exceptional technical powers and individual styles of a number of the company's principal dancers that make them, for everyone but Balanchine, stars, and that he needs for his ballets; they know also that what he makes with the technical capacities and style of one of these stars looks different when it is performed with—adjusted to—those of another; and they do, therefore, come to see a ballet as it is performed by certain dancers they consider more effective in it than others. They did come to see Balanchine's unique achievement with Verdy's style in *Emeralds;* they came to see it and groaned at what they saw instead when he substituted Christine Redpath for Verdy in it; and though they admired what Ashley's dazzling style achieved in it, they perceived that it was not the unique thing Balanchine had achieved with Verdy. Similarly, when Farrell left the company in 1969 they grieved over what *Diamonds* looked like with Mazzo; and though they appreciated Allegra Kent's exquisite achievement in it, they perceived that it too was not what Balanchine had produced with Farrell. And this year they have perceived that other dancers' performances of the roles Balanchine made with Martins that Martins hasn't danced in have been not only different but less effective: Joseph Duell has danced the *Menzies* number in Part 1 of *Union Jack* very well, but without the amusing effect of Martins's dead-pan performance in it; and Duell's Sailor in Part 3 has been engagingly lively, but not as uproariously funny as Martins's. (After the years of effort to make himself the dancer he wanted to be in the roles he wanted Balanchine to make with him, Martins has turned over the roles to other dancers and applied his efforts to his new interest in choreographing ballets, something he does effectively, but not as overwhelmingly as he dances.)

There is a great deal more in the book by this remarkably intelligent and articulate writer—about Farrell, Mikhail Baryshnikov, dancing, the dancer's life, choreography—that I have to leave unreported; but having said he is articulate I should add that his articulateness occasionally runs away with him—as in his concluding statement in Chapter 1, that Farrell's quitting the company in the spring of 1970 left him "without the dancer I was most at ease with (balletically) . . . without a partner, and . . . without a clear function and place in the company." Actually, in the period from December 1967 to the spring of 1969, when she quit the company, he had partnered not only Farrell but other dancers, notably Verdy (to whom he acknowledges his debt for what he learned from her about "phrasing, timing, shaping . . . also partnering"); his dancing and partnering in the ballets assigned to him had been his function in the company; and it continued to be his function after Farrell's departure. His amusing account of his insistence on dancing in one of Balanchine's new ballets for the Ravel Festival, and specifically in *Tzigane;* of Balanchine's statement that this was only a solo number for Farrell, with a few girls coming in at the end, and nothing for a male dancer; of Martins's reply, "I'll come in with the girls and sweep the floor in front of them, or behind them," ends with a dismissal of his actual contribution to it—"I just about make it on the stage before the end"—that is corrected by the photographs of what he does in it included among the large number of superb photographs, most of them large, that provide the adequate and effective documentation of the text that is not provided by the photographs in the books about the New York City Ballet by Lincoln Kirstein and Nancy Reynolds. (*Scandanavian Review*, June 1983)

Note. One learns from Martins's account that Balanchine was capable of cruelty—actually the cruelty not only to an extraordinarily gifted young dancer like Martins, but to a great and dedicated artist like Violette Verdy, and, at a rehearsal I recall, to the minor dancer who burst into tears after something he said to her—all these vulnerable to the power it would have been admirable of him not to use, but he felt free to misuse, in dealing with them.

Kirstein's *The New York City Ballet* was a huge coffee-table version of the souvenir booklet sold in the theater, with photographs that were selected and used with poor judgment and confusedly arranged, seemingly for the purpose not of showing important details of the ballets but of decorating the pages with striking effect. A few of the many examples: page-sized studio photographs by George Platt Lynes of Lew Christensen allegedly in the 1937 *Apollo,* of William Dollar, Marie-Jeanne and Mary Jane Shea allegedly in the 1941 *Concerto Barocco,* of Tanaquil LeClercq allegedly in *Western Symphony,* all shown in positions never seen in those ballets; an action photograph by Martha Swope of a moment in a Verdy-Magallanes *pas de deux* in *Liebeslieder Walzer,* so enormously enlarged on most of two pages as to necessitate cropping that removed the dancers' feet, and reduction to ineffective size of a Farrell-Martins *Liebeslieder pas de deux* on the remaining half-page; a Swope photograph of a moment in Farrell's solo with shepherdess's staff in *Don Quixote,* made ineffective by both extreme reduction of size and cropping of legs; a legless Allegra Kent in the one photograph of *La Sonnambula;* the upper third of Martins in the one small photograph of him in *Apollo;* a striking two-page profusion of girls in the final crescendo of *Symphony in C,* with silhouetted principals' leaps in a void above them for decorative effect, but nothing of the great supported adagio of the slow movement; an unimpressive moment in the *Pas de Trois* of *Emeralds,* but nothing of its extraordinary walking *Pas de Deux;* a page-sized arabesque from one of the early movements of *Tchaikovsky Suite No. 3,* but nothing of its great concluding *Theme and Variations.*

On the other hand the photographs in Nancy Reynolds's *Repertory in Review* were provided for documentation that was complete in the sense that all but a few minor works were represented by at least one photograph; but in many cases the single photograph was insufficient or not the best of those available—a few important examples of poor selection being the ones for *Five Pieces* in *Episodes* and for *Rubies, Diamonds* and *Chaconne,* and the worst of all being the two for *Who Cares?:* This work provided d'Amboise with his most successful role; and his *pas de deux* with McBride was its high point; and 'mindless' is therefore the only possible word for the omission of d'Amboise and the *pas de deux,* and the offering instead of two moments in solos by Bonnefous, an occasional ineffective substitute for d'Amboise, and von Aroldingen. Moreover the photograph for *Five Pieces* was one of the too many that were made ineffective by extreme reduction in size. (The space for many more and larger photographs was used instead for an amount of writing about the ballets, much of it worthless, that exceeded what documentation required.) Croce was critical of the photographs in the Kirstein book in which "sometimes the dancers sprawl past the margins of their space," and the "misguided" silhouetting. But to Robert Garis's perceptive eye, surprisingly, "the quantity and quality of these photographs made the book indispensable;" and the ones in the Reynolds book—"chosen with special care" and "beautifully reproduced"—were "worth the price of the book alone." (Surprising too were the examples he stressed of the text's "exclusion . . . of much of the critical commentary of B. H. Haggin; whoever persuaded Miss Reynolds that Mr. Haggin is not to be taken seriously is not worthy of her trust. One misses his views particularly of *In the Night* and *Who Cares?*" One had to wonder at Garis's not recognizing the important exclusion in the case of *Who Cares?* to be that of Croce's superb article in *Dancing Times* (London), which would have corrected the writing about it that Reynolds published; and the important exclusion in my case to be that of my detailed disagreement with the claims made for Robbins's *Dances at a Gathering* by all the other writers. Reynolds's own values were evident not only in the amount of space she gave to the writing about this work—far more than about any major work of Balanchine's—but in the few lines she gave to the only dissenting view, and in her misrepresenting it by quoting two favorable sentences of mine with her one-sentence summary of my several adverse paragraphs to demonstrate my being merely "not completely satisfied", as against what the two quoted sentences communicated in the context she omitted: that I was not completely *dis*satisfied. And I could be dubious about the benefit to me of a championing which publicized the view of some that I was not to be taken seriously.)

Notable Writing on Ballet

There is general awareness that special powers are involved in, and required for, the composing of a sonata, the performing of that sonata, the writing of a play, the acting in that play, the choreographing of a ballet, the dancing in that ballet. But there is no general awareness that such special powers are involved in, and required for, the critical writing about those artistic activities—that the critic is the professional viewer or listener endowed, supposedly, with special powers of perception and judgment, the exercise of which in his review makes it possible for his non-professional readers to perceive what otherwise they might miss. I say "supposedly endowed" because in the actual critical writing I have encountered in the past fifty years I have found the special powers of the critic to be even rarer than those of the artists whose work he writes about. No one else has written anything like the reviews and essays of Stark Young collected in *Immortal Shadows* (1948), which reported what his eye and ear perceived in the works of theater art placed before him; and until recently this was true also of the writing on dance by Edwin Denby collected in *Looking at the Dance* (1948). But in dance criticism there was a change with the appearance—first, in 1966, in a new quarterly, *Ballet Review* (New York), then also in *Dancing Times* (London), and since 1973 in *The New Yorker*—of writing by Arlene Croce that revealed her as someone, in the field of dance, with the rare gift of the critic's perceptive eye.

This gift made her writing, like Denby's, valuable not only for the illumination it provided with its accurate perceptions and evaluations, but for the correction it provided of other writers' errors. Denby's description in the New York *Herald Tribune* of the extraordinary things there were to see in a Balanchine ballet corrected John Martin's disparaging comment in the New York *Times* that made it out to be not worth seeing. And so with Croce's comments on Balanchine's *Who Cares?* (reprinted in her recent collection, *Afterimages*): her perception that everything in it "has a double impact, with one effect or style imposed on the other—Now on Then, ballet dancing on [Gershwin's] show tunes"; her examples of "the multiple images, the visual punning" that include the d'Amboise solo to *Liza* which suggests "soft-shoe, virtuoso tap, and classical lift and amplitude all at once"; her noting "the tight choreography [that] sustains an almost unbelievable musical interest," and Balanchine's "evident delight in choreographing the countermelodies, cross-rhythms, and abrupt syncopations out of which Gershwin built his compositions." These perceptions and others like them enable a reader not only to see "this wonderful ballet [that] enriches our fantasy life immeasurably, as works of art are meant to do," but to reject Clive Barnes's doubt, in *The Times*, that the Gershwin music "is worth a ballet in our national repertory," and his certainty that Balanchine, whose work in the Rodgers and Hart musicals of the 30s Barnes never saw, was "not a masterly creator in this field" and "this is not his medium."

Here I must mention what I find curious and puzzling: that Croce, who can write criticism as excellent as what I have quoted, appears not to understand the nature of the critic's operation and its relation to the reader. An example of this is her comment on another critic's statement—that it works for someone who sees what this critic sees, but not for someone who doesn't see it, which means for her that his statement is invalid as criticism, when the fact is precisely that the critic reports not *the* truth about a work of art, but the truth for *him*, which becomes true for those others who find it confirmed by their experience of the work.

Thus Croce's writing about Balanchine's *Who Cares?* is true for me because it is confirmed by what I see; and similarly what I see in Jerome Robbins's *Watermill* confirms her annihilating comments on its details and her summary characterization of them as "tedious hokum"; as what I see in his other recent works confirms her statement that "he is fatally attracted to pretentious undertakings" and that "no matter what style the piece is in, the same emptiness yawns from within."

There are numerous other instances of such confirmation; but there are also instances of the opposite. My experience of Balanchine's *Don Quixote* continues to confirm her statement in 1968 that he "has filled an evening-long entertainment with an array of effects employing the full resources of the dance theater, each gripping the attention in a new way," not her statements in 1975 that "it was an interesting failure . . .

when it was new," and that because Suzanne Farrell has outgrown her role in the first two acts the work is "stale and boring" until the dances in the third act, in which she "fully recaptures her old brilliance and adds to it a new gift for dramatization." I recognize the damage Balanchine's changes have inflicted on the first act; but I find that what was astounding and overwhelming in 1968—e.g., Farrell's solo with shepherdess's staff in Act 1, the courtiers' Sarabande and the *Pas de Deux Mauresque* in Act 2—is astounding and overwhelming today. I see in Balanchine's *Bugaku* a fascinating work, not "the nearest thing in the New York City Ballet repertory to a Béjart ballet" that Croce sees. I not only find in *Jewels* the Balanchine masterpiece she says it is not, but am amazed by her disposal of *Emeralds* with the statement that it is "novel in the context of the repertory he has fashioned over the years," not considering even the extraordinarily novel and gripping walking *pas de deux* for Francisco Moncion and Mimi Paul worthy of specific comment—to say nothing of the work's other unmentioned marvels.

So with the writing about dancers. I have seen the Makarova Croce describes who "has a legato rhythm by nature, and . . . loves languishing tempos" (though "languishing tempos" is less than adequate for the extremes of her slow-motion Odette in the Royal Ballet *Swan Lake* two years ago). I have also seen the Baryshnikov who in traditional roles gives "a new urgency to commonplace allegro steps like brisés (in the two speeding diagonals [in Act 2] of *Giselle*)", and invents new steps, such as the "turning *jeté* [jump] in which, at the last second, he changes the foot he's going to land on, and his legs flash past each other in the air." And in the performances of Farrell when she returned to the New York City Ballet in 1975 I saw what Croce reported seeing—the "clarity and composure [of] the shoulders, neck, and head," the "refinement of the arms and the simple dignity of the hands," the "grace of deportment and sensitivity of phrasing." But I saw them as an even more overwhelmingly beautiful amplification of what I had seen in the years before her departure from the company in 1969, not as the striking change from the distortion of "every one of the roles she danced [by] the absurd sky-high penchées, the flailing spine and thrust hips, the hiked elbows and flapping hands" that Croce said she had seen in the performances before 1969. And while I undoubtedly could have missed the small flaws that the eye of a Denby or a Croce would have perceived, I find it impossible to believe that I—and the others I have spoken to—missed the flamboyant distortions Croce described.

She also speaks of the 1963-69 years as the Farrell Years in which Balanchine projected what he saw in her onto the company's other dancers ("today we can see her even in little Gelsey Kirkland"), so that her image became the company norm, the "swinging pelvises, baling-hook arms, and clawing hands" of that image became the company's "new cruel orthodoxy", and the dancers who took over Farrell's roles after she left—Karin von Aroldingen, Sara Leland, Kay Mazzo—became "caricatures of the caricature she had become". I didn't see any of this; and to say Balanchine projected the image of Farrell's tall body and the style of movement it dictated onto the different bodies of other dancers with their different styles of movement is to say he did what seems to me clearly impossible for him to have done if he had wanted to, and what I cannot believe he wanted to, given his known sensitivity to each dancer's individual characteristics of body and movement, and his known practice, when a role is taken over by a new dancer, of modifying the role to fit the dancer, not of making the dancer fit into what the previous dancer did. What he did do after Farrell's departure was to put into her roles in *Don Quixote* and *Diamonds* dancers who were unsuited to them; and what I saw was not caricatures of Farrell that resulted from Mazzo's and Leland's attempts to achieve her image, but the mere inadequacy and ineffectiveness of Mazzo and Leland in the movements—"the great sighing lifts" in Act 3 of *Don Quixote*—designed for the tall body neither of them has.

This is an example of the writing by Croce that doesn't hold strictly to what her perceptive eye sees; and another example worth noting is what she writes about Patricia McBride. I see in McBride an accomplished, and at her best—in *Rubies, Who Cares?*, the final duets of *Liebeslieder Walzer*—an enjoyable and impressive dancer, but one without the exciting emanations of greatness radiated by Allegra Kent or Farrell, among others; which means I don't see in her dancing any basis for Croce's characterizing her as "the most exciting ballerina in America", and the peer of Antoinette Sibley and Makarova in world ballet. But that isn't all: I don't see what in her performances has revealed to Croce that McBride is "the shyest, most tenderly true, bravest, and least corruptible of classical dancers". And I must conclude that something other than what Croce has seen McBride do on the stage is responsible for those statements (and add that in my offstage encounters with McBride she has exhibited no shyness about berating someone whose regard for her dancing is not as high as her own).

I am impelled to that conclusion again by Croce's seeing as "quintessential Verdy" in Balanchine's *La Source* only "firmly profiled arabesques and high relevés-passés that flattered Verdy's pulled-up thighs and sensitive feet," whereas others saw it in the idiosyncratic elegance of her flow of exquisitely inflected bodily configuration enlivened by her subtleties of rhythm. These others include a rising young male soloist of the New York City Ballet whom, recently, I heard observe thoughtfully, "I guess you'd have to say Violette was *assoluta*"; and Edward Villella, who years ago expressed a similar view, which Croce disputes. Asked what his dancer's eye could perceive in Violette Verdy's dancing in addition to what a non-dancer saw, Villella described a few of the "small, delicate things" his eye had in fact perceived: the way she phrased her rising on points and coming down from them; the way—in the repeated *passé, passé*, hold of her solo in *Tchaikovsky Pas de Deux*—"not only the foot and the leg and the body and the arms, but the eyes too [reach] the same point in time perfectly"; the way—at another point in this piece—she stopped after a few turns, but didn't really stop: "as the music continues . . . her arms and fingertips are still going with it, then the air just beyond her fingertips." To Croce—who quotes only Villella's words "stops, but doesn't really stop" without his additional words that made the point of his statement—the aspects of Verdy's style that he described are those "one might as easily find irritatingly mannered as beautiful and impressive." Villella also told how certain lunges in the Symphony Op. 21 of Balanchine's *Episodes* "didn't make choreographic sense" to him until he saw Verdy do them, and "when she lunged and turned I saw a motivation for the lunge and turn—both in visual terms and in relation to the music;" concerning which Croce says that the motivation Villella saw was Verdy's "[acting] the movements with her face and body, as if to imply an emotional context," and that this was "in conflict with the intention of Balanchine's choreography"—which, if true, Villella would have perceived and Balanchine presumably would have corrected. And Villella, finally, spoke of what produced those extraordinary performances: Verdy's physical gifts as a dancer, the fact that she was "a thinking dancer" who worked with her mind as well as her body, her "fantastic discipline . . . fantastic dedication to the essentials that have to be worked at day in and day out;" concerning which Croce's comment is a disdainful "interesting if you are interested in Verdy."

It turns out that with the critic's essential gift of a perceptive eye Croce doesn't have the additional important gift of personal and intellectual discipline. (*Commentary*, August 1978)

Postscript 1981 Croce's comments on Villella's statements about Verdy are in the article *Dancers and Dance Critics*, concerned with what she finds to complain of in the writing about dancers, and in particular the writing I have done about them with, she says, "the full weight of [my] authority as a music critic". My musical knowledge, according to her, led me to my early view of Balanchine as superior to all other choreographers; and one supposes that my "preferences for some of Balanchine's dancers (at the expense of others) . . . are based on the same principles as [my] judgments of Balanchine and the musical artists [I] admire." But (1) instead of the insights of a distinguished music critic I offer only words of praise—e.g. "bodily configuration in motion and pose whose beauty and perfection were achieved with . . . elegance" concerning Fonteyn—that are the same for every dancer I admire, and that work for the person who sees what I see, but not for the person who does not. And (2) I don't deal with dancers in the way I deal with musical artists: whereas I support my judgments of a musician with detailed description of how his powers illuminate or obscure or distort the musical values of what he is playing, I don't offer such description of what a dancer does; and in Verdy's case I resort to statements by Villella to "back up what [I refer] to as 'her unique and exciting combination of exactness, enchanting elegance and style, dazzling brilliance, and dramatic power' "—qualities which are not uniquely Verdy's but "can be claimed for any dancer one happens to find powerful and exciting." Moreover my claim that they are uniquely Verdy's is not supported by the statements of Villella's I choose to quote. And what Croce finds objectionable in all this is that "a bias which would be perfectly acceptable if rendered as such is presented as certified truth."

All these allegations of Croce's are as remote from the realities of what they deal with as the ones about Farrell's distortions and Balanchine's projecting them onto his other dancers. My response to Balanchine's ballets was from the beginning, and continued to be thereafter, primarily that of a non-professional spectator's eye to what it saw, and only secondarily that of a professional musician's ear to what it heard. My first few published paragraphs about them, in *The Brooklyn Eagle* in 1935, beginning with "Ballet is not my field," went on after this disclaimer of authority to report what I had *seen* that had delighted me and might delight my readers: "the unfailing inventiveness, the wit, and the impress of a distinctive mind not only on movement of Balanchine's own devising (and his use of the body as a plastic medium is very much his own) but . . . on traditional material." Only after that did I speak of what, with repeated viewings of the ballets, I had begun to hear: how well Chabrier's *Idylle*, for example, worked with the movements of the *Hand of Fate Pas de Deux* in *Cotillon* that fascinated my eye. (And later it was only after the seemingly unending flow of movement in the Andante of *Concerto Barocco* had repeatedly held me spellbound that I began to perceive how it interacted with the flow of Bach's music like an additional line of counterpoint, each enhancing the effect of the other.)

This reality Balanchine recognized in his comment when—after my first article on ballet in *The Nation* in 1940—I told him of my doubt whether, as someone without professional knowledge, I had any business writing about ballet: "You look; you see; you write what you see; and that's good." And what he said applied to what I wrote about dancers: my statement about Verdy that Croce quotes, and the one in my review about "the idiosyncratic elegance of her flow of exquisitely inflected bodily configuration enlivened by her subtleties of rhythm", describe what I saw; and in the manner of their doing so they are similar to my statement about Schnabel's "playing of Mozart, unique in its subtle articulation of clearly outlined melodic phrase, its delicacy and suppleness, and at the same time its cohesive tension and strength."

Moveover, after concluding my report on the New York City Ballet in the Fall 1965 issue of *The Hudson Review* I began a new paragraph with this statement: "Wondering what the dancer's eye was aware of in Verdy's dancing, in addition to the elegance and style that enchanted the non-dancer's eye, I asked members of the company"—actually only Villella. And in the statements of his I quoted he spoke only about what I had asked him for: some of the things *he* had perceived and had been impressed by in Verdy's dancing that I had not perceived—not about anything *I* had written. Croce's misrepresentation of my explicitly stated reason for quoting him reveals the lack of intellectual discipline that I point out, in my review, in her dealing with his statements.

I note in my review the lack of understanding of the critic's operation revealed in Croce's comment that a statement of mine works only for the person who sees what I see, not for the person who does not. And this lack of understanding appears also in her objections to my alleged "preferences for some of Balanchine's dancers at the expense of others" and my alleged "bias . . . presented as certified truth". In her view, when *she* proclaims McBride "the most exciting ballerina in America" and faults Verdy for aspects of her style that Villella admires, she is exercising legitimate critical judgment; but when *I* report how delightful Verdy makes *Tchaikovsky Pas de Deux* or *Raymonda Variations* with her subtleties—those I perceived myself and those Villella pointed out to me—and how much less enjoyable the performances of those ballets are in which McBride doesn't exhibit such subtleties, I am guilty of preferring one dancer "at the expense of others" and of presenting "a bias . . . as certified truth." (For another instance of this see the note on p. 122.)

Chronicle 1972-75

New York's Metropolitan Opera has the same function as its Metropolitan Museum of Art: to keep valuable works of the art it is concerned with available for interested members of the public. Its presentation of Berlioz's *Les Troyens* in the fall of 1973 was, then, analogous to the museum's putting on view a few years ago its newly acquired Rembrandt painting, *Aristotle Contemplating the Bust of Homer*—with one important difference: a large number of other outstanding Rembrandt paintings have been on view at the Metropolitan and other museums of this country and Europe; but *Les Troyens*, Berlioz's single masterpiece in its singular grand style, remained unperformed anywhere until recently. Rafael Kubelik produced it at Covent Garden in 1957; and as the Musical Director appointed by Goeran Gentele when he took charge of the Metropolitan in 1972, he was responsible for the production there. He was also responsible for the Metropolitan's presenting again, last fall, another singular masterpiece that it had presented in the 50s—Musorgsky's own revised version of his *Boris Godunov*, as distinguished from the complete recomposition of the work by Rimsky-Korsakov that continues to be performed by most of the world's opera companies. And he was responsible for the Metropolitan's presenting again, last fall, for the first time since the 20s, yet another unusual and impressive work—Janáček's *Jenufa*.

These three were the major additions in repertory that Gentele and Kubelik planned for the seasons of 1973-74 and 1974-75; and they represented an artistic understanding and taste that was new in the Metropolitan's operation. *Les Troyens* would have been in several ways an eminently suitable opera with which to open the new Metropolitan

Opera House in 1966; but for Rudolf Bing—confident in his possession of the taste he clearly lacked—*Les Troyens* was "a bore"; and he opened the new house with the *Antony and Cleopatra* he had commissioned from Samuel Barber. Characterizing this work in *The New Republic* as a "pseudo Aida" produced by the "unmemorable operatic talent" that had produced Barber's *Vanessa*, Stanley Kauffmann doubted that Bing really had believed Barber was "a valuable opera composer", and contended that he had commissioned Barber because he had been determined to open the house with an American work. But the man who had commissioned *Antony* for the new house had produced *Vanessa* in the old one, and not only this pseudo opera but Menotti's *The Last Savage*, a work by the preeminent American composer of operatic trash, and one that was astonishingly feeble even in its own terms—which was to say that Bing was someone with no capacity to recognize value or the lack of it, who really did believe that Barber and Menotti were valuable opera composers. Operating without this sense for value, Bing also had wasted productions on other works of little consequence and interest like Cilèa's *Adriana Lecouvreur* and Flotow's *Martha*; operating with no understanding of what was and what was not properly in the Metropolitan's repertory, he had produced European operettas that were no more the proper concern of the Metropolitan than were the American musical shows he did not produce.

True enough, it was Bing who had restored a great work of Verdi, *Don Carlo*, to the Metropolitan repertory; it was he who had given that unique 20th-century classic, Alban Berg's *Wozzeck*, its long overdue first production at the Metropolitan; and it was he who had at last replaced Rimsky-Korsakov's recomposition of *Boris Godunov* with Musorgsky's own work there. Whether he had made the decisions about *Don Carlo* and *Wozzeck* by himself I don't know; but it became clear in time that he never perceived the nature and value of Musorgsky's own *Boris*. He had been persuaded to produce it by the conductors Fritz Stiedry and Max Rudolf; but having no understanding in the matter he had accepted Stiedry's contention that Musorgsky's orchestration needed strengthening to give it carrying power in a theater as large as the old Metropolitan. The strengthening was done by Karol Rathaus, who not only left untouched the musical substance—melody, harmony, rhythm, phraseology—that Rimsky-Korsakov had rewritten, but scrupulously adhered to Musorgsky's choices and combinations of instruments for the tonal images in his mind, and changed only what he thought was Musorgsky's occasionally inexpert employment of the instruments in order to realize those tonal images more exactly. This didn't satisfy Stiedry, who insisted that some passages of extraordinary idiosyncratic writing for winds be made more "effective" by the addition of rich sonorities of strings; and with these occasional Rimskyisms in the orchestration the public heard a little less than the entirety of Musorgsky's own work. But worse was to come a few years later, when, with Stiedry gone and Erich Leinsdorf advising Bing, the Rathaus version was replaced with Shostakovich's reorchestration and partial recomposition of the work. And when, still later, the singer Nicolai Ghiaurov made it a condition of his participation in a new staging of *Boris*, Bing announced a return to the Rimsky version. Thus Bing's dealing with *Boris* illustrated something that is not sufficiently recognized: that we don't always get the right thing in art from the right person and for the right reason; and that we must be glad, of course, to have it even when it comes from the wrong person for the wrong reason, but should realize that what the wrong person gives he may allow to be spoiled and may eventually take away.

Kubelik was a right person; and what he planned with Gentele in addition to *Les Troyens* for their first season of 1973-74, as revised with Schuyler G. Chapin after Gentele's death, included right things like the Metropolitan's first production ever of a major work of Verdi, *I Vespri Siciliani*, and a production of Rossini's long absent *L'Italiana in Algeri*. As for new stagings of standard repertory, I would like to think Kubelik shared my view of the wrongness of the staging of Wagner's *Ring* by von Karajan with the designer Günther Schneider-Siemssen that had been contracted for by Bing, but recognized the necessity of completing it with *Die Götterdämmerung*; and that he also shared my objections to the planned new *Don Giovanni* (in the end canceled for financial reasons)— that the discarding of the old Berman scenery, the greatest I can recall seeing in an opera, was not justified by the arguments that it didn't fit perfectly on the stage of the new house, and that the new *Don Giovanni* would fulfill the promise to Leontyne Price of a new production of an opera for her.

Presumably Kubelik also participated in the discussions leading to the decisions to produce in 1974-75, in addition to *Boris* and *Jenufa*, Britten's *Death in Venice* and Rossini's *The Siege of Corinth*; and again I would like to think his was a voice of dissent. Britten is England's major composer; but one must say of his music what W. J. Turner said of Bach's—that it is not always "as expressive as it is accomplished"; which is to say that Britten, like Bach, operates much of the time as a resourceful inventor of progressions of sounds that go through the motions of saying something while actually saying nothing. There have been exceptions—parts of *Peter Grimes* and *Albert Herring*, and above all *A Midsummer Night's Dream*, one of this century's few impressive achievements in opera. But the exceptions do not include *Death in Venice*, whose musical invention doesn't communicate Mann's prose subtleties and has no purely musical interest in itself. Not only that, but Britten doesn't achieve musical equivalents of Mann's verbal images of the boy Tadzio, but instead leaves it to a choreographer to provide dance equivalents, which possibly no choreographer could achieve, and Ashton didn't achieve with the movements executed by a ballet dancer much older than Tadzio.

As for *The Siege of Corinth*, this is the revision, for the Paris Opera in 1826, of the *Maometto II* Rossini had written for Naples in 1820—a revision which eliminated some of the showy florid writing of the first version and added new writing in the simpler and nobler style of his later serious works. And I would like to believe it was this 1826 revision by Rossini that Kubelik approved, not the version Schippers contrived with his cuts, his patching together of some of the discarded writing of *Maometto* and the simpler writing of the revised work, and the added florid ornamentation that carried excess to sheer absurdity—a version that misused and degraded Rossini's opera for the endless display of Beverly Sills's coloratura pyrotechnics that was itself a misuse and degradation of her long overdue first appearances at the Metropolitan.

The production of this Schippers version of *The Siege of Corinth*, like the earlier productions of the Rimsky and Shostakovich versions of *Boris*, demonstrated that while opera companies have the same function as art museums they don't execute that function in the way museums do. Except for grime and deterioration caused by time; a painting is exhibited by a museum exactly as it was painted originally by the artist, never as altered by someone else; and there is never any debate whether the alterations improve the original work, but instead an understanding that whatever their effect the alterations are impermissible. But for almost 100 years it has been generally accepted that Rimsky's *Boris* is more effective than Musorgsky's and therefore the *Boris* to perform; and only a few—Toscanini, amazingly, not among them—have understood,

first, that no matter how effective, the Rimsky recomposition of Musorgsky's work was impermissible, and, further, that the effectiveness
Rimsky achieved was not the effect Musorgsky intended. What, for
example, Rimsky's orchestral brilliance made more effective was the
Coronation Scene as *he* perceived it, not the scene as Musorgsky perceived it, whose drab orchestral coloring was to convey his perception of
the coronation of Boris as no more a genuine occasion for the down-
trodden Russian people's shouts of joy than his refusal of the throne in
the first scene had been a genuine occasion for that people's visibly
coerced pleas to him to accept it.

(*1983* The foregoing is the reply to Andrew Porter's statement in *The New
Yorker* that "the idea of 'Boris' as a colorful Russian pageant . . . given
dazzling expression in the Salzburg production [of the Rimsky recomposi-
tion] . . . by Karajan . . . is not an untrue idea, but less than the whole truth."
The brilliantly colored Rimsky Coronation Scene to which Karajan gave
dazzling expression is no part of the truth of the scene as perceived by
Musorgsky and realized in his coloring of it. Porter's statement was surprising from someone who insisted that a sonata by Mozart, Haydn, Beethoven
or Schubert was misrepresented by the sound of the piano of today. And
equally surprising was his statement that his hearings of the various musical
texts used at different times in the Covent Garden staging of *Boris*—
including not only Musorgsky's and Rimsky's but a combination of the
two—had "prompted no hard, unqualified conclusions" as to which should
be used, instead of the conclusion one would have expected from him, that
only Musorgsky's could legitimately be used. It was, he said, "in an either/or
choice" that "Musorgsky without Rimsky would undoubtedly be the score
to prefer," which gave the impression of reluctance to have to make that
choice; and in fact he added "but it would be sad never to hear again
[Rimsky's] heady orchestration," revealing that whereas he insisted that the
piano of today misrepresented a sonata by Mozart, Haydn, Beethoven or
Schubert, he didn't recognize that Rimsky's bright orchestral colors misrepresented Musorgsky's somber musical thought, and were something to
hear only in Rimsky's own operas. Though he was to state later (see p. 195)
his belief that a work spoke most effectively in the sounds the composer
intended, he didn't recognize that *Boris* spoke truly only in the sounds of
Musorgsky's orchestration, not in those of Rimsky's. Nor, I should add—
with his mind on those muddled ideas about the work—did he have ears,
eyes and words for the damage to the Kromy Scene from the appalling cuts
and ludicrous staging of its performances.)

Kubelik was one of the few who understood; and having performed Musorgsky's own 1872 revised version in Munich, he reinstated it (with the St. Basil scene of the 1869 version) at the Metropolitan for the new 1974 production. But his resignation from his position of musical director in February 1974 left Schippers free, in the fall of that year, to make cuts which I would have expected Kubelik—after what he had done in his own performances—not to accept. Schippers claimed, in an interview, that whereas Kubelik, in Munich, had "made cuts that I couldn't figure out why," *his* version would be "virtually uncut" and "the most complete performance of 'Boris' ever, ever, ever". But in fact Kubelik's only cut in Act 2—of Feodor's story about the parrot, which delays Shuisky's entrance after he has been announced—was so understandable and right that Schippers did the same; and it was Schippers's additional cut in this act that was incomprehensible and indefensible: the omission of the song which Feodor and the Nurse sing, clapping their hands, in a crescendo of excitement interrupted by the sudden appearance of Boris that frightens the Nurse—an omission which destroyed the intended effect of that entrance. And his damaging cuts elsewhere included the slicing out of a phrase in the dying Boris's farewell to his son, and in the Kromy Scene the omission of repetitions and of the entire reappearance of Varlaam and Missail, which added up to sheer butchery of that great scene. After all this one might doubt Schippers's statement, in another interview, that what he performed "was arrived at between Goeran Gentele, Rafael Kubelik and myself." But I must add that even Kubelik—after telling an interviewer, correctly, that one had to take a work like *Les Troyens* as it stood, without fiddling and cutting—fiddled with a cut of "only about eight minutes or so" of "some nice music" which he said was "a dramatic retardation"—in this not recognizing that in so huge a work the "only eight minutes or so" might as well have been left untouched, and that what he cut was the affecting and dramatically important music of the transition from Dido's quarrel with the departing Aeneas to her decision that she must die.

But it is not only in their dealing with the musical text that opera companies exhibit their lack of the scrupulousness of art museums. No museum would agree that anything had to be done to paintings of past centuries to make them valid for today; but Bing was an advocate of "presenting masterpieces as seen through contemporary eyes"—i.e. the eyes of designer-director teams who used their skills not for the effective realization of the composer's explicitly stated conceptions of the scenes and action of his opera, but instead for striking inventions of stagecraft embodying ideas of their own about the opera that might ignore or contradict the composer's ideas. With Bing's departure there was the hope that the Metropolitan would not again offer anything like the hollowed-out base of an enormous tree that was Schneider-Siemssen's distractingly inadequate and absurd substitute for the interior of Hunding's hut specified by Wagner as the performance area of the first act of *Die Walküre;* or the bullring—embodying Barrault's idea of Carmen and José as antagonists in Spain's erotic ritual of the bullfight— that Jacques Dupont designed in place of the square in Seville specified by Bizet as the scene of the first act of *Carmen.*

However, that hope was disappointed by the very first offering of the new regime in the fall of 1972—the new production of *Carmen* planned by Gentele (himself a stage director) with the designer Josef Svoboda, and staged after Gentele's death by Bodo Igesz. It was announced as a restoration of Bizet's work that replaced the recitatives added by Guiraud with the original spoken dialogue, and reinstated some of the music that had been omitted ever since the first performance. But instead of retaining the crowded, colorful square in Seville that Bizet specified for the first act, Svoboda perversely placed the act in what was in every detail the opposite of such a square: a bare courtyard, enclosed on one side by a severely plain guard house, on the other side by an even more severe windowless wall, and in the center by an iron picket fence with a locked gate, which kept out the passersby referred to in the guards' opening chorus—this being only the first of its disservices to the action. Also some of the restored dialogue was cut—in particular the very first exchange of Carmen and José, whose removal was part of the idea of their first encounter that Gentele substituted for Bizet's. As Bizet has it, Carmen is piqued by José's ignoring her and working at his chain while she sings the Habanera, and at its conclusion jars him out of his indifference with her provocative words and her throwing her flower at him. As Gentele changed it, José, at his first sight of Carmen when she entered, stood transfixed, a doomed man, and continued to stand motionless throughout her Habanera; and as she approached him at its conclusion the stage was darkened except for the spotlights on the two doomed characters who stood confronting each other in silence, until Carmen threw the flower and burst into mocking laughter as she ran away.

Gentele's contrivance was dramatically effective; but so is Bizet's; and *Carmen* is *his* opera, not Gentele's.

It was in *I Vespri Siciliani*, a year later, that Svoboda revealed the full measure of the damage his obsessive idiosyncratic invention could inflict on an opera. *I Vespri*, written for the Paris Opera, was Verdi's version of the large-scale, opulently spectacular grand operas that were presented there. But for this work Svoboda decided on a color scheme for scenery and costumes limited to black and gray, and on scenery limited to the enormous staircase he sees in almost every opera he designs—in this instance a staircase which, flanked by building walls, could be accepted as a street rising from the square in Palermo in the first scene, but could not suggest what Verdi specifies in the scenes that follow: a valley leading to the sea, the study in Monforte's palace, the palace's ballroom, its gardens. (The study was completely bare, with not even a chair for Monforte to sit on.)

But the season of 1973-74 that offered this misconceived *I Vespri* offered also the admirable production of *Les Troyens*. In spite of occasional details that were gimmicky and even damaging—the wolves symbolizing Rome that were hung above the stage; the ineffective film projection of the wooden horse (in Berlioz's score the horse is only referred to, not seen); the fish netting that was hung over the Carthaginian scenes; the chaotic film projections that were added to the embarrassing pantomime during the orchestral interlude *Royal Hunt and Storm*—Peter Wexler's scenery and costumes and Nathaniel Merrill's direction fulfilled most of the requirements of this work in the style of French grand opera that Berlioz ennobled. And except for a few details the production of *L'Italiana in Algeri* designed and directed by Jean-Pierre Ponnelle also served that work well.

Jenufa and *Boris Godunov*, however, fared badly in the season of 1974-75—the first with the ugly sets of Schneider-Siemssen and poor direction of Günther Rennert; the second with the scenic invention of Ming Cho Lee and the direction of August Everding. Lee's imaginative poverty was evident in what he designed as the room in the Tsar's apartment; one of the mannerisms of his invention was exemplified at its worst in the single wall of Marina's boudoir that was placed against the backdrop of foliage for the garden of the next scene; and it got to be irritating in the series of scenes in which the truncated walls of rooms or façades of buildings were all placed against the one permanent backdrop of icons.

Everding, ignoring Musorgsky's stage directions for Boris's last moments, substituted action that contradicted Boris's words. And what Lee and Everding contrived for the Kromy Scene, in place of what Musorgsky specifies, carried confusion to sheer absurdity. (See p. 190.) On the other hand Nicolai Benois provided good traditional scenery for *The Siege of Corinth:* but the hacked-up action defied whatever skill the director, Sandro Sequi, may have had.

A performance of opera in which all the elements are first-rate is rare: in the 30s one ignored the shabby scenery of *Tristan und Isolde,* the insensitive conducting of Bodanzky, and was content with the singing of Leider, Flagstad and Melchior. Today one makes an effort to keep from being disturbed by what operas look like as seen through the eyes of contemporary designers, and listens to the superb musical prformance of *I Vespri Siciliani* achieved by James Levine's conducting and the singing of Caballé, Gedda and Milnes, or the good one of *Boris* achieved by Schippers and the cast headed by Talvela. Recognizing that the Metropolitan can't have all the first-rate singers and conductors it needs, one accepts a performance of *Carmen* or *L'Italiana in Algeri* whose only distinction is the singing of Marilyn Horne; but a performance of *Jenufa* afflicted throughout with the strangulated, strident sounds produced by Varnay is difficult to accept even with the singing of Vickers and Kubiak; and so is a performance of *The Siege of Corinth* with a Sills who can offer an endless boring demonstration of phenomenal coloratura pyrotechnics, but whose voice even in quiet cantilena, by now, is clouded by excessive flutter, and becomes strident with increased intensity. These are what the Metropolitan has offered in the past three seasons, but in addition it offered one example of the rarity I spoke of a moment ago: the performance of *Les Troyens* that was excellently staged, superbly sung by Vickers, Christa Ludwig and Verrett, and admirably conducted by Kubelik.

It was Kubelik who, as Musical Director, was responsible for the Metropolitan's undertaking *Les Troyens, Jenufa* and Musorgsky's own *Boris.* And with the appointment of Levine as his successor one may expect to hear musical excellence at the Metropolitan in the years ahead. What one hopes in addition is that he wants an end of the vandalism of stage designers and directors and will be able to achieve it. (*New Republic,* 16 and 23 August 1975)

Postscript 1983 In addition to the Metropolitan's new productions in those three seasons I heard a few of its repertory performances—three of them in as many weeks in the fall of 1972. Gluck's *Orfeo ed Euridice*, conducted effectively by Mackerras, was ennobled by Marilyn Horne's deployment of her marvelous voice in grandly sustained and shaped phrases. Mozart's *Don Giovanni*, conducted effectively by Maag, offered Edda Moser's powerfully expressive, though not beautiful-sounding, Donna Anna with the more attractive-sounding vocal performances of Teresa Zylis-Gara as Donna Elvira, Edith Mathis as Zerlina, Roger Soyer as Don Giovanni, Stuart Burrows as Don Ottavio, and all these in the heightening scenic context of Eugene Berman's great sets. (They were to have been discarded for the sets of a new production promised to Leontyne Price, but had been saved when financial stringency had forced the Metropolitan to cancel the production—which Price, in an interview, grumbled about, intimating that she had not been treated as an operatic superstar should be.) And Verdi's *Otello*, conducted by James Levine in a manner which revealed the gifts that had enabled him to learn what Toscanini could teach, was made overwhelming by the unique vocal splendor and the volcanic expressive force of Jon Vickers's singing in the title role. (Desmond Shawe-Taylor, who wrote in *The New Yorker* that Vickers's was "the grandest assumption of the role . . . since the time of Martinelli", intended this as a compliment; but for someone who remembered Martinelli's dry, tight voice in the Metropolitan's 1937 *Otello* and had a recording that confirmed his recollection, Shawe-Taylor's statement was absurd. By the evidence of the beautiful voice and eloquent phrasing one hears in the recorded performances of Leo Slezak, including one of an excerpt from *Otello* [in which he sang under Toscanini at the Metropolitan], his was the previous "grand assumption of the role" that Vickers's may be compared with.) And in the spring of 1974 a performance of *Don Giovanni* was made outstanding by Levine's enlivening conducting, to which Leontyne Price added her superb sing-ing as Donna Anna up to the concluding florid last passages of *"Non mi dir"*, which she managed in a sort of vocal shorthand that implied the notes she didn't sing. The title role gained by the magnificence of Sherrill Milnes's voice; but to the eye he presented the incongruity of someone in the get-up of a 17th-century Spanish aristocrat with the swinging, swaying bodily movement of an American cowboy. And to my eye, regrettably, Leontyne Price presented with her Donna Anna the same obtrusive incongruity as previously with her Leonora in *Il Trovatore* and her Pamina in *The Magic Flute* but not with her Aida: when I look at what is happening on a stage my imagination still cannot accommodate itself to a black in the role of a white.

The New York City Opera, in the fall of 1973, provided a first opportunity to hear Delius's opera *A Village Romeo and Juliet*, from which the familiar orchestral piece *The Walk to the Paradise Garden* is taken. I had for many years been aware of the clearly defined ideas and structure exhibited by this extraordinarily lovely piece and a few others by Delius, as against the lack of such clarity of definition in the substance and structure of most of the music of his I had heard. Nevertheless it was astonishing to hear the inexpressive and uninteresting vocal arioso and amorphous orchestral flow that continued on and on until the point near the end where the familiar orchestral intermezzo interjected its few minutes of splendid and eloquent utterance. The musical performance conducted by Bernardi, with John Stewart and Patricia Wells as the young lovers, was good; the stage direction by Corsaro included his usual interpolations of unnecessary and damaging invention and omissions of what the printed text specified.

Notable happenings in New York's concert halls in this period included Janet Baker's performance of Haydn's Cantata *Ariana a Naxos* at a Hunter College recital in the fall of 1972—a musically sensitive deployment of her beautiful voice that was made overwhelming by the intensity of her involvement; and in Philharmonic Hall a few days later the mutually stimulating operation of Baker, Colin Davis and the Boston Symphony that gave extraordinary effect to the great songs of Berlioz's *Les Nuits d'Eté*. In December Solti, in Carnegie Hall, produced an admirable performance of Berlioz's *The Damnation of Faust*—one that was free of the excessive tension and vehemence of some of his performances—with the Chicago Symphony, its chorus, and Josephine Veasey, Stuart Burrows and Roger Soyer. And in January 1973 in Philharmonic Hall Abbado, whose performances of orchestral works are uneven, achieved one of Mahler's Symphony No. 2 that was impressively effective in its dealing with the Philadelphia Orchestra and assisting vocalists and its pacing and shaping of the work.

The Guarneri Quartet's program policy—of offering one great work by Haydn or Mozart or Beethoven or Schubert with two less interesting works by Schuman, Mendelssohn, Brahms, Ravel, Kodály, Berg or Bartók—keeps me from attending most of its concerts; but early in 1974 a program with two major works, Haydn's Op. 20 No. 4 and Beethoven's Op. 131, lured me to the Metropolitan Museum of Art, where I heard the group's instrumental mastery in the service of musical insight achieve deeply satisfying performances of both works. And with Leslie Parnas as second cellist the Guarneri produced another such performance of Schubert's Quintet Op. 163 at a concert of the Chamber Music Society of Lincoln Center. On the other hand the Guarneri's first performance of Schubert's Quartet Op. 161, at the 92 Street YMHA, was made wholly ineffective by the excessively slow tempos of all four movements. Ashkenazy, at Carnegie Hall, played Beethoven's Sonata Op. 109 magnificently. And Michael Rogers began a recital at New York University Medical School's auditorium with admirable performances of several infrequently heard pieces by Mozart; continued with *his* magnificent performance of Beethoven's Op. 109; and ended with an outstandingly perceptive realization of Schubert's posthumous Sonata in A.

One major work of the New York City Ballet's Stravinsky Festival in June 1972 I did not see until the following autumn-winter season: *Pulcinella*, a joint product of Balanchine's and Robbins's gifts for comedy, with the valuable assistance of Stravinsky's engaging score and the imagination of Eugene Berman that produced the scenery and costumes—in particular the fantastic costumes and instruments of the Musicians in the piece. Balanchine and Robbins had been changing the work until the night of the first performance, and continued to change it until the last performance two years later; and this provided a basis for one reviewer's report that it was still only a work in progress, a blocking out of what it would eventually become, and as such lacked the focus, the point of view of a completely achieved work. This made plausible sense in the reviewer's writing, but was not true of what was presented on stage at the several performances I attended, in each of which—however changed from the preceding one—I saw a series of completely achieved happenings, almost all involving Pulcinella, who was therefore its unifying factor, its focus. I saw this in a performance which included a grotesque dance by two Beggars and a quiet solo by Violette Verdy; and in a later performance in which an eccentric dance by Pulcinella replaced the Beggars' dance, and a new lively solo by Verdy replaced her quiet one; and these changes did not make either performance a mere blocking out of an as yet not completely achieved work.

So with Arlene Croce's contention that all the tinkering with *Pulcinella* had not made it right—that Stravinsky's musical jokes, Berman's scenery and the episodic action made it hard to follow, and almost impossible to enjoy if one *could* follow it. This, again, made plausible sense in Croce's words, but was not true of what I saw happening on the stage, which I had no difficulty in following and enjoying.

The dropping of *Pulcinella* after two years was therefore regrettable. And I had regretted the replacement of Verdy's quiet solo in the early performances with the later lively one. I recognized that its quiet elegance was unrelated to the uproarious happenings that preceded and followed; but felt it should have been retained because of its own extraordinarily beautiful use of Verdy's individual style.

With several other Balanchine works of the Stravinsky Festival—*Symphony in Three Movements, Stravinsky Violin Concerto, Danses Concertantes, Divertimento from Le Baiser de la Fée, Duo Concertant*—added to the repertory of the seasons of 1972-73, his one new ballet for the spring season was *Cortège Hongrois*, another reworking of the Glazunov music from *Raymonda* that he had used more effectively in *Pas de Dix* and *Raymonda Variations*. More exciting occasions were provided by Gelsey Kirkland's performances in old ballets, with her sharply defining clarity that made her flow of changing bodily configuration in *Concerto Barocco* as startlingly "fresh and glistening as creation itself", vividly pointed up the *Pas de Deux Mauresque* in *Don Quixote*, and achieved a similar clarifying statement in *Tarantella*.

Balanchine's *Variations pour une Porte et un Soupir*, the next year, was a fun piece, in which John Clifford's every contortion or flinging of himself about was synchronized amusingly with a huge electronic sigh or moan, and every sharply angular movement by von Aroldingen in the get-up of a formidable vampire (including a black robe with wing-like extensions the entire width and depth of the stage) was synchronized, even more amusingly, with the electronic creak or screech of a swinging door. And Kirkland again provided exciting occasions with additional performances in old ballets—the Andante of *Symphony in C, La Source, Theme and Variations*. With her in the *Theme and Variations* I saw, and as outstanding in his distinctive way, was Martins; and I referred earlier to his partnering in *Concerto Barocco* that astonished one by adding to its basic supporting, lifting and carrying, for the first time, the dimension, style and aura of a performance that complemented and framed Kirkland's. And Tomasson's performance in *Tarantella*, less robust and powerful than Villella's, was better suited to Kirkland's than Villella's would have been.

For the fall season of 1974-75 Balanchine's new work was his staging of *Coppélia* with the assistance of Danilova, who was credited only with the accurate retrieving of the second act, but evidently had also coached McBride in the other two acts. This had for me—who had seen Danilova's marvelous performance many times—the consequence that behind McBride, in every movement she had been taught, I saw Danilova doing it with the distinctive verve, gaiety, charm and grandeur she could not teach. But Martins, in the performance I saw, revealed yet another gift—this one for comedy.

American Ballet Theatre, in its 1974-75 season at New York's City Center, had Mikhail Baryshnikov dancing with Makarova and Gelsey Kirkland, who had left the New York City Ballet to dance with him; but I saw him only in *Coppélia* and *Giselle* with Makarova. The best description of him was Croce's statement that he got into a step sequence more quickly, complicated it more variously, and prolonged it more extravagantly than any dancer she had seen, and offered two and three times as much to look at. To this I can add only that he performed his extraordinary feats as if they were as ordinary as walking across a room; and that he exhibited an impressive dramatic gift in *Giselle* and a gift for comedy in *Coppélia*.

At almost the same time as Kirkland left the New York City Ballet Suzanne Farrell returned to it—her first appearance in the Andante of *Symphony in C* made exciting by the new beauty of her slimmer body and the new grandeur of its large movements. She was partnered by Martins, whose slim body, in the six years of her absence, had filled out, contributing to the grandeur of *his* movements, and to his extraordinary force of mere presence. The two were now a wonderfully matched pair, whose operation not only in *Symphony in C* but in the Andantes of *Diamonds*, *Agon* and *Concerto Barocco* was overwhelming. Farrell was also overwhelming alone in her first-act solo with shepherdess's staff in *Don Quixote*, and the one in the third-act ballet. But she proved to be unsuited for *Bugaku*.

The newly engaged Peter Schaufuss revealed impressive gifts in *Swan Lake* and *Raymonda Variations* with Verdy, whom, on the other hand, Anthony Blum's nervous partnering prevented from executing the succession of supported arabesques at the beginning of *Emeralds* with the perfection of her individual style that Conrad Ludlow's secure partnering formerly had made possible. For someone who had seen Kirkland in *Theme and Variations* McBride's performance in it was coarse-grained; and she too was, in her different way, unsuited to *Bugaku*. Of the rising younger dancers Colleen Neary performed beautifully with Farrell in the Allegros of *Concerto Barocco* and in the secondary principal role in *Tchaikovsky Piano Concerto*, in which Ashley, partnered by Martins, was dazzling in her combination of accuracy and speed.

The 1975 spring season offered a revival of Balanchine's *Ivesiana*, in which Farrell and Victor Castelli were delightful in the eccentric movements to the ragtime of *In the Inn*. Also, partnered by d'Amboise, she returned to *Movements*. And Tomasson's finely chiseled classical dancing provided the perfect complement to the elegance and subtleties of inflection and rhythm of Verdy's performance in *La Source*, but a devastating contrast to McBride's in *Theme and Variations*.

As for the Ravel Festival that was the season's major event, the emptiness of the slickly contrived music that defeated even Balanchine's powers of invention also defeated my powers of attention, perception and retention, making it impossible for me to recall what I had looked at. The one exception was *Tzigane*, whose opening solo-violin recitative elicited from Balanchine an impressive recitative-like solo by Farrell, and whose quiet entrance of the orchestra brought Martins onto the stage in slow, sinuous, accenting movements to which he gave a compelling intensity that drew to them the eyes that usually were fixed on the movements of Farrell.

Chronicle 1976-78
(In *The New Republic*)

24 January 1976 One unusual feature of Boulez's first concert in New York with the BBC Symphony 10 years ago, and his first concerts with the New York Philharmonic a few years later, was his manner of conducting. He stood motionless except for the head that turned now toward one part of the orchestra, now toward another, and the forearms and hands that made only minimal movements which were like mere reminders of what he had got the orchestra to do at the rehearsals; and it was this strictly undemonstrative, matter-of-fact physical operation that achieved the miraculously clear textures of sounds of brass, woodwinds and strings that were free of the slightest impurity, and the ensemble precision with which these sounds were attacked, shaped and released. The sounds, textures and ensemble precision revealed his possession of an ear for accuracy of orchestral intonation, balance and execution that was as phenomenal as Toscanini's and Cantelli's; the restrained manner in which he elicited them from the orchestra revealed powers of magnetic compulsion as phenomenal as Toscanini's and Cantelli's; and the superbly shaped performances of three excerpts from Berg's *Wozzeck* and Debussy's *Ibéria* with the BBC Symphony and the overwhelming realization of Stravinsky's *Le Sacre du Printemps* with the New York Philharmonic revealed musical powers also comparable with Toscanini's and Cantelli's.

I speak of the unusual manner of Boulez's conducting because of the misconceptions it led to. Since the programs he devised for the New York Philharmonic when he became its musical director contained very little of the music that interested me I didn't hear his concerts for several years; but I did hear, in those years, the occasional broadcasts of his

111

admirably shaped performances of Berlioz's *Romeo and Juliet* and *Les Nuits d'Été*, Schubert's Fifth Symphony, Beethoven's Second, Mozart's Piano Concertos K. 453 and 467 with the Cleveland Orchestra, and last year a performance of Mozart's Symphony K. 201 with the BBC Symphony that was enchanting in its plasticity and grace. And having heard these I had difficulty in believing the reports in *The New York Times* about the "metronomic approach and emotional tightness" of his "cool, literal performances" of 19th-century Romantic and 18th-century classical music. My guess was that seeing the restrained Boulez manner of conducting, the *Times* reviewers thought they heard a metronomic approach in the performances.

As it happened, Boulez's opening program of this year's Philharmonic season was one that attracted me to Avery Fisher Hall: the Brahms-Haydn Variations, Mozart's Clarinet Concerto, Copland's Orchestral Variations and Stravinsky's *Le Sacre du Printemps;* and the performances added up to one of the great concerts of my experience. The plastically coherent and expressive statement of the Brahms piece impelled me to exclaim in delight at its conclusion. The allegros of the concerto were a little too fast; but the adagio provided Stanley Drucker with an opportunity for subtly inflected large-spanned phrasing of the sustained melody. And the wonderful-sounding and overwhelming realization of *Le Sacre* brought to mind Stravinsky's moving words, "Very little immediate tradition lies behind *Le Sacre du Printemps.* I had only my ear to help me. I heard and I wrote what I heard," and caused me, time after time, to marvel at what that ear had heard, which without it we would never have heard. But in *The Times* I read about the "rather tame interpretation" of the Brahms and the "rigidly controlled style" in which Boulez "put the score [of *Le Sacre*] through its paces like an ace equestrian directing a show horse." And since I had discovered that Boulez's manner of conducting had changed—that he now used vigorous movements of his entire body in his operation with the orchestra—I concluded that the *Times* reviewers were still holding onto their idea of Boulez's "metronomic approach" in the face of the contrary that was to be seen and heard in his performances.

One can apply to the Copland piece that was played in honor of his 75th birthday the words in which the English critic Gerald Larner described Copland's Symphony No. 3: "a most impressive piece of engineering" which "says nothing" and whose "musical effect is small."

It was therefore a cruelty to Copland to perform it before the most extraordinary orchestral work of this century; and it would have been better to honor him with a performnce of excerpts from his opera *The Tender Land*, which offers some of his finest writing in the accessible and attractive idiom of his ballet and other theater scores, as against the inaccessible and unattractive idiom of his "modern" works.

A week later an endlessly boring and deservedly unfamiliar early piece by Wagner, *Liebesmahl der Apostel*, preceded the performance of Beethoven's Ninth whose approach was anything but metronomic. Except for the occasional excessive expansive retardations in the first movement, Boulez's innovations in tempo didn't lessen the effectiveness of his statements of the first three movements; and his magnificent statement of the finale resembled Toscanini's in its expansive and powerfully eloquent treatment of the opening recitatives, and its binding the sectional allegro into a coherent progression to the joyous and exalted conclusion.

The Guarneri Quartet operates on the highest level of instrumental virtuosity, tonal beauty, ensemble execution and musical understanding, but not without occasional flawed musical judgment, which didn't appear in the superb performance of Op. 127 that opened the first concert of the Guarneri's Beethoven cycle at the Metropolitan Museum of Art, but did show itself in the performance of Op. 18 No. 1 that followed. Toscanini used to point out to his musicians that a *p* or an *f* meant one thing in a score of Verdi and another thing in a score of Mozart; and presumably he would have pointed out to the Guarneri that an *fp* of *sfz* doesn't mean in a Beethoven Op. 18 quartet what it means in an Op. 59. For the Guarneri played Op. 18 No. 1 with the occasionally explosive vehemence suitable for the Op. 59 No. 3 that ended the concert. This work it played superbly until the fugal finale, for which it set a tempo too fast for the details to be grasped by the listener's mind or even to be distinguished by his ear.

When Fischer-Dieskau's first recorded performances of German *Lieder* began to be heard in the early 50s there was immediate recognition that his voice, extraordinary in timbre and sensuous beauty, and his musical use of that voice, with its sensitivity and continuity in expressive inflection of phrase, placed him among the greats of this special field. And from the beginning there was also difficulty in understanding—in, say, his distinguished performance of Schubert's *Die Winterreise*—the excessively vehement crescendo, overemphasizing its expressive point, that now and then broke through the limits of his coherent inflection of the vocal line. What, in time, maturity added to vocal beauty and musical distinction in that performance of *Die Winterreise* can still be heard on the records issued 10 years ago (Deutsche Grammophon 2707.028); but those issued two years ago revealed the beginning of vocal deterioration—the loss of bloom and glow, though not of distinctive and moving timbre; and the performance of the cycle in Carnegie Hall this season revealed further losses: the voice still retained its distinctive timbre in quiet passages but lost it in forceful ones—the vehement crescendos now ending in hoarse shouts. There seemed to be more of these outbursts than before; and since I happened to be following the performance with the score I discovered that in a number of instances the vehemence was not called for by any direction of Schubert's or anything in the words or music. But after much that was saddening to hear, Fischer-Dieskau ended well, with a performance of the concluding song of the cycle, *Der Leiermann*, that was free of what has seemed to me an error in nearly all the performances I have heard, including his. The *pp* that Schubert places at the beginning of the song is not modified throughout the vocal part—which I take to mean that he intended the numbness of emotional and physical exhaustion expressed in that vocal part to continue to its last note; yet every singer I have heard, except Hotter, has made the concluding statement an impassioned outburst. It was therefore a gratifying surprise to hear Fischer-Dieskau this time hold the statement to the low dynamic level of what had preceded it, and end his unsatisfying performance of the cycle with this wholly right and moving realization of *Der Leiermann*.

His recital a week later, devoted to a number of Mahler's settings of poems from *Des Knaben Wunderhorn* and a few of his *Lieder aus der Jugendzeit*, provided further gratifying surprises. There were again harshly vehement outbursts, which this time were related to the grim, mordant, macabre texts of the songs about war and death; but the greater number of charming light songs—most of them to tests about nature and love, a couple of them to humorous texts—elicited from Fischer-Dieskau beautiful quiet singing and masterly subtleties of inflection.

28 February 1976 The unending flow of incandescent vocal and orchestral invention in Mozart's *The Marriage of Figaro* makes it one of the supreme wonders achieved by human powers. It has had great performances at the Metropolitan—the ones in 1943 and 1944 with, above all, Steber's Countess, and in addition Sayao's Susanna, Novotna's Cherubino, Pinza's Figaro, Brownlee's Count—performances whose only imperfections were Bruno Walter's slowing down of the second subject of the overture and Cherubino's first-act aria ("When Walter comes to something beautiful," Toscanini commented once, "he melts"). And one listened undistracted by the scenery that Jonel Jorgolesco had been content to make unobtrusively serviceable, or by the stage direction of Herbert Graf, except for one detail in the last act—Susanna's extravagant posturings in the Countess's cloak and hat.

All this as an introduction to the fact that the Metropolitan's new production this year offered not a great musical performance but a good one, with Judith Blegen's beautifully and expressively sung and delightfully acted Susanna standing out above the competent and effective Countess of Evelyn Lear, Cherubino of Frederica von Stade, Figaro of Justinio Diaz and Count of Wolfgang Brendel, and with the high-spirited orchestral context provided by Steuart Bedford. But, as usually happens in the opera house nowadays, one was at times distracted from this good musical performance by the newly thought-up details of the scenic designer Robert O'Hearn and stage director Günther Rennert— what Victor Gollancz, in his book on opera production, *The Ring at Bayreuth*, calls the "visualities" that do not, as they should, "help in realizing the musical-dramatic intention of the work" but, as they should not, "focus . . . attention on [themselves]"— i.e. on their mere novelty, and often their disservice to the work.

Thus Mozart places the first act of *Figaro* in a partly furnished room that is to be Figaro's and Susanna's bedroom, in which, as the curtain rises, Figaro is measuring the floor for the placing of the bed while Susanna, seated before a mirror, is trying on a new hat. But at the Metropolitan the rising curtain revealed a room with the singular feature of two enormous windows in the rear wall through which one saw a flight of stairs rising alongside of them; and one was distracted by the thought that it was impossible to believe a bedroom, or indeed any room, would have such windows alongside a flight of stairs, and by the question what their dramatic purpose could be. The rising curtain also revealed Figaro alone on the stage, carrying in the frame of a bed and

busying himself with its headboard as he began to sing "*Cinque . . . dieci
. . . venti*"; which raised the distracting objection that it made no sense to
sing these measurements of the floor when he was fussing with the
headboard of the bed. And the purpose of the windows and stairs was
revealed when one saw Susanna hurry down the stairs, new hat in hand,
and enter through the door in the rear wall; which raised the further
distracting objections that if, as seemed likely, she was coming from the
Countess she should have entered through the door on the left that led to
the Countess's quarters, and that providing this improbable entrance for
Susanna—and, later, Cherubino's entrance through one of the windows—was not a purpose that justified the outlandish windows and
flight of stairs.

There was more of this sort of thing, of which I mention only the room
decorated for the wedding that Mozart specifies for Act Three. In place
of the usual rear wall there were imposingly tall wooden doors flanked by
tall windows through which one saw the green outdoors; and these
caused one to reflect that if the doors were, as they seemed, the palace's
entrance doors, they should open into an entrance hall, not directly into
one of its principal rooms; and that the doors of a room leading directly to
the outdoors would be not wood but glass. Moreover it was through the
wooden entrance doors that Susanna slipped in holding the purse with
the money to pay Figaro's debt to Marcellina; which caused one to reflect
that she should be coming not from outdoors but from somewhere inside
the palace.

It was the New York City Opera, not the Metropolitan, that started
the vandalism which designer-director teams have been inflicting on
operas the past 30 years, and of which the company's new production of
Wagner's *Die Meistersinger* this year was the latest example of its "opera as
modern, exciting theater." Wagner has the first act begin with Walther
alone on the stage, signaling to Eva in the off-stage nave of Saint
Catherine's Church, in which the unseen congregation is singing the
final chorale of the service; and his approaching her when the congregation files out of the nave. But at the New York State Theater the designer
Carl Toms chose to place the first act *inside* the nave, with Walther, at one
side of it, visible to the singing congregation as he signals to Eva; which
raised in one's mind the distracting question what dramatic purpose was
intended as against the awkwardness and incredibility of what was

achieved. And the continuing action brought further distracting awkwardness: as Wagner has it, Magdalene's having to go back into the nave
repeatedly for the articles left behind by Eva and herself provides time
for Walther's impassioned phrases to Eva; but with the three characters
all inside the nave one saw the awkwardness that resulted from Magdalene's needing little time for the few steps to where she and Eva had sat.
In addition there was the effect of John Cox's innovations in stage
direction, the worst of which was to have Beckmesser, in his hallucinatory whirling about when alone in Sachs's workshop, pick up a hammer
or mallet and bang it against everything in sight; which distracted one
with the question how this noisy clatter could fail to bring Sachs or
David down to investigate.

Nor, unlike the Metropolitan's *Figaro*, did this *Meistersinger* offer a
good musical performance of the work that has some of Wagner's most
engaging and at times affecting writing. The New York City Opera's
director, Julius Rudel, claims for it a personnel that "moves from
Mozart to Weisgall" with unfailing authenticity in every style; but with
the exception of John Alexander's excellent singing as Walther the
performance I heard demonstrated the company's lack of the singers,
orchestra and conductor the work required. Eva was sung by Eleanor
Bergquist with a voice suited for Musetta in *La Bohème;* the Sachs was
Norman Bailey, whose voice, agreeable-sounding in the first and last
acts, was rough and harsh in the lyrical writing of the second; and with
these inadequacies in two of the major roles one heard the lack of
amplitude and richness in the sound of the orchestral context—a result
not only of the orchestra's deficiencies in size and quality, but of the
theater's acoustical deficiencies, and to some extent of Rudel's limitations as a conductor. And this is to say nothing of the damaging and
distracting effect of the substitution of English for the work's German.

Seiji Ozawa obtained beautiful playing from the Boston Symphony,
in New York's Carnegie Hall, in the performance of Berlioz's *Romeo and
Juliet* with the New England Conservatory Chorus and the mezzo-
soprano Julia Hamari, tenor Jean Dupouy and bass José van Dam. And
though Ozawa's pacing of the work was unusually fast he shaped it, in
the faster tempos, with plasticity that achieved affecting expressiveness.
Berlioz's music is what I have heard him conduct with the effectiveness
his performances of Beethoven haven't had—the most recent example

being Beethoven's Ninth, whose flowing variations in the slow movement require the expressive inflection that Ozawa didn't introduce;
whose statements of the string basses at the beginning of the finale must
have the character and expressive effect of vocal recitative that they
didn't have in the strict tempo in which he conducted them; and whose
several sections of the finale must be given the coherence and cumulative
impact that he didn't achieve. And I was led to the thought that the chief
conductor of the Boston Symphony should be someone able to deal with
the major classical repertory.

Having been impressed by the recently formed Cleveland Quartet's
superb recorded performances of Schubert's *Death and the Maiden* Quartet and his less familiar Octet, whose many pages of wonderful writing
make it a work that should be played more frequently than it is, I went to
hear the opening concert of the group's Beethoven cycle in New York's
Alice Tully Hall. The playing exhibited the instrumental virtuosity, the
tonal beauty, the musical sensitivity, the perfection of ensemble of a
quartet of the first rank; but at times—in the opening movement of Op.
18 No. 6, the fugal finale of Op. 59 No. 3, the concluding *allegro* section
of the Great Fugue Op. 133—the tempo was too fast for the music to
make its effect or even, in the finale of Op. 59 No. 3, for its detail to be
heard and grasped. Also, I consider it a mistake to conclude Op. 130 with
the Great Fugue, in which I hear no relation to the first five movements
of Op. 130 in style, substance and expressive content, instead of with the
finale that Beethoven substituted for it, which goes well with those five
movements.

17 April 1976 The repertory the Ballet Russe de Monte Carlo presented when it first visited this country in 1933 included a few poor
ballets like Massine's *Les Présages, Choreartium* and *Union Pacific,* but a
sufficient number of good ones: Fokine's *Les Sylphides* and *Petrushka* and
Massine's *Le Tricorne, La Boutique Fantasque* and *Le Beau Danube,* which
were moving and enjoyable; and on the other hand Balanchine's *Concurrence* and *Cotillon,* which were, for me, made special, apart and fascinating by the idiosyncratic ballet vocabulary and syntax he employed
with the invention, imagination and wit of a distinctive mind. Similarly,
the more than forty years after 1933 brought enjoyable and impressive
achievements by the other choreographers—among them Massine's
Gaîté Parisienne and *Capriccio Espagnol,* Tudor's *Lilac Garden, Romeo and*

Juliet and *Pillar of Fire* (the last of which retained for others the impressiveness it lost for me), Loring's *Billy the Kid*, Lew Christensen's *Filling Station*, de Mille's *Three Virgins and a Devil*, *Rodeo* and *Tally-Ho*, Robbins's *Fancy Free*, *Afternoon of a Faun* and *Les Noces*, Herbert Ross's *Caprichos*, Ashton's *Façade*, *Wedding Bouquet* and *The Dream* (though also many uninteresting ballets of these choreographers as well as MacMillan, Cranko, Cullberg, Butler, Tetley and Ailey). And on the other hand those years brought the succession of Balanchine's works that exhibited individually and collectively a magnitude of developing powers and achievement that, for me, made him stand out above other choreographers as Picasso did above other painters.

The major difference between Balanchine's New York City Ballet and American Ballet Theatre, then, is that one presents a repertory made for it by one of the towering creative geniuses in the arts, and the other does not. This is not to say that Ballet Theatre doesn't have a number of ballets worth seeing—the 19th-century classics, the effective ballets made for it in the early 40s by Tudor, deMille and Robbins, and even a Balanchine masterpiece, his 1947 *Theme and Variations*. Nor is it to say that New York City Ballet has only Balanchine masterpieces: all along it has presented occasional less consequential pieces of his that, like some of Bach's and Mozart's, have represented the mere routine operation of his powers; it has also offered less consequential works of members of his company and uninteresting works of major choreographers like Tudor and Ashton; and in recent years more and more program time has been wasted by the enormous and empty works of Robbins. In the pages of *The New York Times* these Robbins works have provided the creativity of genius that Balanchine was no longer providing; on the stage, however, what they have provided has been interminable demonstrations of the limitations of Robbins's vocabulary and imagination in ballet invention, the unattractive results of the straining for novelty with which he has attempted to transcend those limitations, and his resort to show-biz tricks, cuteness, sentimentality and pretensions to profound meanings. One has had to guess at the explanation of Balanchine's allowing all this; and one of the guesses has been Robbins's box-office appeal. But I recall many empty seats last year and the year before; and what caused the public to fill the theater this year was the return of Suzanne Farrell to the company and the consequent restoration to her roles of the effect they had not had in her absence.

This brings us to a similarity between New York City Ballet and Ballet Theatre where Balanchine sees a dissimilarity. We are disposed to grant an artistic genius the privilege of eccentric ideas about his art—in Balanchine's case the ideas not only stated by him but elaborated in the intellectually fancied-up press-agentry of Lincoln Kirstein's program notes and his book on New York City Ballet. However, the ideas' remoteness from reality is something a critic, when he perceives it, must point out; and I perceive it in the Balanchine ideas about "stars." This word means to him dancers whose exhibitions of their glamorous personalities in popular ballets like *Giselle* and *Swan Lake* bring them publicity, reputations and the drawing-power at the box-office that makes them desirable to companies like Ballet Theatre but not to Balanchine. For him it is the dance movement that is important, not the dancer's "expression of an attractive idiosyncrasy" (Kirstein's words). All this is remote from the realities I see, which begin with the fact that Balanchine's powers of invention are set in operation by each dancer's individual capacities not merely in movement but in the subtleties of timing and inflection of the movements that give them the style that is different, personal, idiosyncratic with each dancer. His greatest dance invention, therefore, has been elicited by dancers with extraordinary physical capacities and dancing styles, which are what most people have in mind when they speak of dancers as stars. New York City Ballet's Allegra Kent, Violette Verdy, Suzanne Farrell, Patricia McBride, Jacques d'Amboise, Edward Villella, Peter Martins and Helgi Tomasson are no less stars, in this sense of the word, than are Ballet Theatre's Natalia Makarova, Gelsey Kirkland, Erik Bruhn, Fernando Bujones and Mikhail Baryshnikov; they exhibit their individual dancing styles in Balanchine's works as Ballet Theatre's stars do in that company's repertory.

New York City Ballet's winter season presented a number of Balanchine's works superbly performed not only by its unacknowledged stars but by gifted younger soloists—Merrill Ashley, Colleen Neary, Susan Hendl, and an outstanding new male dancer, Daniel Duell. There were, that is, not only *Raymonda Variations* with Verdy and Martins, and *Diamonds* and *Agon* with Farrell and Martins, but *Concerto Barocco* with Neary as Farrell's associate in the Allegros in addition to Martins in the Adagio; *Symphony in C* with Verdy in one of her too rare appearances in the first movement, Farrell and Martins in the second, Ashley and Robert Weiss in the third, and Hendl and Victor Castelli in the fourth; *The Four Temperaments* with Bart Cook in the *Melancholic* Variation, Ashley and Duell in the *Sanguinic*, Bonnefous in the *Phlegmatic*, and Neary in the *Choleric; Tchaikovsky Suite No. 3* with Neary and Castelli in the Scherzo and Ashley and Martins in the concluding *Theme and Variations*.

As for Balanchine's new ballets, I was unable to see *The Steadfast Tin Soldier* but did see *Chaconne*, a fine work to the ballet music of Gluck's *Orfeo ed Euridice*, but with the strange feature of an introductory *pas de deux* for Farrell and Martins unrelated in style either to the sustained flute melody from The Dance of the Blessed Spirits to which it was danced, or to what it introduced—the charming dances for the lesser soloists, the incandescent series of variations for the two principals.

Ballet Theatre, this year, offered three new works with Baryshnikov: Butler's *Medea*, Neumeier's *Hamlet: Connotations* and Twyla Tharp's *Push Comes to Shove*. An injury caused the cancellation of the performances I was to see of the first two; but I can report on the third. Baryshnikov had, in *Coppélia*, exhibited a gift for comedy in addition to his gift for casually executed feats of incredible virtuosity; but I wasn't prepared for his achievement, in the Prelude of the Tharp work, of what I would have thought impossible for him to achieve: a very funny take-off of an American vaudeville hoofer's eccentric dance to Joseph Lamb's *Bohemia Rag* (1919), in which his body moved in the twisting, thrusting, strutting style as if it had done nothing else all his life (Baryshnikov is the one who might be able to dance d'Amboise's role in *Who Cares?*). It was also an impressive achievement of Tharp's eye for the style and for Baryshnikov's capacities, and what seemed to me the one major achievement in the work.

Kirkland's distinctive lightness and effortlessly achieved clarity and perfection of changing bodily configuration worked as beautifully in Ballet Theatre's *Giselle, Coppélia, La Sylphide* and *Lilac Garden* as in New York City Ballet's *Concerto Barocco* and *Theme and Variations;* and she was, in addition, amusing and witty in *Coppélia*, charmingly wilful in *La Sylphide*, and moving at its conclusion. I was too far from the stage to be able to report on her dramatic performance in *Giselle*, but near enough for her dancing in *Lilac Garden* to convey its emotional intensity.

The company's fourth new piece was a slight one, a *pas de trois* from

Bournonville's *La Ventana* staged by Bruhn, which Bujones enlivened with his elegantly achieved feats of virtuosity. And these were even more impressive when seen in the context of his effective performance in a *Coppélia* with Eleanor D'Antuono.

Martine van Hamel's Myrtha in *Giselle* must be mentioned, and her Sylphide in an earlier performance of *La Sylphide* than Kirkland's; also Ivan Nagy's James in both performances, and Bruhn's Madge in the second one.

A final observation: If I had written that the plays of Eugene O'Neill did not have now the impressiveness they had for me in my youth, this would have been considered valid as an instance of the revaluation that accompanies one's continuing experience of art; but when I did actually write this about many (but not all) works of Brahms, my statement was said to represent prejudice—i.e. judgment before, or without, or in the face of, experience—which in fact it did not. Or if I had written that the works of Picasso I had seen and the powers they exhibited made him, for me, someone who stood apart from, and towered above, the other painters of this century whom I admired, this too would have been considered valid as a response to my experience; but my writing it about the ballets and the powers of Balanchine was characterized (in a recent issue of the magazine *Ballet Review*)as an indulgence of prejudice for what Balanchine did with his New York City Ballet, and an intolerance of other choreographers' work and other companies, that made what I wrote special pleading rather than criticism. This ignored my appreciative reports of these choreographers' achievements in some of their works—evidence, as I see it, that I had done with each work the reporting and evaluating of what I had seen that was what I had done also with each work of Balanchine, and what I understand criticism to be.

Note 1983 The article in *Ballet Review* (by someone with the improbable name "Cherry Heering" whose writing resembled Arlene Croce's) deplored the exceedingly small number of newspapers and magazines that offered regular reporting by dance critics—in this ignoring the exceedingly small number of writers capable of perceptive and accurate reporting of dance events, and the disservice to the public and to dance by an additional hundred writers incapable of such reporting. In particular, the article pointed out, "the quarterlies offer an occasional Dance

Chronicle by Robert Garis in *Partisan Review*, and B. H. Haggin, . . .
Garis's mentor, holds forth in the *Hudson Review*. . . . Both . . . are
champions of the New York City Ballet and indulge their prejudice
brilliantly . . . Their intolerance of other companies (Haggin has even
used Balanchine as a stick to beat Martha Graham) tends to relegate their
work to the category of special pleading rather than criticism." My
writing did lead Garis to look at ballet; but what he saw, and what he
thought and wrote about it in *Partisan Review*, clearly represented critical
perception and judgment different from mine. Moreover our view of
Balanchine's superiority was also, essentially, the view of Denby and
Croce; and what was criticism when written by them did not become
intolerance and special pleading when written by Garis and me.

19 June 1976 I Puritani, which the Metropolitan produced this year for
two of its stars, Joan Sutherland and Luciano Pavarotti, is Bellini's last
opera, which exhibits his developed powers not only in the melodic
writing that attains its highest point in the aria *"Qui la voce,"* but in its
dramatically meaningful orchestral writing, and in the elaborating ensemble writing exemplified most impressively in the finale of the first
act. While the peculiar timbre of Sutherland's voice below its bright high
range, and the mannerisms of her phrasing, made her singing of sustained melody unattractive to the ear and musically unsatisfying, her
florid singing was spectacular in its agility and accuracy, and her bright
high notes dominated the climaxes of the ensembles impressively. Pavarotti's powerful voice has always lacked the sensuous warmth and ease of
flow this music calls for; and though it rings out clearly in the recently
recorded performance of *I Puritani*, it had an unpleasant rasp in the
Metropolitan performance I attended. It was these flaws in the musical
performance conducted effectively by Richard Bonynge that were disturbing on this occasion, not the stage production and dramatic performance: realistic scenery as imaginatively undistinguished as Ming Cho
Lee's, and singing non-actors as ineffective as Sutherland and Pavarotti,
in performance of dramatic nonsense like *I Puritani*, are the commonplace of opera that one relegates to the periphery of the attention focused
on the music.

The Metropolitan's new *Aida* was another matter. It had special
interest as the first production jointly conceived and carried through by
James Levine and John Dexter, the team of musical director and produc-

tion director newly created not only to work on its own productions but to make the necessary artistic decisions on all Metropolitan productions. I wrote last summer of the musical excellence one could hope for with Levine's appointment as musical director; and this excellence was achieved in large measure in the *Aida*. His conducting shaped the work with a feeling for the Verdi *espansione* controlled by a sense for plastic continuity and coherence in the progression of sound in time. And Leontyne Price, in the title role, astonished one with the beauty of her singing at this late date, except for the strident climactic high C in "*O patria mia*" and some unattractive sounds in the final scene; Marilyn Horne, the Amneris, sang with vocal sumptuousness and dramatic power throughout; and Bonaldo Giaotti was an impressive Ramfis. With these one could accept the constricted sounds produced by James McCracken, the Radames, and the singing of Cornell MacNeil, the Amonasro, that was dramatically effective, but sounded harsh at first and dry even when it became more agreeable.

Much of the time, however, one was distracted from the musical performance by the obtrusively innovative and damaging details of the stage production that represented the kind of re-creative thinking present-day directors and designers feel privileged to do about the composer's work and to impose on it in place of his own explicitly stated decisions concerning the dramatic scene and action. My additional hope last summer was that Levine, since he deferred to the composer's directions about the performance of the music, would want similar deference to what the composer specified about the staging, and would use his power of veto to prevent the sort of thing I have just described. But as it turned out, Levine spoke on several occasions of how Dexter and he, in their discussions, found themselves to be extraordinarily in agreement; and in a joint interview in *The Times* they revealed their agreement in the thinking they had imposed on *Aida*.

Ancient Egypt, in Verdi's mind, was only an exotic place which introduced an element of novelty into what he recognized was a hackneyed dramatic action and provided opportunities for spectacle to enliven it, and as such required no more than scenery and costumes which would represent that place to the eyes of the audience in the theater—in particular what he specified for the opening scene that would represent a hall in the king's palace in Memphis: the set of an interior with colonnades, statues, flowering plants, and a great door at the back through which one would see palaces, temples and pyramids. This, however limited, was all that Verdi needed and used for his musical drama, and all that audiences needed to be moved by it. But the ancient Egypt of *Aida* evoked in the minds of Dexter and Levine a great deal more that didn't enter the mind of Verdi: thoughts of intense religious and social pressures exerted by the priests in the rigidly ritualized society into which the Egyptians were locked; images of grandeur, gigantic scale, enormous space. These were valid as thoughts and images in the minds of Dexter and Levine; but translated into the concrete details of staging that the team introduced into Verdi's opera they were damaging and distracting. To show the Egyptians locked into a rigidly ritualized society the singers were locked into a rigid style of unnatural body pose and arm movement which, throughout the performance, one could not accept as having been employed by any Egyptians but the painted ones in museums. As for grandeur, Dexter and Levine insisted it was not attainable on a stage cluttered "with lots of papier-mâché icons" (in Levine's words), but required the bare sets that would convey an impression of monumental size and space; and so at the beginning of the opening scene the few characters carried on their exchanges not in the intimacy of a palace interior but in what looked like an enormous cavern in a mountain—this despite the Dexter-Levine claim to have staged *Aida* as the intimate opera it really was instead of the DeMille spectacular they said (incorrectly) it had traditionally been misunderstood to be.

There was much more of this sort of thing, which I don't have space for; and I will add only that with thinking concentrated on the insertion into the opera of what Verdi had not put into it, too little or no thought appeared to have been given to things he *had* put into it. Thus, Amneris's apartment didn't merely lack the traditional couch for her to recline on, as her attendants prepared her for the victory celebration, but provided nothing for anyone to sit on; which not only struck one as odd in itself but later produced the distractingly improbable result that instead of being seated in the center of the stage as the dancers performed for her she stood watching them from the side of the stage.

Inserted in *The Times* a few Sundays ago was a brochure with material about "the civilized sights and sounds of a national treasure" that the Metropolitan provided. A paragraph sub-titled *The Promise of a New Era* described how the company's tradition "has now been further enhanced by the talents of two extraordinarily gifted men," Dexter and Levine, who "together . . . have the eyes and ears to see and hear operas in innovative ways, plus the energy to bring them to unprecendented heights." But to me the Dexter-Levine *Aida* promises a continuation of the old era in which production teams' innovative ways of looking at operas have inflicted appalling damage on them.

Equally disappointing—to judge by the announcement for next year—is what the new era promises in repertory. The brochure's cover had a photograph of Martti Talvela in Musorgsky's *Boris Godunov;* but actually this work will not be heard again next year—the reported reason being the one that caused the Metropolitan's board of directors to drop the triumphantly successful production of Berlioz's *Les Troyens:* that it is expensive to perform. But if money is available for next year's new productions of Meyerbeer's *Le Prophète*, Poulenc's *Dialogues des Carmélites* and Alban Berg's *Lulu*, I contend that it should be used instead for additional performances of the long unheard, and then too briefly heard, masterpieces of the 19th century's two great originals, Berlioz and Musorgsky. To drop *Les Troyens* and *Boris* and use what they would cost for *Le Prophète*, *Dialogues des Carmélites* and *Lulu* is equivalent to the Metropolitan Museum's using its money to acquire not the Rembrandt *Aristotle* but works of people like Ad Reinhardt and Andy Warhol.

Explaining the new policy for next year's new productions, Levine stated the "categories of operas in which we should expand the repertory" as "First, basic 20th-century works . . . Second, acknowledged masterpieces that haven't been seen at the Met in many years . . . Third, less-played works by important composers. And fourth, new productions of standard works." The categories are the right ones, but wrongly applied. After 50 years my dim recollection of *Le Prophète* is that it is a work good enough to revive when money is plentiful, but not an acknowledged masterpiece whose claim to be heard is greater than that of *Les Troyens* or *Boris*. Berg's *Wozzeck* (which is in the Metropolitan's repertory) is one of this century's basic works, but his *Lulu*, when the Hamburg Opera performed it in New York in 1967, left me uninvolved and even unbelieving. As for *Dialogues des Carmélites*, which the New York City Opera produced in 1966, its writing had little musical interest or dramatic point. And I would have supposed that those recent performances of *Lulu* and *Dialogues* had sufficed to eliminate any need of their being presented again by the Metropolitan.

Nor is more sense for value exhibited in the rest of next year's repertory. Puccini rates the same number of operas as Verdi's three, and more than Mozart's two; and in place of additional Verdi and Mozart there will be even less valuable works than Puccini's by Giordano, Saint-Saëns and Massenet.

24 July 1976 Some of what the Balanchine eye has seen not only in other dancing than ballet but in other kinds of movement than dance has turned up later in his invention for his own works. Thus, the Diaghilev seasons in London in the 20s gave Balanchine opportunities to see the musical shows and revues playing there, including *Lady Be Good* and *Funny Face*, which charmed his ear with the Gershwin songs and his eye with the Astaire dancing. The vocabulary, syntax and style of American musical-show dancing that Balanchine got to know then he used, soon after his arrival here in the 30s, in dances for the musical *On Your Toes*, with imaginative freshness and mastery which so impressed Rodgers and Hart that they had him perform the same service for their *Babes in Arms* and *The Boys From Syracuse*. And years later, in his ballet *Who Cares?*, he used 17 of Gershwin's show songs as the score for an elaboration, in his personal ballet language and style, of his astonishingly numerous and accurate recollections of the steps and bodily movements that made the dancing in those musicals the distinctive genre it was.

To this marvelous work Balanchine has now added a three-part spectacular, *Union Jack*, in which—using a score fashioned by Hershy Kay out of traditional music, except for one Handel piece Balanchine used in *The Figure in the Carpet*—he elaborates his recollections of other things he saw during his visits to London: the low-comedy routines and dances of the music halls; the ritual maneuvers of the guards regiments at Buckingham Palace; the Scottish military tattoos and folk dances; the hornpipes of the sailors of the Royal Navy. In Part One, six Scottish guards "regiments" of dancers in their clan tartans, and one "regiment" of girls in the tartan of the Royal Canadian Air Force, make successive solemnly slow, swaying entrances, coming to a full stop in the center of the stage, then moving to one position after another in the grouping, and eventually making slow exits—after which they return, one or two at a time, for a succession of dances in which the fast, intricate footwork becomes dazzling, and the fun of the dance of the MacLeod regiment is pointed up by Jacques d'Amboise's stunts of joyous virtuosity. Part Two offers a music-hall comedy act entitled *Costermonger Pas de Deux*, whose high point is the male solo in the comic style Balanchine has retained in his memory all these years, in which Jean-Pierre Bonnefous reveals powers in dance buffoonery that one could not have anticipated. And Part Three brings the sustained fun of the sailors' hornpipes, with outstanding contributions by Peter Martins, d'Amboise and Suzanne Farrell.

This is as much as I can say about *Union Jack* after only one performance; and I strongly recommend a reading of Arlene Croce's *New Yorker* article (May 31) for the perceptions that not only are enlightening in themselves but provide, in effect, correction of other writers' errors. Concerning *Union Jack* it is Clive Barnes's objection—that the cockney music hall he remembers had no dance tradition for Balanchine to use in *Costermonger Pas de Deux*—that is corrected, in effect, by Croce's description of the details of costume, action and dance amplifying her statement that "Balanchine, who evidently spent time in the music halls in the days when he was devising revues for Charles Cochran, has given us a character-mime picture of just such an act as he must have seen then."

One of the things that struck the Balanchine eye in this country was the square dance—its formations, and the wheeling into and out of the formations—which he used first in *Western Symphony*, with a Hershy Kay arrangement of American folk tunes, and a few years later in *Square Dance*, this time with engaging music of Vivaldi and Corelli, but also with an actual square-dance caller to call out what the dancers did: "Otherwise," said Balanchine, "it will be only another ballet, with Vivaldi music." And so the elegant movements were accompanied by jingling words like "Now watch her feet go wickety-wack," which, blared out by the loud speakers, obtruded themselves on one's ears and mind to a degree that made it almost impossible to hear the music and see the ballet. The inclusion of the caller was clearly a mistake, which nevertheless Balanchine repeated in his revival of the piece a few years later. But in this year's revival he eliminated the caller and made revisions in the dances that left almost nothing that referred to the title, making the piece after all "only another ballet, with Vivaldi music," which, excellently performed by Kay Mazzo, Bart Cook and the ensemble, one could enjoy undisturbed.

Despite the amount of thought and work required by *Union Jack*, Balanchine managed to make a few additions to other ballets. *Chaconne* now begins with a slow ensemble piece which introduces the Farrell-Martins *pas de deux* that still is, in style, not an introduction to the ballet that follows. In *Emeralds* two additional Fauré pieces are used—one for a *pas de deux* beautifully made for Violette Verdy's style; the other, after what was the lively finale, for a new slow concluding number that is anticlimactic in effect. And what was the lively finale of *Divertimento from Le Baiser de la Fée* also is followed now by a new slow concluding number—one that is impressive in effect, but is not what the Stravinsky music was originally composed for. In 1972 I felt that the Stravinsky Festival was an occasion that required Balanchine to revive the great dramatic ballet he created in 1937 for the greatest Stravinsky score after *Le Sacre*; and that Balanchine's decision instead to use a few passages of this dramatic score for a new non-dramatic *pas de deux* was a failure in his obligation to Stravinsky. His use now of additional passages for the new conclusion is, I feel, another such failure.

The quietly and precisely achieved clarity and largeness of Peter Martins's movements made them impressive from the start; but they now have in addition a grandeur that is overwhelming. He is, then, the predestined partner for Suzanne Farrell with her similar quietly achieved clarity and largeness of movement to which has been added a similar grandeur. And their operation together is as great as any that can be seen today. Nor is this the only thing of that kind the New York City Ballet offers: the light-as-air operation, singly and together, of young Judith Fugate and Daniel Duell in *Valse-Fantaisie* deserved the storm of applause it got each time I saw it.

15 Janaury 1977　　Claudio Abbado, at the Metropolitan several years ago, produced a performance of Verdi's *Don Carlo* that was made outstanding and exciting by its combination of passion and discipline—a shaping of the work in which he held the impassioned Verdi *espansione* within the limits of unfailing plastic proportion, continuity and coherence. It was another such impassioned but perfectly shaped progression that he achieved with the company of Milan's La Scala in the performance of Verdi's *Simon Boccanegra* in Washington, which National Public Radio made it possible to hear in New York. And I should point out that the greatness of what one heard Abbado produce with the excellent orchestra and chorus and most of the principlas—notably Piero Cappuccilli in the title role and Nicolai Ghiaurov as Fiesco—was not lessened by the vocal inadequacies of the soprano and tenor in the roles of

Amelia and Gabriele: great conductors produce great performances of opera even with less than perfect casts.

A further demonstration of this is provided by the Metropolitan's new *Lohengrin*. James Levine, much younger than Abbado and an American, astonished audiences a few years ago with performances of Verdi's *Luisa Miller* that also exhibited a feeling for the Verdi *espansione* and a discipline which held it within the limits of plastic proportion and coherence. He was clearly—as his subsequent dealing with *Otello, I Vespri Siciliani* and *Aida* confirmed—a superb conductor of Verdi; and his *Lohengrin* shows him to be as superb a conductor of Wagner—one who produced the fine performance I heard with the Metropolitan's excellent orchestra, but with its poor-sounding chorus and inadequate singers in most of the principal roles. The Elsa was Pilar Lorengar, whose basically agreeable voice was made unattractive much of the time by tremolo; the Ortrud Mignon Dunn, whose tremulous voice rose to climactic screams; the Lohengrin René Kollo, who phrased with a musical sensitiveness he hadn't exhibited in von Karajan's recorded *Meistersinger*, but whose voice hadn't acquired luster and warmth or even ease of production; the Telramund Donald McIntyre, who had sung better than he did this time. The one satisfying singer was Bonaldo Giaotti, the King Henry.

Unfortunately one was distracted again from the excellent musical performance by innovative details of the staging by August Everding and Ming Cho Lee that signaled not the new era promised in the Metropolitan's promotion material but the continuation of the old era in which director-designer teams—e.g. Everding and Lee in their dealing with the Kromy Scene of *Boris Godunov* three years ago—were free to substitute what they thought up for what the composer specified in dramatic scene and action. They justify their practice with the better dramatic sense they say the changes make for the public of today, or the sense they claim to be substituting for nonsense; but what the innovations often substitute is new absurdities for the old. And whereas a composer's own absurdities are entitled to our benign indulgence, and their familiarity enable us to treat them with benign neglect, the ones substituted today, which command our attention with their unfamiliarity, have no claim to our acceptance.

In *Lohengrin*, for example, Wagner's having Lohengrin make his entrance in a boat drawn by a swan, to whom, after stepping onto the shore, he turns to sing his thanks and farewell, is something that directors of today insist audiences cannot be asked to accept; and so the Wieland Wagner staging produced at the Metropolitan in 1967 asked audiences to accept the absurdity of principals and chorus peering into the auditorium and singing their amazement at what was not there to amaze them, while Lohengrin climbed out of a depth behind them under a projection of a swan on the backdrop and stepped forward to address his farewell and thanks to the audience. Adapting to this the statement attributed to Hindemith—that music had a face; and if one didn't like it one shouldn't play it; but if one played it one shouldn't change it—I contend that Wagner's *Lohengrin* has a face, and anyone who doesn't like it is free not to stage it, but even his grandson was not free to change it. And whereas audiences of today accept the familiar boat drawn by a swan with only peripheral awareness, Wieland Wagner's unfamiliar substitute compelled attention and full recognition of its absurdity.

As for the new Everding-Lee staging, it is what could be expected from the director who thought up the last act of the Metropolitan's current *Tristan und Isolde* and the Kromy Scene of *Boris*, and the designer who has never, in my experience, produced a set that has revealed imaginative insight or mere skill and taste. And its obtrusive ineptitudes and absurdities begin with the curtain's rise for the opening scene. Even Wieland Wagner's opening geometric tableau on a glowing stage had King Henry, the Herald and Telramund placed prominently in the center, with the chorus in a semi-circle behind them; but what one sees now on the murky stage is a crowd extending from front right around the center and up a ramp that rises to front left; then someone in the crowd high on the left beginning to sing what reveals him to be the Herald; then the Herald yielding his place to someone else whose singing reveals him to be King Henry; then the King making his way down the ramp and coming forward on the stage to a hitherto unnoticed regal seat on the left, where he listens to Telramund who has appeared on the right. Not only is this dramatically unclear and ineffective, but the voices of the Herald and the King don't ring out from the high point on the ramp as they do later from the center of the stage. Still later Lohengrin's arrival is seen by the principals and chorus who sing their amazement as he climbs into view out of some tall weeds on the left to which he turns to address his thanks and farewell. In the second act, which Wagner places in a courtyard of the citadel, Ortrud is directed to rush from the end of Elsa's procession to bar her from the steps to the entrance of the cathedral; but one sees instead a vast interior with flights of steps between its several levels, and Elsa's procession entering on one of these levels with Ortrud holding up the train of Elsa's wedding dress and suddenly dropping it to bar Elsa from the steps leading down to a part of the stage that has no discernible connection with the wedding. If not for its pale blue color one would think the bridal chamber of the third act was designed by Mae West; and in the final scene Lohengrin, instead of sadly greeting the swan who has returned to take him away, addresses his greeting to the tall weeds on the left into which he disappears.

Levine is also an effective symphonic conductor (which not all great conductors of opera are), or at least an effective conductor of Mahler's symphonies. He recorded an excellent performance of the most genial and immediately attractive of those symphonies, the Fourth, and an equally good performance of the First, except for the second movement that he heard not as the lilting *Ländler* that it is, but as the fast waltz it is not. In the New York Philharmonic's pre-season Mahler series this year Levine conducted a performance of the Second, which, when I heard the delayed broadcast in December, I thought was very good.

In that Mahler series Boulez conducted the Third, which he repeated at the orchestra's opening concerts of its subscription season in recon- structed Avery Fisher Hall. My first hearing of this work years ago was Leonard Bernstein's recorded performance, whose distortions of the earlier movements not only made them unattractive but left me unpre- pared for the quiet, control and sustained tension of the performance of the long concluding movement that enabled me to hear in it the grandest and most sublime of Mahler's utterances. Subsequent recorded perfor- mances—by Solti, Abravanel, Horenstein, Haitink—undid Bernstein's damage to the earlier movements, but, surprisingly, did not equal his extraordinary achievement with the finale; and there was no reason to expect anything different from Boulez. But the progression—at once impassioned and disciplined in its plasticity—that seized one's mind with the very first phrases, held it to the last chord of the overwhelming statement of the finale.

I can report in addition that the sound of the orchestra in the recon- structed hall turned out to be superb—a result not only of the expertise Cyril Harris had previously demonstrated in the acoustic excellence of the new Metropolitan Opera House, but of his having made it a condition of his participating in the reconstruction that what he decided was necessary for his acoustic purpose would prevail over what the architect wanted for his esthetic ends. One would assume that this is always so—that the acoustic expert's view is always deferred to; and in the case of the original Philharmonic Hall it was reasonable to think the bad acoustics were the result of mistaken decisions by Leo Beranek. Fairness requires correction of this idea: his original specifications for the hall were not adopted by the architect, who regarded him as someone to contrive good acoustics for the successive sizes and shapes that were considered and the one that was finally adopted. This was the reason for the "clouds" that Beranek devised for the ceiling; and he planned them to be movable, to permit their being adjusted for acoustic purposes; but the Lincoln Center administration, to save money, decided that they were to be immovable; and because of strikes and other delays Beranek had to fix their positions a few months before the hall was completed. I know nothing about Beranek's work except friends' reports of the marvelous acoustics he achieved in the auditorium of Dartmouth College's Hopkins Center; and I am not contending that his original specifications would have produced perfection in Philharmonic Hall, but only pointing out that the actual hall with its bad acoustics was not built in accordance with those specifications. Clearly, Harris was aware of all this, and aware also of the fact that the architect for the reconstruction of Philharmonic Hall, Philip Johnson, had been the architect for the New York State Theater, whose esthetic bad taste had prevailed over the acoustic consultant's recommendations and produced that theater's faulty acoustics. (An associate of the acoustic consultant quoted to me Johnson's statement, "I'm not going to let you spoil my little jewel box!", which actually was not little, and which he himself spoiled as a place in which to see ballet, with its excessive size and its horseshoe-shaped balconies whose center was too far from the stage and whose sides had only a partial view of it.)

12 March 1977 Orchestra players acquire in their rehearsals and performances a doer's knowledge, understanding and perception of what happens in the joint operation of orchestra and conductor that even an experienced listener—even one whose experience includes observation of orchestral rehearsals—cannot have. When Barenboim made his first appearances as a conductor in New York with the London Symphony he was reported in *The Times* to have "a fine feeling for balances, and the clearest, most incisive of beats. . . . His left hand is independent . . . supplementing and not echoing the right." As a listener I was able to hear the lack of even a crude feeling for orchestral balance in the performances of Beethoven's Fifth and Schubert's Ninth that made the works sound like concertos for kettledrums. But my guest at one concert—a bassoonist who had played for 20 years in the Vienna Philharmonic and another 20 in the Metropolitan Opera Orchestra—revealed in a constant nervous movement of his hands the anxiety he said he shared vicariously with the players who, he could perceive, were having to decide which of the contradictory indications of Barenboim's impressively flailing arms to obey. "He is lucky," my guest commented, "that he conducts an orchestra which knows itself what to do."

It was astonishing, therefore, to read, in an article in *The Times* about the New York Philharmonic, that its members—giving their written evaluations of the conductors they had played with, and replying to the question whether or not they would like to play with them again—had said "yes" for Barenboim and "no" for Michael Tilson Thomas, the extraordinarily gifted conductor and musician whom I heard produce with them a marvelously conceived and executed performance of Mozart's Symphony K. 338. Orchestra players, it turns out, occasionally say things that a mere listener can dispute—this because even as possessors of the instrumental expertise they are paid to exercise they vary in musical sensitivity and professional attitude, and as people they vary in intelligence, personal sensitivity, even personal decency. In the Philharmonic they range from the conscientious young cellist who was reported, in the *Times* article, to have been in tears after his first day with the orchestra, a rehearsal with Boulez, which the players' horsing around had reduced to a shambles—from this cellist, and some others like him, to the players whose wrecking of the rehearsal demonstrated their lack of the strict professional principle they claim to be governed by. "We set high standards for ourselves," one player was quoted as saying, in the article, "and we expect the same of our conductors"—which was controverted not only by the wrecked rehearsal but by the "yes" for Barenboim and "no" for Thomas. And there was also a player's statement that with Boulez "it's like performing an autopsy. He understands pitch and rhythmic relationships—not music"—astounding to a listener who had heard, most recently, the moving performance of the finale of Mahler's

Third that Boulez had produced with the orchestra.

Since that performance was moving not only to me but to the 2000 listeners who stood applauding and cheering at its conclusion, I was surprised to find it characterized as "unmoving" by Andrew Porter in *The New Yorker*. His response represented the difference between his idea of Mahler's music as the determinant of the correct way to perform it, and the idea developed by Boulez in an article, "Mahler Now," which Porter had read in a book entitled *Gustav Mahler in Vienna*, and a somewhat revised version of which I read in *The New York Review*. In that article Boulez discusses the characteristics of Mahler's music that he thinks were responsible for the many years in which it was rarely performed and make it difficult to understand even now when it is performed constantly. Since Boulez is, with all his extraordinary musical gifts, an eccentric in his musical composing and thinking, what he says in the article is a mingling of occasional illuminating perceptions with much that I cannot understand. But though I have difficulty in understanding Boulez's words I never had any in understanding Mahler's music. I was impressed immediately by his Symphony No. 2 when I first heard it, performed by Mengelberg with the Philharmonic, in the 20s; and when I fled from Carnegie Hall after an hour of Mengelberg's rehearsal of the first movement of No. 7 it was not because I couldn't understand it but because what I understood was unattractive and, after an hour, impossible to listen to. Further experience increased my understanding of both the earlier four symphonies of Mahler that moved and fascinated me and the later five that I found impossible to listen to. By the time I heard the genial No. 4, performed by Bruno Walter with the Philharmonic in 1944, I could perceive that it was "characteristically expansive and long-winded," but characteristic also in its manifestations of the unfailing alertness and attentiveness of mind that kept the progression freshly interesting—the use of now these few instruments and now those few, of the enormous orchestra, in detail after detail that was strikingly, fascinatingly original; and the daring harmony and counterpoint. (I noted also that Walter's tendency to carry relaxation to the point of slackness was not the weakness in Mahler's music that it was in Beethoven's and Schubert's.) On the other hand, when I heard No. 8 for the first time in 1950 I decided that its frenetic ranting was of no interest to me; and hearing two movements of the uncompleted No. 10 that year, I recognized the difference between the earlier Mahler diffuseness produced by an active, inventive mind and the later diffuseness that was a mere filling in of the huge canvas with endless repetitions of empty gestures and lifeless mannerisms. This, I will add, is what I now hear in the No. 9 that impressed me years ago when I first heard the recording of the historic performance conducted by Walter in Vienna in 1938.

As against these experiences of mine with the music there was what I read about it in the notes accompanying the performances at concerts and on records. They were written by people for whom every work of Mahler was a masterpiece, and who thought it necessary to provide the listener with his every known word, spoken or written, about the performed work, every state of mind and emotion it produced in him as he was composing it—this in the evident belief that what they reported as going on in the tormented composer's mind and life not only made the music he composed understandable, but made it—always—impressive, moving, great. For me, therefore, one of Boulez's most valuable percep-tions in his article is the statement about "how difficult [and by implica-tion how necessary] it is, in the case of Mahler, to steer free of the legend which stubbornly mingles his life and his work—the melodrama and the agony," and the exhortation to "confront directly the uneven monu-ments he left behind." And related to this statement about the music is the later one about its performance: that while Mahler did not intend his many directions in the scores to inhibit "a great subjective re-creation . . . he knew better than to mistake sloppiness for 'interpretation'. He knew that the most demanding kind of freedom actually requires the strictest discipline." For to "succumb to the frenzies of the moment" is both to "trivialize [the music] and empty it of profound content" and to "destroy the subliminal structure which balances the various developments in the work."

That is the issue between Boulez and Porter, who believes that what Mahler's music has to offer, and performance of it must reveal, is "above all 'the expression of feelings,' " and who finds fault with the conductors of today who he says are concerned with revealing the music's structure rather than with "dissolving us into ecstasies and bringing all heaven—or hell—before our eyes." He describes the excellences of Walter's 1938 performance of No. 9—among them "a sense of long-breathed singing and an emotional intensity, expressed in tone color and by accent and rubato within the phrases, that were missing in the Philharmonic per-formance" with Boulez last fall, which he found "unidiomatic both in timbre and in the use of rubato (which Boulez seems to apply in a cosmetic fashion, and not because he feels the music that way)." Quoting a Philharmonic player's complaint about Boulez's requiring only "the right notes at the right times" and there being "never any joy in making music", Porter says that "if to 'joy' we add 'awe,' and even 'terror,' it begins to explain why Boulez's Mahler proves so unaffecting." But I, listening to no one's words, only to Boulez's performance of No. 3, heard rubatos that were genuinely felt as part of an expressive intensity which demonstrated concern with more than the right notes at the right times, in the disciplined shaping of the work that made it deeply moving.

28 May 1977 The statement attributed to Hindemith—that a musical work has a face; and if one didn't like that face one shouldn't perform the work, but if one performed it one shouldn't change it—is an affirmation of the inviolability of an artist's work, a 19th-century composer's no less than a 19th-century painter's or novelist's. The face of Meyerbeer's *Le Prophète* is the music spectacularly sung and the action splendidly staged of a "grand opera" for the Paris Opera; therefore, according to Hindemith, if one chooses to present the work one must present the "grand opera" Meyerbeer envisioned, as the Paris Opera did in 1849, and as the Metropolitan did in 1918, when it had Caruso for Jean, Matzenauer for Fidès and Muzio for Berthe, and had the money for stage splendor; and if the Metropolitan of today doesn't have those vocal and financial resources—if, that is, it has one great singer, Marilyn Horne, whose sumptuous-sounding and expressively moving delivery of Fidès's *"Ah! mon fils"* is comparable with what I remember as Matzenauer's, but has for Jean only James McCracken, whose agreeable tenor voice becomes unattractively constricted and altered in timbre in its upper range, and for Marthe only Renata Scotto, whose every climactic high note is a strident scream, and if it hasn't the money for splendid staging—it shouldn't produce the work. For at best, with those insufficient resources utilized by a stage director who recognized the inviolability of Meyerbeer's work and had skill, taste and intelligence for the task of making it effective on the stage, the result would be an inadequate realization of what Meyerbeer envisioned; and in the actual situation, with those resources utilized by the Metropolitan's John Dexter, who is in every way the opposite of the director I just described, the result is a monstrosity of contemporary operatic stagecraft which should not be presented to the American public as Meyerbeer's grand opera.

Dexter would have produced the same staging of *Le Prophète* even if the money had been available for the splendor Meyerbeer envisioned— which is to say that it represented the ideas about opera production in general and his particular productions that he expressed in the statements quoted in a *Times* interview and a *New Yorker* "Talk of the Town." Staging an opera, for him, is not merely to give effect to what the librettist and composer created: it is to treat their work as material for him to manipulate and change in accordance with *his* ideas about it. If Verdi was content to deal with the hackneyed operatic entanglements of a few characters whom, for the sake of novelty, he placed in ancient Egypt, Dexter was not: his staging of *Aida* was devised to make the audience aware of the rigidly ritualized society into which the ancient Egyptians were locked by the all-powerful priests—something Verdi didn't concern himself with in the opera. Similarly Dexter's staging of *Le Prophète* was intended to get the audience to see "the work [that] exists on a much more profound level" than the immediate spectacular *pièce de théâtre* utilizing the libretto about the historical figure Jean of Leyden and several unhistorical characters—to see, that is, a work in which Meyerbeer, according to Dexter, "[tried] to capture, musically and dramatically, the explosive atmosphere of Northern Europe in the fifteen-thirties . . . when the movement for a populist, instinctive religion had reached the breaking point." To achieve this he replaced the realistic sets for the scenes of Meyerbeer's *pièce de théâtre* with Peter Wexler's single permanent skeletal framework of an uncompleted cathedral extending around the stage "like a huge cage," a symbol throughout the work of the Catholic Church that is a cage enclosing and dominating the people struggling against it. For the rest Dexter—doing away with what for him is the "clutter" of realistic staging—filled the stage with what to my eye is a clutter of wagons, platforms and stairs that are shifted about to provide the successive scenes.

All this he supported, in the interviews, with pronouncements which were received by the awed interviewers (and by his Metropolitan associates) as impressive truth, but which I found to be specious intellectualizing unrelated to the realities of what he professed to deal with. He thought scenery should

> suggest rather than state. You don't try to get the opera to do what the cinema does better. Audiences are not satisfied with seeing a bad attempt at putting Egypt on the stage. Not when they can get the real thing in the cinema. We've got to get back to provoking the imagination of the audience.

But a bad attempt at putting Egypt on the stage is no argument against a good one. And a film of Seville is no more an argument against Eugene Berman's great sets for *Don Giovanni* and *The Barber of Seville* than photographs of Mont Ste. Victoire are against Cézanne's paintings of it: what one wants to see on the stage is precisely the transformation of actual Seville by Berman's imagination. It is this imagined reality that stimulates the audience's imagination; but since it is clearly something Dexter can neither envision nor understand, he will have none of it; and his stimulus to the audience's imagination is the wagons, platforms and stairs in *Le Prophète* that I cannot imagine anyone's imagination being stimulated by.

The title of the *Times* interview was *Dexter—An Artist Who Pinches Pennies;* and the Metropolitan's directors, faced with the company's financial difficulties, may be congratulating themselves on their good fortune in having a Dexter to supply Art at Woolworth prices. But what Dexter supplies for those prices, the *Prophète* that Metropolitan audiences are paying Tiffany prices for, is art of Woolworth quality.

It was interesting to read Vladimir Ashkenazy's statement to an interviewer once that with Beethoven and Mozart he felt "at something of a disadvantage compared with someone like Daniel Barenboim who has been brought up in the classical Viennese tradition," and then to hear him, when he sat down at the piano, play with the disciplined mastery of music and instrument that Barenboim didn't have, and achieve with it the coherently shaped performances of Beethoven and Mozart that Barenboim didn't achieve. (One can hear in the recorded performance of Mozart's Concerto K. 365 for two pianos Ashkenazy's sensitive and elegant statement of a phrase followed by Barenboim's heavy-handed and rhythmically sloppy repetition of it.) Recently, however, Ashkenazy's playing has on occasion sounded as though he had been affected by his listening to Barenboim, and also to Furtwängler, whose undisciplined and shapeless performances Barenboim and Ashkenazy admire. One such occasion was Ashkenazy's recording of Beethoven's Sonata Op. 57 *(Appassionata),* in which he played the hushed opening statements of the first movement as a slow introduction to the outburst in fast tempo a few moments later, and continued to shift back and forth between slow and fast throughout the movement, instead of maintaining, with subtle modifications, the basic tempo of the movement established at the beginning. He dealt with the first movement of

Chopin's Sonata Op. 58 in the same Furtwänglerian manner at one of his recitals in Carnegie Hall this year; and Furtwänglerian too were the excessively long pauses between the opening statements of Chopin's Polonaise-Fantaisie Op. 61 at that recital.

The Quartetto Italiano, when I heard it 25 years ago, produced a marvelously blended ensemble sound, whose fine gradations it employed in a style of great delicacy, sensitivity and elegance that was admirably suited to the writing of Boccherini, Haydn and Debussy, but not to the forceful writing of Beethoven. This continued to be true of the performances I heard on Angel records in the years that followed; and so I was unprepared for the remarkable change a few years ago: the powerful sound and expressiveness of the Italiano's playing of Beethoven on Philips records, first in superb performances of the last quartets, then in equally effective performances of the middle group. A concert at the YMHA in New York this year provided my first hearing of the Italiano in a concert hall after 25 years; and the performances of Beethoven's Op. 132 and Op. 59 No. 2 attained even greater expressive eloquence than the ones on records—to say nothing of their other extraordinary excellences.

As it happened, the first concert of the Cleveland Quartet's Beethoven series at Alice Tully Hall ended with a beautifully played and expressively effective performance of Op. 132, after excellent performances of Op. 18 No. 6 and Op. 59 No. 1.

11 June 1977 In Berg's *Wozzeck*, at the Metropolitan in the fifties, I heard distorted vocal writing which heightened the expressive effect of the powerfully moving words, and discordant orchestral writing which intensified the nightmarish character of the dramatic progression on the stage; but in Berg's *Lulu*, when the Hamburg Opera performed it here in 1967, I heard Lulu's distorted vocal declamation carried to an extreme of voice-wrecking stratospheric screaming that had no expressive relation to the unmoving words and made no other sense, and a similar extreme in the discordant orchestral writing that had no relation to the dramatic situations and actions on the stage; and I heard that again when the Metropolitan produced *Lulu* this year. For me, then, *Wozzeck* is an outstanding achievement in this century's opera, and as such a work which the Metropolitan had the obligation to produce and continue to perform periodically for interested music-lovers; but *Lulu*—contrary to what has been claimed for it—is not. And that the Metropolitan, in its present financial difficulties, spent on a costly production of *Lulu* the money it might have spent on a production, say, of Mozart's *Idomeneo* strikes me as scandalous.

John Dexter's valuable contributions to the production were negative ones: his not pressing his objection to the "clutter" of realistic scenery, which made possible Jocelyn Herbert's admirably imagined succession of interiors for the two completed acts; and his not inflicting on the staging any idea of his about the work's Larger Significance. Lacking Robert Craft's exhaustive knowledge of the text and music I didn't perceive the instances he noted of "the staging . . . frequently in opposition to the music"; but I did perceive that Dr. Goll's sudden collapse and death in the first scene should have been dealt with in a way that would not have provoked the audience's laughter. However, even a better director than Dexter could not have made Carole Farley on the stage of the Metropolitan either the *femme fatale* or the mythic *Erdgeist* of Berg's imagination. Nor could as excellent a conductor as James Levine—given Farley's unimpressive vocal equipment—make her sound like them.

The bare permanent enclosure, with bits of scenery representing the scenes, that David Reppa devised for Poulenc's *Dialogues des Carmélites* cost much less than the sets of *Lulu;* but even that smaller amount was wasted when spent on a work of so little musical value. Dexter's staging on his "uncluttered" stage worked effectively; and the performance conducted by Michel Plasson—with Maria Ewing as Blanche, Régine Crespin as the dying Prioress, Shirley Verrett as the new Prioress and Mignon Dunn as Mother Marie—was a good one. As always the orchestral sonorities prevented most of the words of the English translation (by Joseph Machlis) from being understood, so that a reading of the text in advance was necessary; and one might as well have read it in preparation for a performance in French.

The 20th century will be better represented at the Metropolitan next season by Debussy's *Pelléas et Mélisande* and Britten's *Peter Grimes;* the work of the past revived after long neglect will this time be one worth hearing, Donizetti's *La Favorita;* and not only Mussorgsky's *Boris Godunov* will be heard again but Tchaikovsky's *Eugene Onegin* (and in Russian). But returning with these two major works will be also Cilea's *Adriana Lecouvreur;* French opera will be represented not by Berlioz's *Les Troyens* but by Massenet's *Thais;* with the newly staged early *Tannhäuser* of Wagner there will be not one work of his matured powers; and the three operas of Puccini will be given, but only one of the four master-pieces of Mozart. I cannot imagine the Metropolitan Museum removing any of its Rembrandts or Cézannes to make room for the equivalents of *Thais* and *Adriana Lecouvreur;* nor can I recall at the Museum any equiva-lents of such items of the standard operatic repertory as the works of Massenet, Cilea, Mascagni, Leoncavallo, Giordano or even Puccini. The standard operatic repertory (like the standard orchestral or piano reper-tory) includes low-grade works that are listened to respectfully by people who would not read or look at their equivalents in literature or painting.

6 and 13 August 1977 "Don't perform; just do the steps," I heard Balanchine say to Violette Verdy when he was making *La Source* with her (the equivalent of which would have been Bernard Shaw's telling Mrs. Patrick Campbell to just say the words in *Pygmalion*). But Edward Villella, replying some years earlier to my question what his dancer's eye perceived in the Verdy operation, mentioned "the amazing way Verdy understands a new role . . . as soon as it is started [and] brings something to it while she is learning the steps. . . . I remember when a dancer was showing her the steps of a role: when Verdy repeated them they weren't just the steps anymore, the way she suddenly brought them alive and made things happen and explode." One of Villella's examples of what Verdy brought to a role was her use of her eyes in the series of *passés* (the toe of one foot raised to the knee of the other foot) in her solo in *Tchaikovsky Pas de Deux:* "When she does this *passé-passé*-hold, it's not only the foot and the leg and the body and the arms, but the eyes too, with everything reaching the same point in time together"—the effect of which "very few [dancers] realize . . . and understand . . . but Verdy does." And as photographs of this repeated *passé-passé*-hold sequence in a Dance Horizons booklet about Verdy show, what Villella meant by "the body and the arms" was the changes in tilt of the head and in configura-tion of exquisitely inflected arms, wrists and fingers that were uniquely hers. Those photographs don't show the subtleties of timing and rhythmic inflection that made the enchanting movements breathtaking; but it is such photographs with their limitations that are all we will have from now on to recall to us the unique marvels she made of what she performed—the roles Balanchine made expressly for her in *Tchaikovsky Pas de Deux, Episodes, Liebeslieder Walzer, Emeralds, La Source,* and the ones originally made for other dancers. For her departure from the New York City Ballet last fall, as it turned out, ended the possibility of ever seeing their living realities again on the stage.

What Verdy had performed (like the role of Eliza Doolittle after Mrs. Campbell's era) was performed this past year by others, and—whether poorly or well—performed differently. The first *Emeralds* had Christine Redpath "just doing the steps" unimpressively (which, incredibly, she had been assigned to do several times the preceding year in place of Verdy when she was still with the company); the next one had Sara Leland doing no better; but then the outstandingly gifted Merrill Ashley made the supported arabesques and lifts of the opening scene, and the turns and other details of the following solo, beautiful and effective in her own style (which Verdy used to characterize enthusiastically as "so legal!"). In *La Source* Kay Mazzo performed prettily, which was not enough for anyone who had seen Verdy's performance. And concerning *Tchaikovsky Pas de Deux* I will report now what I forgot to report a year ago: that after having been danced for years by Melissa Hayden and Patricia McBride with little more than the necessary technical virtuosity that excited audiences, it was transformed into something overwhelmingly grand by the flow of Suzanne Farrell's large movements and the similar movements of Peter Martins's new solo.

Because of injuries Villella was another of the company's older great dancers whose performances of his roles in Balanchine's ballets were not seen this past year, and may never be seen on the stage again. As it happened, Helgi Tomasson was a handsome Oberon in *A Midsummer Night's Dream* who danced the solo to Mendelssohn's Scherzo with his elegance and clarity; and Robert Weiss danced it with his exciting elevation; but what both lacked was Villella's power of presence on the stage and power of spacious movement in the air. Merely to do the difficult and taxing steps of the Villella role in *Rubies* as well as Peter Schaufuss and Weiss did them was an impressive achievement; but what they did not achieve was the additional effect of those steps—not just the vigorous ones but the occasional delicate twisting movements—being done by Villella's powerful body. Nor did Schaufuss and Weiss achieve Villella's humor at certain points: not only in the episode of his sly misleading and eluding of the pursuing boys near the end of the last movement, but in his return to the stage in the middle of the slow movement—the manner of his debonair high-stepping past McBride with an unseeing glance, his sudden stop and double-take, and his dash to her for the resumption of their *pas de deux*.

Of the other two older greats of the company Allegra Kent, in one of her rare appearances, again created in *Bugaku* the image she maintains of a remote figure going through a ritual of passion that no one else—neither McBride nor Mazzo nor even Farrell—achieves. And Jacques d'Amboise astounded one with several of his dazzling performances in *Union Jack* and *Who Cares?*—after which Adam Lüders did the steps in *Union Jack* and Jean-Pierre Bonnefous and Martins demonstrated the inability of an impassioned Frenchman or an elegant Dane to look and dance like an American musical-show hoofer in *Who Cares?*

Nor could either of the young dancers who were substituted for Francisco Moncion in the extraordinary walking *pas de deux* in *Emeralds* make of his part what his powerful presence and dramatic mask used to make of it. However it was the company's numerous gifted young dancers who produced superb performances of several great Balanchine classics: *The Four Temperaments* with Bart Cook in the *Melancholic* Variation, Ashley and Daniel Duell in the *Sanguinic*, Bonnefous in the *Phlegmatic*, Karin von Aroldingen in the *Choleric*; *Symphony in C* with Colleen Neary in the first movement, Ashley in the second, Heather Watts and Schaufuss in the third, Kyra Nichols in the fourth; *Divertimento No. 15* with Ashley, Neary, Nichols and Maria Calegari in addition to Farrell and Martins. And it was the young dancers who astounded one in *Bournonville Divertissements*—the one new work of the winter season shortened by the orchestra's strike.

Bournonville Divertissements was a staging of five numbers from ballets of the 19th-century Danish dancer, teacher and choreographer whose teachings, and the ballets in which he used what he taught, are preserved as the basic tradition of the Royal Danish Ballet. The numbers were a *ballabile* from *Napoli*, danced by Nichol Hlinka and Daniel Duell with a group of the corps; a *pas de deux* from *Kermesse in Bruges*, danced by McBride and Tomasson; a *pas de trois* from *La Ventana*, danced by Ashley, Nichols and Weiss; the well-known *Pas de Deux* from *Flower Festival in Genzano*, danced by Farrell and Martins; and a *pas de sept* from *A Folk Tale*, danced by Neary, Lüders, Victor Castelli, Muriel Aasen, Wilhelmina Frankfurt, Watts and Jean-Pierre Frohlich. They were chosen and staged by Stanley Williams, a former soloist of the Royal Danish Ballet who teaches in the School of American Ballet, and whose coaching of the young Americans resulted in performances which not only gave to the virtuoso showpieces an exciting life and charm that the recent Ballet Theatre performance of the *pas de trois* from *La Ventana* had lacked, but enabled me—even before I read Svend Kragh-Jacobsen's program note—to recognize in the difficult movements simpler forms of what I had been seeing in Balanchine's work. (It was not merely a matter of Balanchine's coming into direct contact with the Bournonville style, as Jacobsen mentions, when he came to the Royal Danish Ballet as guest choreographer in 1929: what he had learned years earlier in the Imperial Ballet School in St. Petersburg had been a blending of the Bournonville style, taught in the school by his pupil Christian Johannson, with "the Italian virtuosity that was added . . . when Cecchetti was appointed dancer and teacher in 1890.")

The spring season's new ballet, Balanchine's *Vienna Waltzes*, had scenery, costumes and waltzes to music of Johann Strauss, Franz Lehar and Richard Strauss that made it suitable for the festive atmosphere of the annual gala benefit at which it was given a preview. The waltzes were of course skillfully contrived and orchestrated on the stage, and therefore pleasant to look at; but they were not a creative achievement on the level of Balanchine's *Liebeslieder Walzer*. Two pieces of invention rose above the rest: the humorous steps of the fast *perpetuum mobile* to Johann Strauss's *Explosions Polka;* and the episode in the final scene in which Farrell, alone on the stage in a low-cut long white ball dress, displayed the beauty of her body and its movement in a slow walk to stage center, where she stopped, bowed low to an imagined partner, and began to move and turn with arms circling above her head, joined after a few moments by Bonnefous and then by other dancing couples for the final waltz.

After Glen Tetley's *Sargasso*, a monstrosity of modern-dance-style contortion and distortion that American Ballet Theatre presented some years ago, one thought the company would want no further works of his; but in the past year it offered two more. One, *Le Sacre du Printemps*, was a *perpetuum mobile* of frenetic writhing, leaping and worse that misused Stravinsky's score and the unfortunate dancers; the other, *Voluntaries*, was a quiet *perpetuum mobile* of ballet movements—to Poulenc's Concerto for Organ, Strings and Percussion—whose sequences and groupings were uninteresting from first to last. Thinking of the succession of worthless new works that Ballet Theatre had been presenting, I remembered the awful works of De Valois, Helpmann, MacMillan and others presented by Sadler's Wells Ballet in its early visits, which had been occasions to point out that the company's service to us was not its offerings of contemporary English works—except for Ashton's comic masterpieces *Façade* and *A Wedding Bouquet*—but the opportunities it provided to see authentic and effective productions of the classics of the past—notably Nicolai Sergeyev's staging of *The Sleeping Beauty*, with Oliver Messel's beautifully imagined scenery and costumes, the dancing of the well-trained and rehearsed company, and Margot Fonteyn's enchanting Aurora. One could say the same of Ballet Theatre, even though it had presented a poorly designed *Giselle* in which Makarova had been free to make damaging changes in the choreography of the second act, and a poorly designed *Swan Lake* in which she dictated damaging tempos for her slow-motion performance. And for this year's *Sleeping Beauty* the company was having Mary Skeaping reproduce the Sergeyev staging and Messell duplicate his scenery and costumes for it. I looked forward, therefore, to seeing again the reality and totality of what my mind retained as a few dimly remembered fragments; and I was shocked by costumes whose garish colors I knew I had not seen years ago; a backdrop of a palace that I knew had not looked as drab as it did now; choreography that was less effective, not only because of the changes but because it was not executed as well; a lack of the over-all distinction that I remembered—to say nothing of the interpolation of the scene in *La Sylphide* in which Madge and the other witches brew their mischief, in place of the three sinister old women knitting that I saw in the first act years ago.

As it happened, these impressions were confirmed and accounted for by two pieces in the latest issue of *Ballet Review*—an interview with Skeaping and a review by David Vaughan. Skeaping said she had been unable to complete her task because of Ballet Theatre's inability to provide the necessary rehearsal time; Vaughan said, specifically, that in the limited rehearsal time she "could just about teach the dancers the steps, but could hardly begin to teach them *how* to dance them." This was because the company hasn't "a recognizable classic style shared by all the dancers," whereas "when the then Vic-Wells Ballet first began to dance *Beauty* in 1939 . . . a style was already in the process of being formed on the basis of the nineteenth century classics as produced by Sergeyev"—the style that, by the time Sadler's Wells first performed *The Sleeping Beauty* here in 1949, gave the dancing the effectiveness, and the performance the over-all distinction that I remembered. Vaughan considered the company's eclectic repertory-building policy "not conducive to homogeneity of style, particularly when there is apparently no one in authority who will say no to dancers who change choreography to suit their whims"—by whom he meant Makarova, who "in *Beauty* on opening night performed various passages according to the Kirov version she was used to." In the much later performance I saw, Cynthia Gregory performed the prescribed movements of the Rose Adagio and the final *pas de deux* with impressive security and perfection, though she presented the image of a serenely mature woman instead of an impulsive young girl.

Paradoxically it was the ruthless will of the Makarova who introduced Kirov movements into the Sergeyev-Skeaping *Sleeping Beauty* that enabled her to get the girls slowly coming down the ramp, at the beginning of *La Bayadère*, to exhibit in their succession of arabesques a style shared by all that was beautiful and exciting to see not only in this sequence but in what followed. In the first performance I saw Makarova danced with her exquisite fluidity, and Fernando Bujones soared into space with his contained elegance; in the second Gelsey Kirkland exhibited her sharply defining clarity of configuration, and Mikhail Baryshnikov not only added personal warmth and spontaneity to his virtuosity but demonstrated again that to do the phenomenal things he does on the stage is as natural for him as swimming is for a fish.

The new *Nutcracker* was not a new staging of the original Petipa-Tchaikovsky ballet, nor even, like Balanchine's, an invention of new choreography for the original Petipa scenario and the music Tchaikovsky fitted to it. Baryshnikov used the music for a scenario of his own that is unsuited to it. Tchaikovsky's score is a marvelous evocation of a child's real world, seen in the first-act Christmas party, and a child's imagined world, seen in the dream of little Clara that follows the party—the dream of the two children's visit to the Kingdom of Sweets, in which the divertissements for their entertainment culminate in the *pas de deux* of the Sugar Plum Fairy and her Cavalier with its impassioned supported adagio. Baryshnikov's Clara, a grown-up young girl, dreams of being taken by her grown-up young Nutcracker-Prince to his palace, where it is they who dance the impassioned supported adagio that is interfered with by a Drosselmeyer attempting unsuccessfully to take Clara away from her Prince. And after the final waltz all the characters disappear, leaving Clara alone in the morning sunlight that streams into her room. As one watches all this one is aware that the music is incompatible with it; and I find it hard to understand Baryshnikov's *not* being aware of this. The performance I saw had Makarova and Bujones dancing the little they were given to dance very beautifully.

One must be grateful to Ballet Theatre for the opportunity to see two historic Diaghilev classics, *Firebird* and *Petrushka*. The *Firebird* was as nearly as possible the original Fokine version fitted to Stravinsky's spacious and luxuriantly orchestrated 1910 score—which is to say that it was this version as restaged in 1926 with scenery by Natalie Gontcharova, as restored by Serge Grigoriev and Lubov Tchernicheva for the Royal Ballet, which presented it here in 1955, and as duplicated now by Christopher Newton. As in 1955, I liked the general effect of greater amplitude in music and story line, and found the *pas de deux* of the captured bird struggling to free itself from Ivan Tsarevitch as impressively original, imaginative and effective as when I first saw it in 1916; and in the expanded scene involving Kostchei and his subjects it was interesting to see what had been impressively imaginative in 1910 even if it was less effective today. The Firebird's animated entrance solo called for what Gregory's technique could give it; and she was impressive also in the *pas de deux*.

The *Petrushka* was Yurek Lazovsky's reproduction of the last Fokine version that Ballet Theatre presented in the 40s with Lazovsky's great performance in the title role; and the choreographed portions were identical with those Lazovsky had reproduced for the Joffrey Ballet; but the production—including even the unchoreographed milling about of the crowd—looked better spaced out on the large Metropolitan Opera stage than squeezed onto the stage of the City Center. With Marcos Paredes's Blackamoor and Karen Brock's Dancer, both good, I was fortunate in seeing Erik Bruhn's Petrushka—interesting in its casting off the traditional mask of chalk-white face with zigzag black mouth, so that one saw a human face with the puppet's movements. The combination of the choreographed portions with Stravinsky's music struck me again as one of the masterpieces of 20th-century ballet that should be in the repertory of every ballet company.

3 September 1977 The Vienna Philharmonic bassoonist whose comments on Barenboim's conducting I reported a few months ago made an interesting point once about Bruno Walter, under whom he had played in concerts and opera. The flaw in Walter's symphonic conducting, he said, was its rhythmic weakness—the liberties in tempo that destroyed coherent structure in a symphony of Beethoven or Schubert; but this weakness did not prevent him from producing highly effective performances of opera. It is normal for opera singers to take the liberties in tempo—e.g., the liberty of prolonging a phrase excessively—that are destructive of rhythmic coherence; and whereas Toscanini—as insistent on coherent shape in an opera of Verdi as in a symphony of Beethoven or Schubert—held the singers' expressive plasticity within the limits of that coherent shape, Walter fitted his own liberties around those of the singers so skillfully that his performances of the operas of Mozart and Verdi in the 20s and 30s were outstanding.

As it happened, I had observed a similar inequality in the work of the conductor Zubin Mehta. I had heard him produce effective performances of opera at the Metropolitan, and had therefore been surprised by his ineffective performances of orchestral works on records; but these hadn't prepared me for a performance of Beethoven's Ninth with his Los Angeles Philharmonic in Carnegie Hall that was the worst orchestral and musical operation in my experience since Barenboim's with the London Symphony. Like Barenboim, Mehta did not achieve the orchestral balance required for good sound and clear texture, or give the progression enlivening inflection and coherent shape; so that one heard an opaque mass of coarse sound that was drowned every now and then by the thunder of kettledrums, in shapeless statements of the work's four movements. Trying to account for the earlier good performances of opera, I found the explanation in the fact that at the Metropolitan he had conducted an excellent orchestra which, after years of rehearsal and performance of the repertory, was able to perform adequately in *Aida* or *Il Trovatore* even with an ineffectual conductor, and which, in addition, was accustomed to listen to the singers, and on occasion to go along with their singing when it was more persuasive or compelling than the movements of the conductor's baton; so that while the movements of Mehta's baton had presented an image of assured mastery in the operation, he could actually have been fitting them to what was being done by the singers and orchestra.

It is several years since that performance of Beethoven's Ninth; and Mehta has been appointed Boulez's successor as Musical Director of the

New York Philharmonic. Interested in what he would achieve with this major orchestra, I went to hear the one program he conducted it in last March; and as it happened the opening work was the Mozart Symphony K. 338 that I heard Michael Tilson Thomas perform with the orchestra a few years ago. I can best describe Mehta's performance by saying that as a mere technical operation of conductor with orchestra it did not produce the finely drawn lines of luminous sound balanced in clear textures that Thomas produced, and as a musical operation it did not impart to the work the lightness, grace and verve, the style in phrasing, of Thomas's performance. And the performance of Berlioz's *Symphonie Fantastique* that ended the concert revealed Mehta's total lack of the sense for correct proportion in change of tempo and sonority. Crescendos were excessive even in the quiet introduction; and the climaxes in the Allegro that followed brought explosions from the kettledrums which were nothing compared with the deafening noise of brass and percussion in the March to the Scaffold. Recalling the beautiful-sounding *fortissimos* that Boulez had produced in Mahler's Third at the Philharmonic's opening concert last fall, I didn't agree with the reviewers' charitable conjecture that Mehta hadn't yet adjusted to the acoustics of reconstructed Avery Fisher Hall: they didn't need adjusting to; and Mehta had produced his noisy Beethoven Ninth in Carnegie Hall.

At the Philharmonic's final concerts of the season, which ended Boulez's connection with the orchestra, his parting gift to the public, to remember in the years ahead, was the sound he got the orchestra to produce in a beautifully shaped, lyrical and warmly expressive performance of Berlioz's *The Damnation of Faust*—a sound the public is not likely to hear from that orchestra again in the near future. Randall Jarrell once quoted Goethe as saying, "In the face of the great superiority of another person there is no means of safety but love." Not for the Philharmonic players faced by Boulez, who found their safety in dismissing him as concerned solely with the correct note at the correct time, not, as *they* were, with the making of music. Nor for the critic who found his safety in citing these players' assessment in support of his own view of Boulez as one whose "coldly correct musical manners" were "unsuited to a romantic, picturesque score"—Mahler's Third last fall, and now Berlioz's *Damnation*, of which Boulez had produced an "unemotional, prosaic account."

A concert of the Philadelphia Orchestra in Carnegie Hall game me my first experience of the conducting of Riccardo Muti, who is expected to succeed Ormandy when he retires. The one major work of the program was Berlioz's *Romeo and Juliet*, of which five instrumental sections were performed: Introduction, *Romeo Alone—Sadness—Festivities at the Capulets', Love Scene, Queen Mab* Scherzo, *Romeo in the Tomb of the Capulets*. These present difficulties of execution—above all in the Queen Mab Scherzo—that call for a virtuoso orchestra led by a virtuoso conductor; and the performance demonstrated Muti's ability to obtain from the orchestra the phenomenal playing it is capable of. They present also difficulties of musical realization that demand a conductor on the highest level of musical insight, judgment and taste; and the musical progressions revealed Muti's sense for coherent shape, but also a tendency to play what Berlioz marked *poco f* or *poco sf* or *poco cresc.* as *molto f, molto sf, molto cres.*, which in the *Love Scene* destroyed the expressive effect Berlioz's markings were intended to produce—the delicacy of feeling in the young lovers' *"premiers transports, premiers aveux, premiers serments."*

And finally, I attended a concert of the Guarneri Quartet in Alice Tully Hall to find out whether the group had made any changes in its performance of Schubert's Quartet Op. 161 in the few years since I heard it at the YMHA. The work, though rarely played, is fully as great as the familiar *Death and the Maiden* Quartet, and exhibits its greatness in the way all of Schubert's major works do—in the alternation of deeply affecting quiet writing with outbursts of overwhelming power. And the only recorded performance I know is the Budapest Quartet's on the mono record issued in the 50s and now reissued on an Odyssey record. It was the Budapest performance from which I formed my idea of the work—an idea that derived its authority for me from the rightness of expressive effect the four movements had in the tempos that were the ones prescribed by Schubert: I. *Allegro molto moderato*, II. *Andante un poco moto*, III. *Allegro vivace*, IV. *Allegro assai*. At the YMHA a few years ago, therefore, I was unprepared for—and left unconvinced by—the Guarneri's slow tempos for the first, second and fourth movements—a tempo for the first that was slower than any conceivable *allegro*, a tempo for the second that was slower than any conceivable *andante*, and a tempo for the finale that reduced the *perpetuum mobile* rush, breathtaking in its driving energy and momentum, to a leisurely saunter. At Tully Hall last spring, I am glad to report, the first and second movements were played more animatedly and therefore more effectively; but the finale was again the ineffective saunter.

My recollection is that the Schubert quartet was preceded by a superb performance of Haydn's Quartet Op. 77 No. 1; and the concert ended with Fauré's Piano Quartet Op. 15, which I found as uninteresting this time as when I last heard it 30 years ago at a Harvard Fauré festival, but in which Anton Kuerti added extraordinarily beautiful playing of the piano part to the equally outstanding playing of Dalley, Tree and Soyer.

26 November 1977 The choice of Musorgsky's somber *Boris Godunov* for the festive social occasion of the Metropolitan Opera's opening night of the season might be interpreted as evidence of the management's recognition of the work's greatness, were it not for the contrary evidence: the retention of the damaging cuts that Thomas Schippers made three years ago. In the first (1869) version of Act Two Xenia is lamenting the death of her fiancé when Boris enters and begins to comfort her; in the revised (1872) version of the act performed by the Metropolitan Musorgsky contrives a more dramatically effective episode in which Feodor and the Nurse try to divert Xenia with songs and hand-clapping whose crescendo is interrupted by the entrance of Boris, and the startled Nurse's exclamation causes him to ask her if he is a frightful wolf. But Schippers omitted the songs, and with them the effect of Boris's entrance and the reason for his question. Even worse was Schippers's butchery of the superb final Kromy Scene with his snipping out of repetitions, his omission of the reappearance of Varlaam and Missail, his abbreviation of the passage sung by the two Jesuits—all of which made the individual episodes and the entire scene too brief to have the effect and impact they should have (a result aggravated this year by Kazimierz Kord's excessively fast tempos). And what Schippers omitted three years ago the Metropolitan's Musical Director couldn't be persuaded to restore this year.

   To the musical damage Schippers inflicted on the Kromy Scene August Everding added the damage of his senseless and ludicrous staging, which also was left unchanged this year. One saw again the crowd pile up logs around the captive Boyar, then, for no evident reason, take them down; one saw again Dimitri make his entrance not, as Musorgsky specifies, on a horse from which he addresses the crowd and on which he makes his exit, but standing precariously on a platform carried by a few soldiers, who lower it for him to step onto the stage where he addresses the crowd and then makes his exit on foot. Nor was there any change this year in what Everding contrived for Boris's last moments in the preceding scene in place of what Musorgsky specifies.

The performance too was less than what the festive occasion called for. Martti Talvela's voice retains its power but has lost all sensuous warmth and capacity for delicate inflection; and his singing most of the time was an uninflected hard-sounding *forte* that was inexpressive as well as unattractive. Paul Plishka's beautiful singing as Pimen suggested that he be allowed to sing the title role. He doesn't have Talvela's gigantic stature; but that stature accentuates Talvela's awkwardness in movement; and Boris has been played effectively by singers of normal height. Marius Rintzler, the Varlaam, couldn't be heard above the orchestra in his boisterous song in the inn scene; but Wieslaw Ochman as Dimitri, Robert Nagy as Shuisky and James Atherton as the Simpleton sang well. And except for his rushing of the Kromy Scene Kord paced the work effectively.

What the occasion demonstrated again about Musorgsky's *Boris* was that it maintains its power and greatness undiminished through all defects and inadequacies of performance. My companion at the performance I attended—a non-professional music-lover, with no knowledge of Russian and only the meager information about the action provided in the program—was electrified by what she heard, and was still electrified two weeks later; and the audience stayed almost until midnight to cheer after the end. As for me, playing through the vocal score for the first time on an out-of-tune piano in a Maine village 25 years ago, I was able to hear the unfailing rightness and expressive effect, achieved with completely assured mastery, of every note in the moment-to-moment invention, and the extraordinary powers operating with incandescent adequacy for every dramatic point they were required to deal with; and now—as on each previous occasion when I have heard the work after an interval—that invention and those powers struck me with new and overwhelming impact.

The Metropolitan's revival of Tchaikovsky's *Eugene Onegin* used the good Rolf Gerard sets of the 1957 production, with one welcome change—the room in the Gremin mansion specified in the score in place of Gerard's outdoor set for the final scene. That 1957 production had the excellent Onegin of George London and Gremin of Giorgio Tozzi, but was fatally flawed by the Tatiana of Lucine Amara and Lenski of

Richard Tucker—this in addition to the damage from being sung in English (which should be read in the libretto before a performance, not heard during the performance with the music of Tchaikovsky, Musorgsky, Verdi or Mozart). This year's revival not only gained by being sung in Russian, but was made outstanding by the superb Tatiana of Teresa Zylis-Gara and Lenski of Nicolai Gedda. Though Zylis-Gara sang well and with moving expressive power in the *Letter Scene* and the final duet with Onegin, it was her dramatic performance—above all the image she projected in the first act, of the shy, withdrawn, silent girl, and of this girl shaken by the impact of what she took Onegin to be—that was extraordinary. And on the other hand, though middle-aged Gedda achieved a remarkably lifelike image of the young and volatile poet, it was his singing that was astounding and, in Lenski's final monologue, produced the sensational high point of the performance. The uniquely great performance of that monologue, in its vocal beauty and musical phrasing, has been for me the one recorded early in this century by Leonid Sobinov; and a close approximation of it is the one recorded shortly before his death by Jussi Bjoerling; but Gedda manipulated a less beautiful voice than theirs with such skill, in phrases so marvelously imagined—in his *pianissimo* repetition of the piece's opening statement, his dwelling on the little figure whose repetition builds up to the piece's climax—that the performance, in the end, was one of those in which one is aware of having heard a great operation of extraordinary human powers.

The Onegin was Sherrill Milnes, who employed effectively a voice that no longer had its former ear-ravishing luster and warmth, but retained its steadiness and power; and who projected an impressive image of the bored sophisticate of the early scenes, but was less convincing in the agitation that expressed itself in the swinging about of his body and arms in the last scenes. I had the good luck of hearing Plishka in place of Talvela in the sustained melodic flow of Gremin's aria; but the off-stage duet of Tatiana and Olga at the beginning of the opera was spoiled by the unpleasant-sounding voice of the Olga, Isola Jones, who fortunately had very little to sing thereafter. And James Levine conducted with his unfailing sense for continuity and shape.

What I found to be true a few years ago of Britten's setting of Thomas Mann's *Death in Venice* I found to be true also of Thea Musgrave's *The Voice of Ariadne*, which the New York City Opera produced this year:

that whereas the characters, situations and action of the Henry James story from which the opera is derived are made believable to a reader by the prose that presents them to his imagination, the ones of *The Voice of Ariadne* were not made believable to me in the New York State Theater by what Amalia Elguera's libretto and Musgraves's music presented to my eye and ear. It was my first experience of her music, in which I heard no expressive relation to the words and nothing of musical interest in itself.

Since what is musically valuable in the New York Philharmonic's activity in the years ahead will have to be provided by guest conductors, it was a heartening experience to hear the two concerts at which the orchestra was led by the impressively gifted young English conductor Andrew Davis. Regrettably, thinking it necessary, as a visiting Englishman, to show interest in American music and to inform his American audience concerning English music, he opened his first program with Ives's *Decoration Day* and devoted the first half of his second to Elgar's Concert-Overture *In the South* and Britten's Violin Concerto. In the Ives piece a long stretch of quiet dissonant writing that conveyed no musical sense to me was interrupted briefly by a raucously discordant texture of the various sounds of holiday celebration, after which the quiet dissonant writing returned to end the piece; and its one point of interest was the precise and beautiful-sounding playing Davis was able to get the orchestra to produce. This fine playing in the next work, Mozart's Piano Concerto K. 466, provided the perfectly matched context for playing of the solo part by young Emanuel Ax that was admirable in its shaping of phrase with exactly the right combination of delicacy, cohesive tension and strength—most notable in the piano's long, wide-ranging episode of quiet sustained melody in the second movement. And the orchestral playing attained virtuoso caliber after the intermission in a performance of Berlioz's *Harold in Italy* that was the most understanding and effective since Toscanini's, which in fact it closely resembled in over-all shape, sensitive inflection of phrase, clarity of texture and brilliant sonority.

Elgar's *In the South*, at the second concert, offered a large amount of his characteristic richly scored diffuse orchestral doodling, with two episodes that were made unusual by their clearly defined melodic ideas. And Britten's Violin Concerto turned out to be one of the arid products of his ability to put unattractive sounds together in seemingly endless uninteresting progressions; and as such was a waste of the efforts of the conductor, orchestra and soloist, Rodney Friend, the orchestra's concertmaster. As for Beethoven's Symphony No. 7, which completed the program, it was admirably paced; and if I had sat again on the left side of Avery Fisher Hall the loud passages undoubtedly would have had the same balance of strings, woodwinds and brass as those of Berlioz's *Harold* the week before. But I sat this time in row BB on the right side, where the brass and kettledrums in the big tuttis were not only unpleasantly loud in themselves but made the violins inaudible. Apparently the new hall has at least one acoustic bad spot.

It must have been puzzling and discouraging for Davis—after giving Berlioz's *Harold* a shape whose accuracy extended to its every subtle inflection in tempo and sonority—to read in *The Times* the next day that the work was "not yet for him. He caught the main outline, but not its subtleties"; and that "part of the trouble was flabby rhythm. There were too many accented upbeats." As puzzling and discouraging as it must have been for other distinguished musicians to read in *The Times* about the "sloppy metrics" caused by "accented upbeats" in their performances. It puzzled *me*, a mere listener, to read in *The Times* a few years ago about the accented E-flat on the upbeat of the opening statement of Mozart's G-minor Symphony that I hadn't heard in Giulini's performance with the Philharmonic. Or about what was described as having happened, that I hadn't heard, in bar 3 of Berlioz's *Les Troyens* in Kubelik's performance at the Metropolitan: the accent on the first note of the "ascending scale passage starting on the [unaccented] second [eighth] of the [six-eight] measure," the result being that "instead of (ONE) two three FOUR five six" the passage had come out as "a flurried ONEtwothreefourfive, and the whole metrical scheme [had gone] off the rails." However, when I listened to Giulini's recorded performance of the Mozart G-minor I found that there was no accent on the initial E-flat; and on my tape of Kubelik's performance of *Les Troyens* at the Metropolitan the ascending notes in bar 3 were perfectly even. So I am no longer puzzled, and Giulini, Kubelik and Andrew Davis can rest easy: those accented upbeats occur in the columns of *The Times*, not in the performances in concert hall and opera house.

7 January 1978 A performance of Beethoven's *Eroica* Symphony by Lorin Maazel with the Philadelphia Orchestra some years ago, in which his pacing of the work, as someone remarked, made it sound more like Beethoven's *Erratica*, kept me away from further performances of his until this season, when interest in what he would achieve as guest conductor of the New York Philharmonic led me to attend a concert in which they played the Suite No. 1 from Handel's *Water Music* and Mozart's Symphony K. 551 (*Jupiter*). A striking feature of his conducting on this occasion was his idiosyncratic waving of his baton in circles in all directions, in which my eye could see no relation to what was happening in the music or what was being done by the orchestra, and to which he added exaggerated pantomimic indications of *decrescendos* and other details. I had the impression that there had been communication at the rehearsals, which had established the orchestral balances, tempos and dynamics that the experienced orchestra was able to produce at the concert without the explicit guidance it didn't get from the circlings of Maazel's baton. The playing was good, but without the impress of musical distinction that the conductor must provide and Maazel didn't provide. And he still exhibited a lack of the sense for correct tempo: he made the majestically proclamatory opening of the Handel piece ponderous in its excessive slowness; the Bourée much too fast for its proper effect.

Having heard excellent performances—of Mozart Serenades among other things—conducted by Edo de Waart on records, I welcomed the opportunity to hear him conduct his Rotterdam Philharmonic in a Beethoven program at a concert of Carnegie Hall's International Festival of Orchestras. The orchestra, it turned out in the opening piece, the *Leonore No. 3* Overture, was not of the virtuoso caliber of the Amsterdam Concertgebouw or the great American orchestras; but it played with precision and good sound in the unusually fast tempo de Waart set for the *Allegro* of the piece—so fast that it could not be made faster for the concluding *Presto*. The Piano Concerto No. 3 followed—a work by the young Beethoven, of the same period as the Symphony No. 2, several years before the dramatic *Eroica*, all of which I mention because both de Waart and Paul Schenly, the soloist, dealt with it as if it were a later dramatic work. I cannot recall ever having heard in it the extremes of *fortissimo* Schenly produced in contrast with the *pianissimos*; and he didn't persuade me that they were not excessive. But they didn't sound unpleasant; and his quiet phrases were ear-ravishing in tone and beautifully shaped. The Symphony No.7 that completed the program *is* a powerful work of Beethoven's later years; but de Waart, who shaped it effectively, exaggerated its power to a degree that made the orchestra's sound in the finale unpleasantly noisy.

A Vanguard recording of Liszt's *Transcendental Etudes*, which didn't change my belief that *Paysage* is the one fine piece among them, introduced me to the playing of Russell Sherman, which I found so impressive in its command of the piano and its dealing with the music that I went to hear him play Beethoven's Sonatas Opp. 7, 31 No. 2, 57 *(Appassionata)* and 109 at the Metropolitan Museum of Art. I heard again a completely assured operation of a sense for shape that included freshly thought-out details, and a command of the piano that served his every musical purpose, but also, to my surprise, the extreme, and to my ears excessive *fortissimos* that I mentioned hearing in Schenly's performance of the Concerto No. 3. These excessive *fortissimos*, produced on Sherman's bleak-sounding piano, were unpleasant to the ear in the sparsely occupied Balcony where I sat; but may have been pleasanter in the well-filled Orchestra.

James Levine's contribution to the Metropolitan Opera's new *Rigoletto* is his superbly conducted musical performance that offered, the night I heard it, the excellent singing by Placido Domingo as the Duke and Ileana Cotrubas as Gilda, with singing by Cornell MacNeil in the title role that was still affected by his previous illness. This musical performance is best listened to with eyes closed that prevent one's being distracted by John Dexter's contribution—the stage production that is another of his acts of vandalism.

With the new production there was the usual talk, confidently mindless, not only by Dexter in a *Times* interview with Peter G. Davis of the paper's musical staff, but by Levine in an interview with Tony Randall during an intermission of the televised performance. I use "mindless" as the accurately descriptive term for the statements of both men that made no coherent sense and had no relation to any realities of what they professed to deal with. In a part that I missed of the Levine interview he was quoted as saying that they had benefitted from previous productions they had seen, and had perhaps achieved "greater fidelity to what the composer wanted". But the productions they had seen undoubtedly included the Metropolitan's previous one designed by Eugene Berman, concerning which I wrote in 1952 that the décors of the first three scenes were "the most astoundingly beautiful and effective I can recall seeing in opera," and that by effective I meant "not only their extraordinary living presence as setting for what is seen and heard, but the way the first-[scene] palace interior, with its levels and windowed galleries, provides the means for the profusion of activity created by Herbert Graf." Clearly, this first scene designed by Berman was the *"sala magnifica nel palazzo Ducale"* that Verdi specifies, which the "great decaying Renaissance tower" (Dexter's words) occupying the center of the stage in the new production doesn't even suggest. In the part of the interview with Levine that I did hear he repeated their nonsense about the public accustomed to seeing the real scenes of movies and television not wanting to see papier-mâché imitations of them in opera, in which one should present instead what conveys the work's essential dramatic reality—in the new *Rigoletto* the tower whose increasing dilapidation in the successive scenes relates to the decadence of Mantuan society that the work really is about. I call this nonsense because what the public sees in movies and television includes sets of interiors and exteriors that are made of the same materials as the sets of opera, including the tower in the new *Rigoletto;* and because what that tower in scene after scene impresses one with is its lack of any relation to what one sees happening in the work, and the distracting awkwardness and absurdity it creates in the happenings.

In the first scene, for example, the tower leaves too little performance area on stage for the activity of a ball; and the necessary prominence of the Duke is achieved implausibly by placing him on a balcony with little space for movement, where he sings *"Questa o quella"* to Borsa, embraces a couple of female companions, is joined by Rigoletto, and looks on as Rigoletto clambers down to the stage to make sport of Monterone. And in the second act there is added—to the built-in absurdity of Monterone's being led to prison through the Duke's apartment—the absurdity of this being done on the tower's balcony, from which he addresses the portrait of the Duke on the stage below that he cannot see.

Dexter, in *The Times*, told Peter G. Davis that to stage *Rigoletto* as it was done originally—which is to say with realistic sets that placed it in the period of its dramatic action—"would be a disservice to the opera because we no longer have a direct cultural relation to the 19th century." By this he meant I don't know what, but certainly nothing that would convince those who saw Berman's realistic sets for *Rigoletto* that they were a disservice to the opera. Works like *Le Prophète* and *Rigoletto*, Dexter went on, "have to be presented in a practical way that suggests the piece and allows the audience to use their imaginations"—this practical way being the skeletal framework of an uncompleted cathedral and the clutter of wagons, platforms and stairs in *Le Prophète*, or the crumbling tower in *Rigoletto*, that suggests nothing the spectator's imagination can relate to the work's drama. And all he could deal with, said Dexter, was "practical, technical problems. If something esthetically interesting arises out of the solution, that's wonderful. But you don't go to a piece with an esthetic approach—you go with a technical approach." That is what you do if you are a John Dexter; but if you are a Eugene Berman your approach to an opera is esthetic. For Davis the Dexter *Rigoletto* showed "how a practical solution might well lead to a heightened esthetic experience"; but it didn't demonstrate that to me.

The Metropolitan has been urging the public to experience the sights and sounds of the operatic treasures of our civilization, not recognizing that what Dexter does to the sights of *Aida*, *Le Prophète* and *Rigoletto* constitutes their destruction by one of the barbarians who rule the staging of opera today.

A word about televised opera: I think it is a mistake to have television present the singing actors as they would be seen by someone standing two feet away from them on the stage, where he couldn't avoid noticing things like Rigoletto's false nose and his eye on the prompter; and that it should instead present in the living room what is seen by the person in the opera house sitting at some distance from the stage, to whom Rigoletto's nose seems real and his eye on the prompter is less noticeable, and to whom he is part of the large stage picture.

(4 February 1978) The war for Musorgsky's own *Boris Godunov* may never end; but battles occasionally are won. Moscow's Bolshoi Theater and London's Royal Opera are among the companies which, after performing the Musorgsky original, reverted to Rimsky-Korsakov's recomposition of the work, and Karajan chose the Rimsky version for Salzburg; but the Metropolitan, which came close to reinstating that version in 1968, presented the original again a few years ago; and a major victory now is the first recording of it, issued on Angel records, which will make possible the repeated hearings that will result in its becoming as well

known to the musical public everywhere as the Rimsky version. Such knowledge will lead to additional stage productions and to recordings of better performances than the Angel, which offers good singing by Talvela, Gedda, a number of Polish singers and the Polish Radio Chorus of Krakow with good playing by the Polish Radio National Symphony, but pacing by the conductor Semkow that is damaging to the music's significance and effect.

Whereas the long fight for Musorgsky's *Boris* has achieved these successes, the fight for his *Khovanschchina* hasn't even begun: with effort concentrated on the rescue of *Boris*, there hasn't been an awareness that the *Khovanschchina* we have heard is also a product of Rimsky's rewriting. While orchestrating the work Musorgsky had left unorchestrated, Rimsky said, he "had occasions here and there to put a little order into the choral parts, and to retouch the solo parts now and then, as they were written somewhat unevenly by Musorgsky himself," and to "eliminate certain passages which . . . were musically weak." As it happened, a Vanguard record years ago offered two excerpts from Musorgsky's original version that I thought were magnificent music; and not surprisingly all of the first and part of the second were among the passages Rimsky eliminated because he found them musically weak. I discovered the omissions when I listened to the Belgrade Opera recording of the Rimsky version with the Lamm text of the Musorgsky original before me; and this text enabled me to perceive also the changes that were more numerous and substantial than Rimsky's words "a little order" and "retouch" conveyed—changes that were as impermissible and outrageous as his similar rewriting of *Boris*. Hearing his *Khovanschchina* again recently, after many years and without the Lamm score, I was struck by the Musorgskyan character and expressiveness that the music retains even as adulterated by Rimsky—in particular the expressive power of the arioso writing in which so much of the dramatic dialogue proceeds. But that power would be even greater with the adulteration removed.

The dramatic dialogue in Britten's *Peter Grimes*, which I heard broadcast from the Metropolitan, also proceeds mostly in arioso, which differs from Musorgsky's in having no expressive relation to the words; and writing that merely carries words and action without expressive relation to either is what one hears much of the time in Britten's operas. There are also occasional pages of effective invention for the words and dramatic situation: in *Albert Herring* Lady Billows's grand announcement to

Albert of his election to be King of the May, the dirge for the supposedly dead Albert; in *Peter Grimes* the anguished outbursts of Grimes, the affecting introduction to the third act. And in *A Midsummer Night's Dream*, which the New York City Opera produced in 1963, all the music works effectively with the text on its three levels—the supernatural level of Oberon and Tytania, the real-world level of the lovers, the low-comedy level of the artisans. This is the work of Britten that the Metropolitan should have produced rather than his *Death in Venice;* the work of his that the New York City Opera should have kept in its repertory rather than *The Turn of the Screw*. But the repertory decisions of both companies are beyond my powers of rational understanding.

The "largest repertory of contemporary works available anywhere" that Julius Rudel of the New York City Opera boasts of actually includes the many works dropped after one season that didn't merit production at all, as well as a few—Alban Berg's *Wozzeck*, Britten's *A Midsummer Night's Dream* and *Albert Herring*—that did merit retention in the repertory but have not been repeated. Of the endless succession of works by Americans that the company has presented the only one of high musical quality that justified production in 1954 and further hearing thereafter was Aaron Copland's *The Tender Land;* but it was inferior works by Menotti, Douglas Moore and Carlisle Floyd that were repeated, not Copland's work. And though the company wasted productions on those works of Menotti, Moore and Floyd and others by Giannini, Beeson, Rorem, Weisgall, Blitzstein and Weill, it did not produce Virgil Thomson's *The Mother of Us All*.

As for the Metropolitan, which claims to present the operatic treasures of our civilization, Wagner's *Tannhäuser*—though a work by a man whose matured powers produced such treasures—is itself not one of them, but an early product of musical gifts which do not yet operate even as interestingly as in *Lohengrin* a few years later. It is, then, a work for a company to present *in addition* to *Tristan und Isolde* and *Die Meistersinger*, but not instead of them; and it is shocking that Wagner should be represented at the Metropolitan this season by not even one of the works of his maturity, but only by a musically boring early work. Its interest for me was that of the performance I attended—of James Levine's impressive conducting, the excellent singing of Grace Bumbry as Venus and Bernd Weikl as Wolfram, Leonie Rysanek's alternation between tremulous and steady singing as Elisabeth, James McCracken's constricted-sounding singing in the title role, his loss of his voice in the finale of Act 2, his partial recovery of it for Act 3, and such features of the staging as the ludicrous erotic choreography contrived by Norbert Vesak for the Venusberg scene, the handsome Hall of Song designed by Günther Schneider-Siemssen.

In an article about music criticism two years ago I wrote concerning Robert Craft's collection of critical writing, *Prejudices in Disguise*, that to credit him with the critic's essential equipment of perception and judgment was to say that I found a great deal in the book that was confirmed by my experience as a listener and that outweighed the occasional statements my experience contradicted. And that applies now to *Current Convictions*, a new collection of his essay-reviews of books and performances written for *The New York Review of Books*. A number of them deal with other subjects than music; but the majority give us Craft's perceptive comments on the creative powers and works of Mozart, Verdi, Wagner, Strauss, Liszt, Ravel, Ives and Schönberg, and his evaluations of the Bayreuth productions of Wagner, the Metropolitan's productions of *The Marriage of Figaro*, *Parsifal* and *Der Rosenkavalier*, the Paris Opera productions of *Figaro*, *Otello* and *Faust*, the last group being the occasion for another demolition of Harold Schonberg's confident pronouncements in *The Times*.

An example of a perception of Craft's being confirmed by my experience is his statement that James Levine, "charging through the score" of *Der Rosenkavalier*, failed "to hesitate on upbeats in [the] waltzes"—which describes what I heard Levine do in the *Ländler* movement of Mahler's First Symphony. On the other hand Craft's belief in Solti's infallible musicianship is contradicted by the way Solti "charged through" Tchaikovsky's *Pathétique* Symphony on a record I heard recently. More important, whereas Craft finds in Charles Rosen's book on Arnold Schönberg manifestations of "the awesomeness of his intellect" and "language of such precision and elegance as virtually to defy . . . paraphrasing," I, in my reading of Rosen—e.g. of *The Classical Style*—have found that the precise-appearing words that produce for Craft awesome intellection produce for me statements whose imprecision defies not only paraphrasing but understanding. (And not only I: the reviewer of Rosen's book on Schönberg in *Perspectives of New Music*, Elaine Barkin, began with the question "What is it about Charles Rosen's 'short account' of Schoenberg that baffles and perturbs?" and the answer, quoted from *Alice in Wonderland*, "Somehow it seems to fill my head with ideas—only I don't know exactly what they are," which she then proceeded to apply to passages in the book.) Or when the statements are the understandable ones a reader quoted to me from the preface of the book on Schönberg— "Today we are no longer under any obligation to persuade listeners of his importance, or even to assess it. . . .Schoenberg's achievement appears to many musicians an uneven one, but it has seemed to me of very little interest to say which works I like best and which I think least successful. In any case, that will be perfectly clear in what follows; but the exercise of taste for its own sake makes for dubious criticism"— they are not only wrong but, in their lofty ex cathedra assurance, comically wrong. (There is more that needs to be said about Rosen; but I limit myself here to what relates to Craft's statements.) (Not published)

Note 1983 A musician wrote to me in February 1974 about the lecture, *Schumann and the Romantic Movement*, that he had heard Rosen give at the University of Massachusetts. After demonstrating how passages in Schumann's Impromptu on a Theme of Clara Wieck were more effective as originally composed and published than as revised by him years later, Rosen had embarked on an erudition trip about Romantic philosophy, art, architecture, poetry ("everything but Schumann", said my correspondent): impressive-sounding but unclear phrases, interspersed with quotations in their original French or German of passages by writers my correspondent didn't know and wasn't interested in—writers, moreover, who were not of Schumann's early-nineteenth-century period but of the 1780s. And after this hour-long digression Rosen had jumped to the 1830s ("And so we come to Schumann") and repeated his point about the revisions of the unfamiliar Impromptu on a Theme of Clara Wieck, which, my correspondent said, were interesting, but not as interesting as Schumann's revisions of his great Fantasia Op. 17 would have been. And this Rosen performance had succeeded in its purpose of leaving the audience—except my correspondent and another musician who later gave me the same report—overwhelmed by what it thought it had learned about Schumann.

(4 March 1978) Before her recent recital in the Great Performers at

Lincoln Center series in New York's Avery Fisher Hall I had heard the
mezzo-soprano Christa Ludwig at the Metropolitan Opera in the Wieland Wagner staging of *Lohengrin*, in which her Ortrud was that of a
singing actress of compelling vocal and dramatic power, and in the
broadcast of Berlioz's *Les Troyens*, in which her singing as Dido was
extraordinary in its tonal beauty, affecting expressiveness and grandeur.
With these exceptions I had known her work only from records, of which
a recent one offered songs of Brahms in which the beauty and power of
her voice were undiminished. I was therefore unprepared, at the recital,
for the absence of its usual warmth and amplitude that made it almost
unrecognizable in the opening group of songs by Beethoven. It had
regained a little color in the last song of the group, *Ich liebe dich;* and the
gain continued in the songs of Schubert and Wolf that followed, producing increasingly effective performances which culminated in singing of
Wolf's *Kennst du das Land* that was overwhelming in its restored vocal
beauty and power. In full command of her resources she now produced
superb statements of three of Mahler's Rückert songs, and wasted those
resources on the inexpressive vocal writing of Alban Berg's *Seven Early
Songs*. But one of her encores was a grand proclamation of Beethoven's
Die Ehre Gottes aus der Natur.

(In a *Times* interview two days before the recital Ludwig said that
having begun in 1946 she was now singing less and giving up roles that
put a strain on her voice. She should in addition do the longer warming
up her voice now requires *before* the recital instead of during its first two
groups.)

In the forty years before Toscanini began to conduct the New York
Philharmonic in 1926 he fulfilled his obligation to perform what the
major composers were creating—*e.g.* Strauss's tone poems and *Salomé*,
Debussy's *Pelléas et Mélisande*, *La Mer* and *Ibéria*, Stravinsky's *Petrushka*.
He thought it reasonable that what he had done in his youth should now
be left to his young contemporaries, who had an understanding and
feeling for the new music that he didn't have, while he increased his
insight into the great music of the past. As it happened this music of the
past included a few great works which the public was unacquainted
with; and my generation of music-lovers learned to know Berlioz's *Romeo
and Juliet* from the performances Toscanini began to give in 1928, Verdi's
Requiem from the performances he began to give in 1931, Beethoven's
Missa Solemnis from the performances he began to give in 1934. Other

conductors began to perform them after him; and their performances had to stand comparison with his—which is to say, specifically, that the shapes the other conductors gave to the works, and the expressive meaning conveyed in those shapes, had to stand comparison with the shapes and expressive meanings of Toscanini's performances. Guido Cantelli produced an equally great performance of Verdi's *Requiem;* but although Colin Davis's and Ozawa's performances of Berlioz's *Romeo* and Jochum's performance of Beethoven's *Missa* were good, they were surpassed by Toscanini's.

In Beethoven's *Missa,* for example, no other performance in my experience imparted to the hushed orchestral Prelude to the *Benedictus* the raptly mystical character it has in Toscanini's recorded performance. Nor in any other performance were the numerous changes of tempo in the *Gloria* and *Credo* made with the sense for relation and proportion that achieves the continuity and coherence the two progressions have in his performance. And Kubelik, in his recent performance with the New York Philharmonic, failed in these matters as the other conductors have done. In addition one didn't hear in the performance the finely chiselled detail and the exact orchestral execution that Toscanini achieves. Kubelik's baton technique does not, like Toscanini's, communicate explicitly and immediately to an orchestra what he wants it to do; and the excellent playing he obtains from his own Bavarian Radio Symphony that is accustomed to his conducting style he could have achieved with the New York Philharmonic only with more rehearsal than was available—to judge by the playing that got poorer as it got nearer to the end. The soprano Benite Valente, after a rough-sounding start, sang beautifully; the tenor Robert Tear and bass-baritone John Shirley-Quirk also sang well; but the contralto Birgit Finnilae produced unattractive sounds; and I have heard better singing by the Westminster Choir.

Verdi's *Otello* is in fact one of the treasures of our civilization that the Metropolitan Opera claims to offer—one whose greatness was fully realized in performance there when Toscanini conducted it and Leo Slezak sang the title role, and not again in comparable degree until Jon Vickers sang it in the performances conducted by James Levine a few years ago. Those performances should have continued in the years that followed; but it was not until the current season that the Metropolitan presented the work again, offering seven performances of this masterpiece as against the ten of *Adriana Lecouvreur*, the eleven of *Thais*, the thirteen of *Cavalleria Rusticana* and *Pagliacci*, and of those seven of *Otello* only four with Vickers. Having heard one of the four, I can report the overwhelming impact again of the musical performance conducted by Levine, the expressive power of Vickers's employment of his lustrous voice, the beautiful and affecting singing of Katia Ricciarelli as Desdemona, with the effective singing of Cornell MacNeil as Iago, the adequate singing of the rest of the cast, the excellent playing of the orchestra.

It was, however, another performance to listen to with closed eyes, in order not to be distracted and outraged by what is presented to the eye in place of what the text and Verdi's directions call for. The Zeffirelli stage production—which Andrew Porter found to be a "basically conventional approach" with "clever solutions to the tricky points of stage disposition (the garden chorus, the overhearing scene)"—is on the contrary a monstrosity of wholly perverse innovation that creates the "tricky" difficulties Porter credited it with solving. No difficulty arises from what Verdi prescribes for the second act: a room on the ground floor of the castle, with glass doors at the back through which Desdemona can easily be seen in the garden outside, surrounded by the women, children and sailors paying her homage; but difficulty *is* created by Zeffirelli's transferring the desk, map and books of Otello's study to outdoor battlements extending across the back of the stage and leaving only a small opening on the left through which Desdemona can be seen crowded into a corner with a few women and children. Nor does any difficulty arise from what Verdi prescribes for the third act: the great hall of the castle, with columns on the right behind which Otello conceals himself to observe and overhear Iago and Cassio in the foreground; but Zeffirelli creates sheer absurdity by placing the act in an armory (to make possible the innovations of Otello pointing a sword menacingly at Desdemona, and Iago and Cassio playing with a sword as they converse) and perversely concealing Iago and Cassio behind the rack of weapons with Otello visible in the foreground.

The additional appearances that Vickers might have made in *Otello* he made in *Pagliacci*, which is not one of the treasures of our civilization that are the only legitimate concern of an institution like the Metropolitan. Neither is *Cavalleria Rusticana* or *Adriana Lecouvreur*, in this season's repertory, or last year's *Andrea Chénier*, or *Francesca da Rimini*, which Levine told Peter G. Davis of *The Times* he was "dying to do" and had been "all set with a production three years from now, but the proper singers were not available. With luck, we will be able to schedule it for the future." He was "also on a campaign to do more Mascagni," and "eventually you will be seeing more verismo operas," which he admired for the same reason as he did Hitchcock films: "the strong melodramatic approach, the technical skill in manipulating the emotions of the audience. . . . Sure, the man who holds Beethoven's Op. 131 String Quartet as the epitome of music will reject all this. . . . I love Op. 131 but I love 'Andrea Chenier' too, and I feel sorry for people who must arbitrarily set limits that exclude one or the other."

Levine spoke with his usual confidence; but what he said, in reply to those who object to the *verismo* operas he is determined to have the Metropolitan produce, was his usual mindless esthetic pronouncements which misstated the objection they replied to. What I as a music-lover require of the musical writing I listen to—writing of any genre, any style, any expressive level—is intrinsic musical value. And the music I love—the music that satisfies my requirement—is not only Beethoven's last quartets but works of less exalted expressive content, like Tchaikovsky's symphonies and ballet scores, Strauss's early tone poems, Dvořák's *Slavonic Dances;* the show music of Kern, Gershwin, Rodgers and Hart, Porter, Arlen, and the jazz improvisations of Louis Armstrong, Bix Beiderbecke, Jack Teagarden; in opera not only Beethoven's *Fidelio* and Mozart's masterpieces, but works of Rossini, Bellini, Donizetti, Verdi, and of Verdi not only his incandescent mature writing for the melodramatic libretto of *Otello* but his unsophisticated early writing for the melodramatic libretto of *Il Trovatore*. What I have no interest in is writing of little or no intrinsic musical value, like the later tone poems and operas of Strauss, the works of Rachmaninov, Ravel, Shostakovich, Puccini, and the even lower-grade *verismo* operas Levine assures us we will be seeing. The objection to the Metropolitan's producing these operas is, then, not that in intrinsic musical value—properly the determining factor in the production of any opera—they aren't on the level of Beethoven's last quartets, but that they are too far below the level of the operas of Rossini, Bellini, Donizetti and Verdi. And any similarity to Hitchcock films has no relevance in the matter.

By now it is clear that for whatever pertains to musical performance Levine has exceptional gifts which have greatly benefitted the Metropolitan and its public; but for what lies outside musical performance, like repertory or staging, he has a muddled mind filled with current rubbishy ideas that has contributed to disasters like the *Aida*, *Le Prophète* and *Rigoletto* inflicted on the Metropolitan and its public in the recent past, and that promises more such disasters in the future. (Not published)

Note 1983 Shortly before the appearance of my article of 7 January 1978 the unexpected arrival of a parcel of *New Republic* letterheads with "B. H. Haggin" printed above "Music" seemed to indicate that *The New Republic's* literary editor, Roger Rosenblatt, was satisfied with the accommodation of our different ideas in my writing for the magazine. In my previous writing for *The Nation* I had alternated extended discussions of a single subject with chronicles of two or three musical events that I had dealt with more briefly; and after my long first article on the Metropolitan Opera for *The New Republic* in the summer of 1975 I had written Rosenblatt that I would like to write an occasional chronicle like the ones from *The Nation* that I enclosed, as well as an occasional article dealing at length with one subject. I had suggested several subjects for long articles, of which he accepted two; in the fall he had accepted my suggestion of a chronicle of three concerts; and he had continued to accept suggestions of chronicles as well as articles. In a handwritten note in February 1976 in which he had welcomed the suggestion of an article on Van Cliburn he had added that the chronicles were useful and pleasurable to a great many readers, but that many other readers were equally interested in critical essays on single topics; and a few months later he had written that he considered the single-topic approach to be better than asking a reader to make too many leaps in thought. But since no reader had ever complained about any difficulty in making the one or two shifts from one topic to the next in a chronicle, and Rosenblatt had not mentioned the matter again, I had continued to write both the chronicles that he had said interested many readers in addition to the single-topic essays that other readers were equally interested in and he preferred. And the letterheads seemed to indicate that he had been satisfied to accept both.

Also, in September 1977 Rosenblatt, in connection with my commenting on books, had cautioned me against using my column to disparage the work of other critics, conceding that a little of this was healthy, but contending that too much was boring to readers. He would not have written this to an anthropologist or an economist commenting on the ideas in books of other anthropologists or economists, or even to a literary critic commenting on the ideas of other literary critics: only a music critic's comment on the ideas of another music critic is regarded as improper and a misuse of his publication's space for a personal quarrel (the editor of *The Nation* thought it proper for him to publish his disagreement with an editorial in *The Times*, but not for *The Nation's* music critic to publish his disagreement with an article by *The Times's* music critic). In reply to Rosenblatt I had quoted Bernard Shaw's statement that "musical criticisms . . . are of low average quality simply because they are never discussed or contradicted," and his advocacy of the formation of "a Vigilance Committee of musicians for the exposure of incompetent critics." And since there was no such committee, I had said, "as long as I continue to encounter ideas I think are wrong I will consider it part of my job as a critic to correct them. None of my readers have written to say they found this boring; whereas many . . . have told me it has been one of the most valuable of my services as a critic." Concerning this too Rosenblatt had raised no further objection.

But if Rosenblatt was satisfied *The New Republic's* publisher, Martin Peretz, was not. Late in February 1978 he wrote me that the chronicles I had sent for February and March 4 would not be printed, and why. He said he had reread my correspondence with Rosenblatt and the articles *The New Republic* had printed; but the inadequacy of his reading was evident in the letter's postscript with his parting shot that if I didn't close my eyes at the Metropolitan's performances I might think differently about the one of *Tannhäuser*—what his reading had made of what I had said after describing what my open eyes had seen in the stagings of *Rigoletto* and *Otello*: that the musical performances of these two operas were best listened to with eyes closed. It was evident also in his major charge—that in the face of Rosenblatt's repeatedly expressed preference for articles focussed on a single topic I had continued to write the unfocussed chronicles that allowed me to take the easy course of merely stringing together my immediate impressions and judgments with my recollections and grudges into a succession without coherence—which overlooked or misread my exchanges with Rosenblatt on that matter and my numerous extended discussions of a single topic. And it was evident in his finding in my comments on other critics' ideas a misuse of my space to engage in intra-professional wars that he likened to intra-university politics.

Peretz wrote that he had read me for years; but in our telephone conversation in May 1975 in which we discussed my writing for *The New Republic* he had not brought up anything he objected to in what he had read; nor had he objected to anything in the copy of my previously published book *A Decade of Music* that I had sent him after our conversation. In fact I had not heard from him again after that telephone conversation until his letter in February 1978. In May 1975 he had talked like a person of good sense and good manners; in his letter he wrote with neither; and so my reply—in which I declined his offer to let me continue if I met his requirements—began with this statement:

> It isn't only I who respond negatively to your objections to my operation as a music critic but, in effect, the countless readers who, in the forty years of that operation, have written me about their profit and pleasure from it. . . . They have included *New Republic* readers, some of whom protested when Harrison dropped [my record column] in 1966, and welcomed me back in 1975; and I cannot see myself even trying to change what has worked successfully with my readers for forty years, to satisfy a publisher with a mistaken belief that those readers share his weird ideas about criticism, and about my criticism in particular—a publisher, moreover, with the further mistaken belief that he is privileged to express his dissatisfaction with my operation in terms not only wrongheaded and factually inaccurate but personally offensive.

Chronicle 1978-83

Notable happenings in the concert hall early in 1978 included the pianist Paul Schenly's first solo recital, in which he revealed his possession of not only the technical powers demanded by Brahms's *Variations on a Theme by Paganini*, but the musical gift that achieved an impressively effective realization of Schubert's writing—now grandly proclamatory, now poignantly lovely, now hair-raisingly powerful—in his posthumous Sonata in A, and admirably shaped performances of Schubert's Impromptu Op. 142 No. 3 and a Nocturne and Mazurka by Chopin.

A recital by the pianist Maurizio Pollini, whom I had previously known only from records, gave me my first opportunity to hear him in a hall. After recording, at the age of eighteen, the remarkable performance of Chopin's Concerto No. 1 that is still available on a Seraphim record, he had withdrawn from public view for further study; and in the recorded performances that had signalized his reappearance several years later one had heard an operation on the highest level of instrumental mastery and musical insight—a disciplined operation, moreover, in which, as in Toscanini's performances, expressiveness was contained within coherently proportioned shape by an unfailing plastic sense. This operation I now heard in Carnegie Hall in his performances of Beethoven's last three sonatas; and it made them strikingly different from the performances by Ashkenazy that had begun to trouble me with what seemed to represent his agreement with Furtwängler that expressive profundity in performance was increased by slower tempos, expanded *ritardandos*, and lengthened silent pauses. The hushed opening statements of the first movement of Beethoven's *Appassionata* Sonata, for example, were played by Ashkenazy not in the *allegro assai* tempo

Beethoven prescribed for the movement, but as a slow introduction to the outburst in fast tempo a few moments later; and he continued this alternation of slow with fast throughout the movement, instead of maintaining Beethoven's *allegro assai* as the movement's basic tempo, with the modifications Beethoven specified, and the additional slight modifications that articulate the musical progression in a performance. And whereas Pollini was content with the *maestoso* character of the introductory pronouncements of Beethoven's Sonata Op. 111 played in tempo, Ashkenazy, to make them more majestic, slowed them down to the point at which the distention in time distorted their shape and made them ponderous.

As it happened, I heard an excellent performance by Ashkenazy later in the spring at the first of the concerts in Carnegie Hall at which Haitink conducted his Concertgebouw Orchestra in Beethoven's nine symphonies and his five piano concertos with Ashkenazy as soloist. The concert was preceded by a brief hall rehearsal of a few passages in the *Egmont* Overture and *Pastoral* Symphony, at which I marveled at the sound and sensitivity of the orchestra that I was hearing live for the first time. And after these passages a few points in the Concerto No. 1 were checked with Ashkenazy. Haitink's recorded performances of the nine symphonies (regrettably not with the Concertgebouw but with the London Philharmonic) had been the only recent ones I had found to be well conceived; and at this concert his pacing and shaping of the *Pastoral* was admirable except for a slackening of tempo, damaging to momentum and continuity, in one passage of the second movement. Admirable also was the powerful performance of the *Egmont* Overture. As for Ashkenazy's performance in the concerto, it could be that he didn't feel any impulse to make this early writing of Beethoven's more profound, or that he was restrained by his having to play within the orchestra's framework; but a major factor in the performance must have been what Ashkenazy had told an interviewer before the performances in Washington that preceded the ones in New York. When he had recorded the concertos with Solti and the Chicago Symphony the "tremendous energy" that was "the main thing with Solti" had "resulted in very tight and very exciting performances" in which "I myself became very excited, and perhaps overdid it;" whereas "with Haitink—I've already played the concertos with him in Amsterdam—I feel a tremendous amount of warmth and expansiveness . . . a very humane way of making music"—the result of which was the relaxed and beautifully sensitive working together of soloist, conductor and orchestra that I heard at the concert. (Which is to say, as justice to Ashkenazy requires, that I did not hear at any point what Andrew Porter reported—that "Haitink and Ashkenazy did not mate well;" that Ashkenazy, for one thing, did not have Haitink's "command of . . . 'molded' tempo;" and though Haitink was "content to accompany, yet occasionally pianist and orchestra got out of time.")

Another important visit was that of John Nelson with his Indianapolis Symphony and Symphonic Choir. In Carnegie Hall in 1971 Nelson had conducted his chorus from New Jersey, an assembled orchestra and good soloists in a five-hour concert performance of Berlioz's *Les Troyens* that had had for me the same effect of revelation as Toscanini's performance of Berlioz's *Harold in Italy* with the New York Philharmonic in 1929: hearing what Nelson's performance had presented as *Les Troyens*, I had apprehended and been deeply moved by what had not been communicated through previous performances. And the mastery of the musical work and of his performing forces that he had exhibited on that occasion he exhibited in Carnegie Hall again in 1978 in Berlioz's *Requiem*.

The renown of the Leipzig Gewandhaus Orchestra, which I heard for the first time in the fall of 1978, led me to expect playing comparable with that of the other renowned German orchestras. What I failed to take into account was the fact that an orchestra's players and conductors change, and so do therefore its playing and its sound. The Gewandhaus Orchestra that Kurt Masur conducted in Carnegie Hall was not the one Nikisch had made renowned fifty years before, and might play and sound differently; and from what Szell had said about the New York Philharmonic's playing under Toscanini in Europe in 1930—"This was orchestral performance of a kind new to all of us"—it was entirely possible that the orchestra Nikisch conducted had not been the equal of the Berlin or Vienna Philharmonic of today. Certainly the one I heard in Carnegie Hall was not: it was a good orchestra with which Masur produced respectable performances of Mendelssohn's *Italian* Symphony, Mozart's Sinfonia Concertante K. 364 and Beethoven's Fifth.

Even the sufficiently rehearsed performance of Tchaikovsky's Symphony No. 5 that Abbado recorded was made unacceptable by its traditional distortions of tempo that falsified expressive content; but his performance of the work with the New York Philharmonic in the spring

of 1979 sounded as if it had had only a single run-through after almost all
the rehearsal time had been used for the other two works on the program.
A lot of time must have been required by the fifteen or twenty minutes of
delicate sonorities of Ligeti's *Lontano*—"these tender, intertwined, almost fluid crystal formations . . . associated in my mind with a sense of
great spatial and temporal distance", the program notes quoted him as
saying—that conveyed no musical significance to me. And much time
evidently had been devoted to achieving the beautiful playing by the
orchestra and its precise integration with the playing by Pollini, in the
performance of Beethoven's Concerto No. 4 that appeared to hold
everyone else spellbound as it did my companions and me. (Again, in
justice to Pollini this time, I must say that I did not at any time hear what
Andrew Porter reported—that "the ensemble between the soloist and
the orchestra was often imprecise," and that in Pollini's playing as in his
performances of Beethoven's last three sonatas a year earlier—"nothing
happened." The playing, nerveless and without cohesive tension, in
which *I* heard nothing happen was Alfred Brendel's—in Mozart concertos, Schubert sonatas, some of Beethoven's sonatas—in which Porter
reported hearing marvels like Schnabel's.)

Pollini's program at a later recital included Schumann's Sonata Op.
11, which in my early years of concert-going ranked as a major work of
the piano literature, and as such was played frequently. Hearing it now
after many years I found that the impassioned declamatory introduction
was as impressive as the impassioned opening of Schumann's Fantasy
Op. 17, but the *allegro vivace* first movement it introduced didn't fulfill
the expectations it created; and that the second movement's melodic
writing was exquisite and deeply affecting, but the remaining two
movements were much less interesting. And the five pieces of Schumann's *Gesänge der Frühe* Op. 133, which I had never heard before, were
interesting only as examples of his individual style of writing for the
piano. These works, and Chopin's Fantasy Op. 49 and Sonata Op. 35,
Pollini performed very beautifully; but the records I played at home after
the recital confirmed my recollection of Cliburn's performances of the
two Chopin works—his greater perception and articulation of detail in
the coherent shape that emerged with the grandeur he imparted to
whatever he performed.

Ashkenazy too played music by Schumann and Chopin at a recital
which began with an excellent performance of Beethoven's rarely heard

Sonata Op. 31 No. 1. The Schumann work was the superb set of imaginative pieces, *Davidsbündlertänze*, of which Ashkenazy shaped the meditative ones with admirable sensitiveness, but, surprisingly, rushed and banged the lively and vigorous ones as if they were mere vehicles for bravura display of virtuosity. And he did this also with Chopin's Fantasy Op. 49, Ballade Op. 47 and Scherzo Op. 39.

Pollini provided additional memorable experiences with his performances, in March 1980, of Schubert's Sonatas in C minor, A major and B-flat major. Composed in September 1828, a month or so before his death, they are the last of his major instrumental works, concerning which one can say what J. W. N. Sullivan writes about Beethoven's last sonatas and quartets: that Schubert's use of the medium of music reveals him as a great musical genius, and what he communicates through that medium reveals him as a great spirit. What one gets from the statement of the theme at the beginning of the second movement of Beethoven's Sonata Op. 111—a communication of long experience mastered, profound lessons learned, inner illumination and superearthly exaltation attained—one gets also from the two meditative statements with which Schubert's Sonata in B-flat begins, from later pages in this sonata, from pages in the other two final sonatas. This, and everything else the works communicate, Pollini's performances made overwhelming. A year later he offered superbly effective performances of Schubert's Sonata Op. 42, Schumann's Fantasy, and Chopin's Nocturnes Op. 48 and Polonaises Opp. 44 and 53. And in 1982 he began a recital with poised and admirably articulating statements of Mozart's Fantasy K. 475 and Sonata K. 457; continued with another such statement of the Adagio K. 540; but then played the first movement of the Sonata K. 576 in a tempo too fast for clear articulation of passage work, and did this again with the finale. Though one heard his normal beautiful playing after that, it was in lesser pieces by Schubert—the three Impromptus titled *Drei Klavierstücke* D. 946, and the *Wandererfantasie*—that are mostly uninteresting.

Early in 1982 I heard in Carnegie Hall—after several years in which I had heard it only in recorded performances—the singing of Janet Baker. I was prepared for losses after those years; but miraculously none were revealed on this occasion. I heard now what I had heard years before: the singularly beautiful voice whose bright, clear timbre was as distinctive as the timbres of Rethberg's, Ponselle's and Flagstad's voices had been; the security in its production that enabled it to do with no apparent effort whatever it was required to do; the sense for coherent shape in the flow of sound it produced; the unerring musical intelligence and taste evident in the subtle inflection of phrase; the personal involvement and intensity that made deeply affecting her realizations of the songs of Schubert, Schumann, Mahler, Strauss, and the closing group of unfamiliar and attractive songs by Gounod, including one, *Prends Garde*, in which she employed her gift of humor. And after all this her final encore was a triumphant performance of Handel's spectacular *O Had I Jubal's Lyre*.

And in the fall of 1982, also after several years, I heard one of the concerts of Karajan and his Berlin Philharmonic in Carnegie Hall. What struck the eye immediately was the idiosyncratic movements that did not, like Toscanini's, have a visible compelling relation to the orchestra's every sound, but instead constituted a plastique of curving arms, hands and fingers accompanying the flow of sound, with only an occasional clenching of fist for a climactic *fortissimo*. Nor was the compulsion exercised by his eyes, which most of the time were closed. It was the compulsion of mere presence that elicited the marvels of precise execution and beautiful sound that had been worked out in rehearsal. Interesting in addition was the fact that the sound of this orchestra did not—like that of Stokowski's Philadelphia or Koussevitzky's Boston Symphony— have a distinctive character analogous to the various distinctive timbres of the soprano voices of Ponselle, Rethberg, Lotte Lehmann and Flagstad, the tenor voices of Caruso and Bjoerling. As for the musical operation, I was agreeably surprised by Karajan's steady tempos and coherent shaping of the first two movements of the Brahms Fourth, but then disappointed by his different treatment of the concluding passacaglia. Its theme was stated not *allegro energico e passionato*, as Brahms directs, but rather slowly and deliberately without energy and passion; this slowness continued in the successive variations until the point— after the solemn pronouncements by brass and woodwinds in Variations 14 and 15—at which the theme returned, this time *allegro energico;* but after several variations there was an excessive slowing down for the *fortissimo* proclamation of Variation 24. And such distortions of tempo and shape in the Brahms Second included the excessive slowing down of the *tranquillo* episode in the development of the finale.

A notable happening in Carnegie Hall a month or so later was the performance of Mozart's Piano Concerto K. 482 by Richard Goode with the conductorless chamber orchestra Orpheus. I was there because of their performances of the Concertos K. 453 and 488 on a Nonesuch record, in which Goode's playing was made outstanding by its combination of sensitiveness with the strong enunciation that one heard in Schnabel's playing of Mozart but one usually doesn't hear today, and by the fact that the force with which Goode began a phrase was sustained to its conclusion instead of diminishing to the usual pallid whisper; and this playing was admirably integrated with the beautiful and sensitive context provided by the small orchestra. In the similar performance of K. 482 Goode's playing, scaled to the size of the orchestra, did not have in the large space of Carnegie Hall the impact it had at the microphone's close range on the record.

At Janet Baker's recital in Carnegie Hall early in 1983 one heard again the moving operation of musical intelligence, taste and intensity of involvement, but their effect lessened this time by diminished vocal resources. The voice had its distinctive timbre and glow in its middle range, but less amplitude and power; and high notes that formerly had rung out with thrilling clarity and force were produced now—in Wagner's *Wesendonck Songs*, for example—as effortful *pianissimos*.

A great occasion at the Metropolitan Opera House on a Sunday afternoon in March was the performance of Schubert's *Die Winterreise* by Christa Ludwig and James Levine. One could expect Ludwig's mezzo-soprano voice—by now a little thin and cold at its top, but still opulent lower down—and her matured musical and dramatic powers to produce deeply affecting singing; but I did not foresee that Levine would demonstrate at the piano the remarkable gift for collaboration with a singer that he had revealed in his conducting of opera, in playing that anticipated, complemented, supported, intensified Ludwig's every sound. The manner of their working together, and the realization of Schubert's great work it achieved, were an overwhelming experience.

At Avery Fisher Hall a couple of weeks later I remarked to a friend before Pollini's performance of Beethoven's *Diabelli Variations* that the crucial test would be whether in Variation 20 Pollini would—as only Schnabel had done with his infinitely slow and still performance of it—take us to what J. W. N. Sullivan had called the "strange seas of thought" of Beethoven's last works. And it turned out that Pollini did hear in that variation what Schnabel heard—in addition to everything else his enlivening and expressive performance communicated. For

Andrew Porter, who found Pollini's performance "immaculately polished but lacking in wit, humor, fantasy, and suddenness", it also demonstrated that "Beethoven's indicated dynamics are literally unobservable on a modern Steinway grand, with its mighty sustaining power." But I heard Beethoven's indicated *p* and *pp* in Variation 20 produced by the Steinway piano, whose sustaining power made it possible for me also to hear the chords connected as Beethoven indicated, which I would not have heard if Pollini had played them on the early 19th-century fortepiano with little sustaining power, as Porter advocates. I cannot accept the contention of the fortepiano cultists that since Beethoven had to accept, in the fortepiano available to him, its lack of sustaining power necessary for a legato in *cantabile* analogous to that of the human voice or a violin, the non-legato is not only what *we* must accept but what *he* would prefer to the legato made possible by the modern piano. I find it impossible to believe he would not have welcomed the modern piano's legato in *cantabile* if it had become available in his lifetime, or would object to it if he could hear it today. (And as a professional user of words I object to the misuse of them—in phrases like one writer's "legato machine" or Porter's "mighty sustaining power"—to give the piano's strengths the appearance of grave and unacceptable weaknesses and the fortepiano's weaknesses the appearance of highly desirable strengths.)

The Metroplitan Opera's advertisements and brochures have exhorted opera-lovers to experience "the flame of genius"—kindled "somewhere between the glorious music and the grand theatre, the immortal composers and the incredible artists"—that ignites "fiery emotions . . . evening after evening;" but in reality this is something opera-lovers have in recent years been able to experience only on occasional evenings. "The flame of genius" is not what one hears in the operas of Leoncavallo, Mascagni, Giordano, Cilea and their like—and, for my ears, Puccini—that form a major portion of the Metropolitan's repertory; that flame in Beethoven's *Fidelio* and Wagner's *Tristan und Isolde* has been extinguished by Erich Leinsdorf's leaden conducting; and the fiery emotions ignited by the vandalism John Dexter's staging inflicted on Verdi's *Aida* and *Rigoletto* and Meyerbeer's *Le Prophète* were outrage and fury. What the new production of Smetana's *The Bartered Bride* offered in the fall of 1978 was not the flame of genius but only an engaging work conducted well by James Levine, with the distinguished but middle-aged Nicolai Gedda in the role of young Jeník and the lustrous voice of Jon Vickers wasted in the role of the stuttering Vašek—this acceptable musical performance with an obtrusively ineffective staging designed by Josef Svoboda and directed by Dexter. On the other hand the performance of Verdi's *Otello* with the new Otello of Placido Domingo a year later did provide an experience of that flame, but only in what one heard—Verdi's music and the performance superbly conducted by Levine, with Domingo's beautiful and powerfully expressive singing—and though what one heard included the unfocussed voice of Gilda Cruz-Romo, the Desdemona, making it necessary to apply to the performance what Tovey said about the flaws in Schubert's major instrumental works: that "the highest qualities attained in important parts of a great work are as indestructible by weaknesses elsewhere as if the weaknesses were the accidents of physical ruin."

Another experience of the flame of genius solely in what one heard was provided by the new production of Verdi's *Don Carlo*, of which I attended a performance in the theater and watched a televised performance in the spring of 1980. One experienced it first of all in the new version of the opera that was performed. The Metropolitan did not offer again Verdi's four-act revised version of 1883, the one performed in most opera houses thereafter (though recorded performances have included the first act that Verdi in 1883 omitted from the original five-act work performed in Paris in 1867). Nor, fortunately, did it offer what it had originally announced for production—that original five-act work, which would have satisfied the musicological interest of a few, but would have deprived music-lovers of Verdi's incandescent new invention for the 1883 revision. Instead it not only added the 1867 first act to the revised four acts of 1883, but restored to that first act what Verdi in 1867 dropped before the first performance and omitted from the published score—its orchestral introduction and opening scene. They remained unknown until a few years ago, when Andrew Porter unearthed them in the parts used in Paris in 1867. And so music-lovers heard for the first time at the Metropolitan the orchestra's powerful statements that seized one's mind and held it fast with their developing progression, and, when the curtain rose, the poignant phrases of the suffering peasants in their encounter with Elizabeth in the forest of Fontainebleau.

And of this marvelous product of Verdi's matured powers the performances I heard offered another superbly paced and shaped progression achieved by Levine with the unequal contributions by the performers available to him: the admirable singing by Sherrill Milnes as Rodrigo and Tatiana Troyanos as Eboli, the expressively phrased but at times strident singing by Renata Scotto in the televised performance and less attractive singing by Cruz-Romo in the live performance as Elizabeth, the ineffective singing by Vasile Moldoveanu with Scotto, and Giuseppe Giacomini with Cruz-Romo, as Carlo, the hoarse-sounding singing by Nicolai Ghiaurov as Philip, the acceptable singing by Jerome Hines as the Grand Inquisitor. (I should mention that Cruz-Romo, for whatever reason, did not sing at all but only gesticulated meaninglessly in Elizabeth's opening-scene encounter with the lamenting peasants.)

Again what was presented to the eye—the scenery of David Reppa, imaginatively inadequate when it was not senselessly innovative, and Dexter's direction—included much that one did best not to look at. Listening with eyes open one was distracted by what was at times obtrusively awkward and questionable in the action deployed in, and accommodated to, the singular interior of the Monastery of St. Just; and one was outraged by the omission of the cathedral in the *auto-da-fé* scene, which eliminated a striking moment in the action and defeated the purpose of the music Verdi wrote for it—the moment when Philip, crowned and robed, should have made his impressive entrance through the cathedral's portals high above the square, but instead had to enter unimpressively from the wings on one side of the stage. The ineptitude Dexter revealed here he demonstrated also in his deployment of the singers in the second scene of Act 2—above all in the placing of Elizabeth, Rodrigo and Eboli when Rodrigo described Carlo's suffering to Elizabeth: what Verdi intended him to confide to her, unoverheard by Eboli, Rodrigo declaimed in the center of the stage as if to both Elizabeth at some distance from him on his right and Eboli at the same distance on his left. (One had to wonder at Levine's apparent consent to this absurdity.)

It was not Dexter again but Covent Garden's Elijah Moshinsky who produced the damagingly innovative staging of Verdi's *Un Ballo in Maschera* early in 1980 and expounded the questionable ideas it represented in a *Times* interview the day before the première. What was damaging was the unit set designed for Moshinsky by Peter Wexler, which obtruded its unchanging ugliness not only in the various interior scenes but in the one exterior scene, increasing the difficulty one had in seeing it as a credible representation of the desolate plain at midnight envisioned by Verdi. And the idea represented by this set was explained not by Moshinsky in *The Times* but by Andrew Porter in his *New Yorker* review: as one who had seen Moshinsky's stagings of *Peter Grimes* and *Lohengrin* at Covent Garden Porter could write that "Mr. Moshinsky has a 'method.' He stages operas in a plain, severe box, endeavoring to throw all emphasis onto the actors." This implies that the scenery Eugene Berman provided years ago for *Don Giovanni* and *The Barber of Seville* drew attention away from the singers; but in fact it did what scenery should do, which is to provide a heightening context for what is done by the singers whom one's attention is concentrated on. And actually it was Moshinsky's unchanging ugly box that—as Porter said of all such "minimalist" scenery—drew "attention to itself more insistently, more obtrusively, than even the most elaborately realistic décor does."

What one saw happening on the stage was itself not obtrusively and distractingly innovative: it was mostly what one had always seen and one could, as always, pay little attention to—if one looked at it without knowledge of what Moshinsky had said in *The Times* and Porter had written in *The New Yorker*, and therefore did not attempt to see in it an embodiment of their ideas about it. As the dramatic action of *Don Carlo* is a revision of a play in which historical figures—Philip II of Spain, his wife and his son—appear with attributes and motivations imagined by Schiller in the imagined situations and happenings of his plot, so the dramatic action of *Un Ballo* is a revision of Scribe's libretto (described by Verdi as "vast . . . grandiose . . . beautiful") for Auber's opera *Gustavus III, ou Le Bal Masqué*, which used the historical fact of the assassination of Gustavus III of Sweden by a noble of his court in 1792 as the basis of an imagined sequence of what Julian Budden, in his book *The Operas of Verdi*, characterizes as "striking situations and *coups de théâtre* [offering] opportunities for a display of the most intense and varied emotions." In Verdi's opera the varied emotions are revealed immediately in the opening scene as those of a high-minded ruler exercising his power with concern for the welfare of his subjects, privately troubled by his passion for the wife of his close friend and adviser, yet, by the end of the scene, planning an occasion of gaiety; and on the other hand the hatred of two conspirators motivated by personal grievances—one by the seizure of his ancestral castle, the other by the murder of a brother (acts hardly consistent with the ruler's previously attributed characteristics). When the Neapolitan censorship, in 1857, prohibited the assassination of a king in the opera and insisted on his being replaced by a duke "anywhere in the north except for Norway and Sweden" and in an early century, and Verdi's librettist Somma suggested a Duke of Pomerania in the twelfth century, Verdi rejected the twelfth century but accepted "the need to find a princeling, a duke, some devil or other—all right, in the north— who's seen a bit of the world and had a whiff of Louis XVI's court. Once the drama's finished you can think about this at your leisure." And in 1858 he wrote to Somma that the Roman censor "would like the scene removed from Europe. What would you say to North America at the time of the English domination? If not America, somewhere else; the Caucasus perhaps?" Somma chose North America; and at the première in Rome in 1859 the assassinated ruler was Riccardo, Earl of Warwick, governor of late-seventeenth-century Boston. Budden characterizes the revised libretto as "a preposterous story transferred to an inappropriate setting" (late-seventeenth-century Boston as the location of ancestral castles seized by its governor); and to account for Verdi's not transferring the action back to Sweden in later European productions Budden suggests that this colonial governor brought with him from England a whiff of the court of Charles II—the "gaiety and sophistication . . . by which [Verdi] set such store."

Whatever the wider political implications of the actual historical assassination of Gustavus III, Budden's account establishes that in the fashioning of *Un Ballo* Verdi was concerned only with its fictional characters' "intense and varied emotions" in the fictional "striking situations" culminating in the assassination of a fictional governor of late-seventeenth-century Boston by fictional conspirators in revenge for their various fictional personal grievances. This was what he embodied in his opera for audiences to perceive and respond to; what they did perceive and respond to at the première and in many productions since then; what they were familiar with and expected. And since the "preposterous story transferred to an inappropriate setting" was familiar they could treat it as they treated the preposterous stories of other operas—according it a minimum awareness that prevented its distracting their minds from the music that interested them. But for people at the Metropolitan's performances of *Un Ballo* in 1980 who had read the Moshinsky interview, what he said they were to perceive in the work as staged by him was not familiar and required attention—the attention which brought only the discovery that it introduced extraneous matters into Verdi's opera that did not merit the distracting attempt to perceive them.

"The assassination of Riccardo in 'Un Ballo in Maschera'", the interview began, "bears an uncanny relationship to the assassination of John F. Kennedy—it symbolizes the passing of an era. For that reason the action of the opera must be set in a period that the audience recognizes and knows to be a historical turning point." The Kennedy assassination did not, in historical fact, symbolize the passing of an era; Verdi's reasons for placing the assassination of Riccardo in *Un Ballo* in late-seventeenth-century Boston, described and quoted by Budden, include nothing about this being what audiences would recognize as a historical turning point; the Metropolitan did not, before 1980, consider it necessary to relocate the opera in such a period for its audiences; and for its audiences in 1980 there was no need of transferring it to "the time . . . just before the American Revolutionary War", regarded by Moshinsky as "the recognizable turning point in history" in which "the destruction of [Riccardo] . . . symbolizes the passing of an age of culture as the British rule ends and constitutional government begins." The end of British political rule did not end the culture in Boston represented in visible details of Moshinsky's staging; and there was no need to transfer to "the eve of the Boston Tea Party" an assassination which in Verdi's opera was not an act of political or cultural significance in relation to this or any other time, but an act of personal revenge, perceivable as such whatever the period it was placed in, for an audience at any time or place. It was surprising to find Moshinsky saying in his concluding paragraph, "But in the end the physical surroundings are not that important—the basic emotions that Verdi depicts remain the same and speak to everyone whether the action takes place in Sweden or in Boston" (and, one may add, whether late in the seventeenth century or the eighteenth), since this truth expressed in his words did not guide his staging of Verdi's opera.

Similarly distracting for some members of the audiences was what they had read in Andrew Porter's *New Yorker* article. Having learned that Moshinsky's training had been "writing a thesis on Alexander Herzen, for Isaiah Berlin," Porter considered it significant in connection with *Un Ballo* that "Herzen, like Verdi, was Paris-based in 1848, the year in Europe in which history took a new turn." Not that he had "found any contact between the two men," or could remember "any of Herzen's books . . . in Verdi's villa." But "both were concerned with the way individual temperament could affect the fate of nations. (The passages in Herzen's memoirs about his encounters with Mazzini and Garibaldi are useful reading for any Verdian.) And both . . . Herzen's fictions and Verdi's operas . . . pressed the theme of individual responsibility." Therefore "Herzen can open a way to 'Ballo'." And therefore also "the new Met production . . . shows Verdi's opera to be (in Shaw's words for Wagner's 'Ring') 'frightfully real, frightfully present, frightfully modern'." Specifically, "the Met directorate may not have deliberately intended [—] at a moment in America's history when potential rulers' actions in a time of personal stress must color voters' decisions whether or not they are fit to rule [—] to throw its voice into the public debate, but willy-nilly it has done so"—which was to say that the Metropolitan production related *Un Ballo* to the 1980 presidential election campaign that was in audiences' minds. ("Serious opera," Porter added to this absurdity, "has always been a political art.") Placing *Un Ballo* in eighteenth-century Boston on the eve of the Revolution, said Porter, satisfied Verdi's requirements of a time when "great issues were stirring," and a society of an elegance attested to by Hawthorne's description, in his *Legends of the Province House*, of "a spectacular masked ball in the governor's mansion" that hid "the distress and danger of the period . . . under an ostentation of festivity." And more of same.

All this represented what Porter stated (in the introduction of his collection *Three Seasons of Music*) as a major consideration in his writing about a work—"the historical, social, political . . . considerations that may have determined the form it took; its place within a composer's oeuvre; the place it can hold today within a particular society and culture . . . the sense of the past playing upon, shaping, and providing ways of understanding the present . . ." And the suitable comment on it is E. M. Forster's at the Harvard symposium on music criticism in 1947 (reprinted in his *Two Cheers for Democracy*)—that the primary aim of criticism was esthetic: to consider the work of art as an object in itself, and report the life perceived in that object; that an only subsidiary aim was to report "the relation of the work of art to the rest of the world . . . the conditions under which the work of art was composed, the influences which formed it (criticism adores influences);" and that "when criticism strays from its central esthetic quest to influences and psychological and historical considerations" the contact established "is no longer with the work of art." (In an article in 1939 I said that Mozart didn't write his Symphony in G minor to teach a lesson in history; and I would add now about that symphony what Isaiah Berlin was reported to have said about Verdi's operas—that to apprehend what Mozart intended his work to communicate one needs no outside information.)

Budden's account of what went into Verdi's fashioning of *Un Ballo* includes nothing that supports Porter's statements: the opera he produced was concerned not with "great political issues" but with personal ones—the love of Riccardo and Amelia, the desire for revenge that this love aroused in Renato, the other conspirators' desire of revenge for the seizing of an ancestral castle, the killing of a brother; neither the political thinking of Herzen nor thought about the 1980 presidential election was needed to "open a way" to the work for the Metropolitan's audiences; nor did it require, for its manifestation of Boston society's elegance and gaiety, the transfer of its masked ball from late in the seventeenth century to the eve of the Revolution. Porter's statements did not, for his readers, "open a way" to what Verdi intended to be perceived and responded to in his opera, but instead introduced into their minds extraneous, irrelevant distractions from it. Forster would have said that those who applied to the Metropolitan's *Un Ballo* in 1980 Porter's statements about great political issues and Herzen's political thinking and the 1980 presidential election were in contact with these historical considerations of Porter's, not with the opera of Verdi.

The musical performance of *Un Ballo* conducted by Patané, with Pavarotti's Riccardo, Ricciarelli's Amelia, Quilico's Renato, Blegen's Oscar and Bianca Berini's Ulrica, did not provide an experience of the flame of genius.

William Dudley's permanent set for the performance of Britten's *Billy Budd* that I attended in the spring of 1980—a cross-section of all the decks of the ship which provided the particular deck or cabin or cell required by each scene—was impressively effective; but in the Prologue and Epilogue it was visible, as it seemed to me it should not have been, behind the room in Vere's home in which he meditated on the happenings he had participated in. Dexter's direction this time made sense; and Leppard conducted a well-shaped musical performance to which Richard Stilwell and James Morris contributed excellent vocal and dramatic embodiments of the central roles of Billy and Claggart. But I must add that the allegorical characters and issues presented by Forster's adaptation of Melville's novel are, for me, as unconvincing as the melodramatic ones of *Il Trovatore, Rigoletto* and *La Forza del Destino;* and they do not, like the Verdi librettos, elicit music I find interesting, except for Billy's final soliloquy. *Billy Budd* is not as musically arid a work as *The Rape of Lucretia* or *The Turn of the Screw;* but it hasn't even as much good writing as *Albert Herring;* and the mystery remains why the Metropolitan did not at last produce instead Britten's one musically effective opera, *A Midsummer Night's Dream.*

The new production of Verdi's *La Traviata* early in 1981 did offer one of the infrequent experiences of the flame of genius—a performance of the uncut work superbly conducted by Levine and made distinguished by the beautiful and expressively phrased singing and the convincing acting of Ileana Cotrubas, the Violetta, and Domingo, the Alfredo. One was grateful for the scenery of Tanya Moiseiwitsch that was not innovative; and though it was surprising to see, at the beginning of Violetta's elegant party for barons and viscounts, a coatless man pursue a woman across the stage and push her onto a divan, Colin Graham's direction offered no distracting surprises after that.

The review in *The Times* revealed that Cotrubas had contributed more than her performance to the production: she had withdrawn from it because of her disagreement with Dexter's ideas for the staging of the work, and had returned to it only when he had been replaced by Graham. One learned later that she had withdrawn from the production of *Don Pasquale* the year before and had *not* returned; and in an interview she stated what impelled her to these actions: to the director who said "Many things in the opera are just too weak, and we have to help them," her reply was "No, don't! Do them as they are, because the composer and the librettist knew what they had done . . . If you cannot believe in it, leave it to other people to do, people who are better than you for this opera"—better that is, than the "director who is good for dramatic theater" but in an opera house "will be disastrous" because "he doesn't love music, he doesn't understand it . . . doesn't know what to do with singers." A distinguished singer had at last spoken out against, and acted to prevent, the vandalism inflicted on operas by stage directors that Rudolph Bing had described approvingly as "presenting masterpieces as seen through contemporary eyes."

Graham's stage direction was a major contribution to the production of Mozart's *Così Fan Tutte* early in 1982 that was one of the outstanding examples, in my experience, of a performance of a great opera in which all the elements were distinguished and worked perfectly together. That is, he contrived for the singers as they sang—in the scenes created by the quick changes in Hayden Griffin's ingenious arrangement of attractive movable panels—movements and gestures that seemed to flow out of the phrases they were singing. And though these phrases were produced by Maria Ewing, the Dorabella, and Kathleen Battle, the Despina, with voices more beautiful than those of Pilar Lorengar, the Fiordiligi, David Rendall, the Ferrando, Lenus Carlson, the Guglielmo, and Donald Gramm, the Don Alfonso, they were shaped with sensitiveness and moving expressiveness by all the singers, and—even when the singer was not looking at Levine—fitted perfectly into the sensitively and expressively shaped orchestral context he provided. It was a seamless ensemble operation that held one spellbound, and not the less so for one's awareness of the impressiveness of two of the participants—Lorengar, the expressive force and grandeur of whose singing made up for what it lacked in tonal beauty; and Ewing, whose extraordinary comic gift Graham used for invention that made her Dorabella a delightful character never seen in this opera before. And so it was astonishing after this to read in Andrew Porter's review of the earlier performance he had attended that Levine had "rushed through . . . many numbers at breakneck speed. Recitatives were gabble-gabble and gobble-gobble, not witty discourse. The first three trios and the aria 'Ah lo veggio' (which Mozart marked allegretto but Mr. Levine took at an allegro assai) were the most disconcertingly rapid. Mr. Levine's Mozart is often graceless, despite his evident affection for the music. With a stick, he beat out every beat of the score, emphatically, insistently. The effect was breathless, unilinear, not shaped to the words and their sense, and not taking life from—but, rather, inhibiting any eloquence in—the singers." The recitatives I had heard had been no faster than those in previous performances, and had elicited the usual chuckles and laughter from the audience; the tempos of the first three trios and the aria "*Ah lo veggio*" had been those I was accustomed to and heard again when I played Colin Davis's recorded performances of the pieces as a check. Moreover, my eye had shifted several times from the singer who was shaping phrases sensitively and expressively, to Levine whom I had found each time shaping the orchestral context, with supple movements of his stick, sensitively and expressively around the singer's phrases. Since the singer at times wasn't looking at Levine it was clear that they were doing together what they had arrived at in rehearsal and must have done at the performance Porter had attended and described inaccurately. It was not his first such inaccurate report; and the first had not been about Levine's Mozart: I recalled being astonished some years earlier by the statement that Levine's performance of Verdi's *I Vespri Siciliani*, which I found to be paced as effectively as his other performances of Verdi, had sounded to Porter as if Levine wanted to get through the work as quickly as possible. Nor is it only Porter's inaccurate perceptions of Levine's conducting of Mozart and Verdi that have led me to conclude—as I did many years ago about Virgil Thomson—that what he writes cannot be read with confidence in its being a correct perception and evaluation of what was presented to his ears.

The new production of Rossini's *Il Barbiere di Siviglia* replaced the delightful Berman scenery with Robin Wagner's gingerbread set for the opening scene, and used the revolving stage for a couple of brief scenes not in Rossini's score that were part of John Cox's fussy staging. The musical performance conducted effectively by Andrew Davis had Kathleen Battle's Rosina as its only vocal asset. And Catherine Malfitano's Violetta was the one distinguished feature of a performance of *La Traviata* I heard that was conducted capably by Roscigno.

The revival of Musorgsky's *Boris Godunov* in the fall of 1982 was entrusted to James Conlon, who achieved the best-paced and shaped performance of the work since the one conducted by Tibor Kozma (substituting for Stiedry) in the 50s. Conlon also restored to the final Kromy Scene all the passages Schippers sliced out of it in 1974, but not what he sliced out of Act 2—the crescendo of singing and clapping of hands by Feodor and the Nurse building up to Boris's entrance. A reader who had written to Levine about the cuts reported his reply that his own policy was to perform opera without cuts, as he had done with *La Forza del Destino*, *Don Carlo* and *Tristan und Isolde*, and he was sure Conlon would open the cuts in *Boris* that his rehearsal time and discussion with his producer would allow. It seemed to me that Levine, the Metropolitan's Musical Director, should have done for *Boris* what he did for the Verdi and Wagner operas he mentioned: provide the rehearsal time needed to restore to Act 2 the dramatically important passage Schippers omitted.

And as necessary as the restoration of the music Schippers cut from the Kromy Scene is the elimination from it of the distractingly senseless details of Everding's stage action: the crowd, early in the scene, for no evident reason carrying in and piling up big logs, and a little later taking them down and carrying them out; and the Pretender, at the end, entering not on a horse, as Musorgsky prescribes, not on foot, not in a sedan chair, but standing and struggling to keep his balance on a platform carried by soldiers, from which he steps onto the ground to address the crowd, and then exits on foot. What also should be eliminated are the changes introduced by Everding in Boris's last moments in Act 4. Boris, at the climax of Pimen's narrative, has risen and tottered from his throne into the arms of several Boyars who have placed him in the chair in which, left alone with Feodor, he has sung his farewell to his son and his plea to God for mercy. In Musorgsky's score the Boyars now enter with the chanting monks, causing Boris to struggle to his feet exclaiming "I am still the Tsar!"; then he falls back into the chair, and pointing to Feodor he exclaims "There, there is your Tsar! . . . Forgive me, Lord . . . Forgive me . . ." and dies. Performance tradition—established, if I remember correctly, by Chaliapin—has had him not fall back into the chair but stagger toward the throne with the exclamation "I am still the Tsar!", and, still on his feet when he dies, fall down the two or at most three steps from the throne. Everding increases the number of steps to six or seven; and he has Boris, while still alone with Feodor, conduct him up those steps to the throne, on which he seats Feodor and himself, then addresses from the throne his exclamations to the Boyars when they enter, and dies in a fall made more sensational by the six or seven steps. What Musorgsky prescribes achieves the dramatic sense and effect he wanted, and should be restored. And in Act 2 Feodor should, as Musorgsky directs, remain on the stage absorbed in his maps while Boris sings his first troubled monologue and after Shuisky's entrance, until the point at which Shuisky's mention of the uprising led by the Pretender causes Boris to order Feodor to leave: Feodor should not, as Everding directs, leave the room when Boris begins his monologue and return, absurdly, a few moments before Boris has to order him to leave.

The senseless and distracting eccentricities of design and direction with which Jean-Pierre Ponnelle's staging had damaged Monteverdi's *L'Incoronazione di Poppea* and Mozart's *La Clemenza di Tito* created apprehensions about what he would do with Mozart's *Idomeneo*, which, incredibly, the Metropolitan presented for the first time. But he was content for once to place the action credibly on a large assemblage of platforms and pillars, with painted backdrops for the successive scenes, through which on occasion one saw a huge mask of the Neptune who is the work's dominating dramatic force; to dress the characters, as at the opera's first performance in 1781, in handsome eighteenth-century costumes, with the exception, for no apparent reason, of the flowing white robe worn by Ilia; and to limit the eccentricities of his stage direction to providing arias, duets and trios—again for no evident reason—with the distracting visual counterpoint of entrances and movements in the background by characters who had no part in the scene.

These flaws in staging did not dim the flame of genius in Mozart's opera and in the performance conducted by Levine. *Idomeneo* is the twenty-five-year-old Mozart's first major work for the theater—"the sphere," E. J. Dent points out in his great book on the operas, "in which Mozart is most completely himself; his concert works . . . [being] all fundamentally evocations of the theatre." Mozart's passionate sense for the theater is evident in the text he contrived out of the dull and clumsy conventional *opera seria* libretto supplied by Varesco, and in the music he wrote for that text—music which seizes the listener's mind with the overture that, in Dent's words, "indicates the heroic plane on which the drama is to move," and which holds that mind thereafter with the expressive orchestral writing in the recitatives, the noble style of the arias, the novel dramatic character of the great quartet, the inspired use of coloratura for the climactic phrases of the demented Electra's final aria. We hear in this work a sustained dignity and grandeur, Dent points out, which we don't hear in Mozart's later operatic masterpieces, and which make it literally the "grand opera" those later masterpieces are not. It is to *Idomeneo*, says Dent, that "we must turn to see the young Mozart at his greatest heights:" the "monumental strength and . . . white heat of passion that we find in this early work of Mozart's" we "never find again." And Levine produced a fulfilling realization of this writing in the orchestral context he shaped sensitively and expressively, as always, around the beautiful and expressively phrased singing by Cotrubas as Ilia and Frederica von Stade as Idamante, the powerful singing by Hildegarde Behrens as Electra, the musically admirable singing Levine obtained incredibly from Pavarotti in the title role. But in what was for me another overwhelming musical experience Andrew Porter again "sensed" Levine insistently "beating the time to his soloists on the stage and in the pit "; in addition he objected to Electra's singing both her final aria and "the fiery recitative that Mozart composed to replace it" (as she does also in the 1956 Glyndebourne performance on records, presumably because of the recitative's effectiveness as an introduction to the aria); and he ended with a complaint—buttressed by musicologists' certifications of necessity—about the "many necessary appoggiaturas [that] are missing." On the other hand he made the surprising comment that while in theory one wanted to hear and see the ballet omitted from Metropolitan's *Idomeneo*, "current opera-house practice" made one glad to have been spared it—surprising from someone I recall disapproving more than once of the omission of the ballet from an old opera.

The Metropolitan's new production of Verdi's *Macbeth* retained the ballet music he inserted for the Paris production, which it should have omitted for the same reason that it omits the ballet music Verdi inserted for the Paris production of *Otello*—that the ballet destroys continuity and tension in the dramatic action; but also for the reason mentioned by Porter—the "current opera-house practice" that foretold the laughably inept and boring ballet choreographed by Stuart Hopps. Distractingly questionable in addition were details of John Bury's scenic design and Peter Hall's stage direction—among them Hall's having Scotto seated for Lady Macbeth's impassioned opening aria, and in other obtrusively unsuitable positions in later numbers. All this made the performance another to listen to with eyes closed. But what one heard—though it included effective singing by Milnes in the title role and Paul Plishka as Banquo—included also Scotto's managing to get by with what her diminished vocal resources could produce: singing in her lower range that was agreeable-sounding and expressive, but fine-spun *diminuendos* to *pianissimo* high notes in place of the impassioned *crescendos* to climactic high notes demanded by her role. However one heard this singing in a performance shaped by Levine whose effect—for me, whose last previous experience of the work had been provided by the 1976 La Scala recording—was to reveal anew and with increased impact the magnitude of what Verdi's powers achieve in this early work of his, and, in so doing, also the magnitude of Levine's powers in the conducting of opera.

What Porter wrote this time was strikingly revealing too—not about the performance but about his critical writing. In dynamics, he said, Levine "phrased carefully, but his 'phrasing in time' was rigid, unnatural, unbreathed," bringing to mind, for Porter, Giulio Ricordi's likening the young Toscanini's conducting of Verdi to a "mastodonic player piano". Levine's actual conducting—as distinguished from what Porter describes as his conducting—does resemble Toscanini's actual conducting, which was described correctly, after his Beethoven series with the BBC Symphony in May 1939, by W. J. Turner, who in the 20s and 30s provided London with the most perceptive and distinguished musical journalism after Bernard Shaw's, and who wrote in his review of the series:

> It is a great mistake to think that Toscanini keeps strictly to metronomic time. One of his greatest virtues is his subtle variation of tempo; but always in the service of shape . . . derived from the rightful expression of the music. It is in discovering this rightful expression and hence the perfect shape that Toscanini is supreme among living conductors.

What Turner described was Toscanini's style of performance not just in symphonic music but in whatever music he conducted, including opera. Its distinctive characteristic was its unfailing coherent plasticity, achieved by a beat that was never anything but flexible in relation to the music, and was unyielding in relation to the singer only in compelling him or her to operate expressively within the coherently shaped flow it was creating in the music—as Gadski, Destinn, Slezak and Hempel did at the Metropolitan, Lotte Lehmann, Roswaenge and Kipnis did in Salzburg, and Albanese, Nelli and Vinay did at NBC (Alfred Wallenstein reported to me Vinay's speaking of his singing in Toscanini's 1947 *Otello* as the greatest of his career). And what I have just described is what Levine did in his conducting of *Macbeth*. Porter's statement about it, and his previous statements about Levine's conducting of operas by Verdi and Mozart, reveal him to be one of the people Turner was replying to, who—presented with Toscanini's or Levine's "subtle variation of tempo . . . always in the service of shape"—can hear it only as a "[keeping] strictly to metronomic time", or, in Porter's words, a " 'phrasing in time' [that] was rigid, unnatural, unbreathed".

In this mis-hearing of Levine's performance as "rigid", as of similar performances by Pollini in which Porter reports "nothing happened"—performances by musicians who operate with the discipline that keeps expressive flexibility contained within plastically coherent shape created by subtle inflection of steady basic tempo—in this I find a deficiency of critical perception, judgment, taste. And I find this deficiency exhibited conversely in his advocacy of the performances by musicians operating

without that discipline—the performances of symphonic music by
Furtwängler, the performances in opera by singers of the distant past, in
which the liberties with tempo and phrasing destroy the music's continuity of flow and tension, its coherent shape. Rethberg, Elisabeth Schumann, Thorborg, Flagstad, Jurinac, Schipa, Roswaenge, Bjoerling,
Bergonzi, and in earlier years Farrar, Hempel, Homer, Slezak, Urlus,
Jörn—whose deployment of their exceptional voices reveals them to
have been scrupulous and distinguished musicians—are not the singers
whom one hears about from Porter, and whom he holds up as models for
young singers today. Reviewing a performance of *La Traviata* by a newly
founded group in Norfolk, Virginia, in which he said the "three young
principals . . . gave talented and touching accounts of their roles," he
went on to advise the tenor to listen to Alfredo's *"De' miei bollenti spiriti"*
sung on a record by Fernando de Lucia. But Toscanini, on one occasion,
said he had something for me to hear—a record Horowitz had insisted on
lending him; and while his son went to get the record he sat down at
the piano and accompanied himself in a burlesque of what I then heard
on the record: de Lucia's performance of Alfredo's aria, which Toscanini
listened to laughing at the self-indulgent spinning out of the voice in
what he found to be ludicrously mannered phrasing. Also, in his review
of Vickers's first performance in *Otello* at the Metropolitan in 1972 Porter
was not content to state his view on the right tempo at one point and to
support it with Verdi's metronome marking, but wrote that "from
Tamagno [who sang the title role at the première in 1887] Vickers might
well adopt a broader approach to . . . *'Ora e per sempre addio'*. Verdi's
marking . . . is just about Tamagno's basic tempo on each of the three
records he made of the excerpt, but the basic tempo he freely holds up in
order to stress particular words and notes, with wonderfully brilliant
results." One thing to say about this is that whereas it probably was
Tamagno who set the tempo for the performances he recorded years
later, it probably was Levine who set the tempo for Vickers at the
Metropolitan. More important in Tamagno's "broader approach" is his
"freely" holding up the tempo "to stress particular words and notes" that
Porter so strongly approved of—as he did of Melba's similar slowing
down, for similar stress, of the notes of the phrase *"unico raggio di bene"* in
the duet *"Dite alla giovine"* from *La Traviata*, for Porter a striking example
of her "stylish use of portamento and rubato" that impelled him to ask
"What modern conductor would allow his soprano to sing the phrase so

eloquently?" But actually what she did was, like what Tamagno did, a self-indulgent distortion of the phrase's shape, obtrusively over-emphatic in expressive effect, which I have never heard from any other singer (in particular not from Hempel, whose coherent phrasing in her recorded performance achieves an expressive eloquence never equaled in my experience). And this distortion that Porter strongly approved of Verdi strongly objected to.

Moreover, in his biography of Toscanini Harvey Sachs reports concerning the 1887 première of *Otello* that "Tamagno did not satisfy Verdi or a large segment of the public." He also reports that in order to participate in the preparation of the première supervised by Verdi Toscanini got himself hired as second cellist in the orchestra for the entire season, which enabled him—when he was preparing his revival of *Otello* at La Scala in December 1899—to dispute Tamagno's claim that he was singing as Verdi had taught him in 1887. And Sachs quotes Alfredo Segre's account of how Toscanini confirmed his claim that *his* tempos were the ones Verdi had requested at the rehearsals by taking Tamagno to Verdi, who congratulated Toscanini for the accuracy of his memory. Tamagno's tempo in *"Ora e per sempre addio"* hasn't, therefore, the authority—or even relevance—for a singer today that Porter ascribed to it.

Neither has his holding up that tempo to stress particular words or notes. In a letter shortly before his death Verdi refers to "the calamity of the 'rondos' of the prima donnas" when he began, and "today . . . the tyranny of the conductors"; and in the earlier letters in the volume I read years ago he objected repeatedly and vehemently to singers' and conductors' liberties with phrasing and tempo. The distorting of shape of phrase by Tamagno in *Otello* and Melba and de Lucia in *La Traviata*—which Porter cites as authoritative and to be learned from their recordings by young singers today—is, then, what Verdi battled against all his life. This makes Porter's advocacy astonishing not only in itself but in its inconsistency with what he stated (in the introduction to his collection *Three Seasons of Music*) as one of the major ideas governing his writing: his belief that "the music of any age speaks to listeners most clearly, most directly, with the tones and accents and in the forms that its creator intended;"—which, as amplified in other statements of Porter's, I understand to mean that if a work is to speak to listeners today what it spoke to those of its composer's time one must ascertain, use in performance, and inform listeners of the text, the performing forces, the

manner of their performing, and all other discoverable facts of not only
the first performance but the performances since that one, for "what
the past can tell us about it"—including for Porter even such facts as
the one, reported in a review of a concert performance of Verdi's *I
Masnadieri*, that the cello solo in the overture was "composed for Alfredo
Piatti, who led the section at Her Majesty's" at the première. This belief
produces the Porter review of a performance of an opera that fills pages of
The New Yorker with facts of the work's history; and the facts Porter
considers necessary for performers and listeners to know about *La Traviata* and *Otello* include the performances recorded by Tamagno, de
Lucia and Melba. But the forms the opera's creator intended include the
shapes of its phrases; and the distorted shapes of the phrases in *La
Traviata* and *Otello* in those recorded performances are *not* what Verdi
intended and performers and listeners need to know today: they are what
those singers and others of their time insisted on doing regardless of his
objections; and in them it is not Verdi who speaks, but those singers who
misspeak, what he intended the phrases to say.

The statement of Porter's I quoted may, then, be persuasively reasonable as concept, but has no relation to the realities of what it deals with.
Titian's portrait *Young Man With Glove* does, in the Louvre today, speak
to us with the colors and forms he put on his canvas, as George Eliot's
Middlemarch does with the words she wrote that we read in the book.
Bournonville's ballets, on the other hand, we cannot see performed by
the dancers for whom he made them; and in the photographs of early
performances we see bodies and styles strikingly different from those of
the Royal Danish Ballet's dancers today; so that even with the photographs to help them the present Royal Danish dancers could not, with
their bodies and styles, reproduce those early performances if they tried
to. Moreover, one must doubt that the photographed performances that
spoke intelligibly and impressively to the audiences of their time would
do so to the people today with eyes and minds accustomed to the ballets
and performances of the recent forty years or so. And I find it impossible
to believe that Bournonville, if he saw the Royal Danish performances of
today, would not recognize his ballets in them and would not accept
them. I consider this to be true also of performances today of plays of the
past—even in the face of what a reader reported having heard Porter say
at a CUNY panel on criticism: that we wouldn't ever understand

Shakespeare properly until we saw his women played by boy actors.*
And it is true of performances today of music of the past. We can hear
Haydn's piano sonatas played on the fortepiano for which he wrote
them; but we have no recording that enables us to hear *how* they were
played on that instrument in Haydn's time (and reading what was
written about eighteenth-century performance by those who did hear it
is not equivalent to hearing it, though it can be useful for other purposes—when, for example, the music critic of *Queens Quarterly* in
Toronto, Thomas Hathaway, points out that although "Mozart wrote
no crescendos between a *piano* here and a *forte* several measures later, . . .
taking that to mean he expected abrupt alternations of two dynamic
levels ignores the fact that in his youth the aesthetic of expressive
diminuendo and crescendo was strenuously promoted in the writings of
his mentor, C. P. E. Bach, and others"). Malcolm Bilson's remarkably
perceptive playing of the sonatas on the fortepiano is that of a sensitive
musician of today, and would be equally perceptive if he played them on
the piano of today. And I cannot believe that if Haydn heard Bilson play
them on the piano he would find the sensitive melodic inflection unacceptable, or would reject the full and mellow sound of the powerful
bass chords and insist on the fortepiano's shallow metallic clatter instead.
As for operas of the past, the earliest recordings of excerpts from them
were made at the beginning of the century by the singers whose liberties
in phrasing and tempo were denounced by Verdi; and of the performance of *Otello* by Toscanini in 1899, whose tempos elicited Verdi's
congratulation, we have no recording.

However, in Verdi's case—as against Donizetti's or Bellini's or Rossini's—there are a very few exceptions: we do have on records the broadcast performance of *Otello* conducted by Toscanini in 1947, which one
would expect Porter to cite as establishing the tempo of *"Ora e per sempre
addio"* for Vickers in 1972, and Toscanini's broadcast performances of
Act 4 of *Rigoletto, La Traviata, Falstaff* and *Un Ballo in Maschera.* These we
can regard as speaking to us with the sounds and forms Verdi intended,

---

*This reader, only a few months out of Bryn Mawr College, wrote, astonishingly, about
the "sort of self-imposed blindness" in Porter's "categorical dismissal of what he called the
'sensitized plate school of criticism' . . . just as theoretically minded literature students are
terrified by what they call 'impressionistic criticism';" and about what she perceived, at
that panel, as "his intense, nervous, articulate fantaticism".

by virtue not only of the tempos he approved of in the incident involving *Otello*, but of the "phrasing in time" he approved of in another incident reported by Sachs in his biography. In 1898 Toscanini, preparing a performance of the *Te Deum*, found it necessary to speak to Verdi about "slight tempo modifications . . . which he felt were implicit in the music at certain points, but which Verdi had not indicated in the score." Playing the piece for Verdi on the piano, Toscanini slowed down slightly at one such point, at which Verdi said "Bravo"; and when he stopped playing to ask Verdi why he hadn't written the *rallentando* in the score, Verdi answered: "If I had written it, a bad musician would have exaggerated it; but if one is a good musician, one feels it and plays it, just as you've done, without . . . having it written down."

Porter did write once, in a review of a Karajan recording of *Otello* in *The Gramophone*, that there could "never be another performance so authentic . . . in its expression of Verdi's intentions" as Toscanini's in 1947; but he did not mention this performance of Toscanini's in his review of the Metropolitan's performance in 1972: what he cited to Vickers was the Tamagno performances with the distortions Verdi had battled against. And ten years later, in his review of the Metropolitan's new *Macbeth*, he wrote that Levine's rigidity brought to mind Giulio Ricordi's likening the young Toscanini's conducting of Verdi to "a mastodonic player piano". Given Porter's obsessive involvement with the historically distant, one could understand his going back to the turn of the century to quote the opinion of a noted musician or critic, but not of a publisher, and particularly not the publisher Giulio Ricordi, in the light of the facts recounted by Sachs.

Those facts begin with the "terrible battles" which the conductor Giulini, in conversation with Sachs, said "Toscanini fought . . . in order to achieve things which everyone today takes for granted." What Toscanini fought against was the "lethargy of routine" in opera houses that produced the performances in which the works were falsified by an accumulated "tradition" of singers' and conductors' liberties with text, tempo and phrasing; and the lethargy of the public that wanted to hear the performances it was accustomed to hearing. What he battled for was authentic performance of what he found in the composer's score; and it was not until his fourth Scala season that he felt he had built up enough support and good feeling in the public to risk presenting such a performance of what Sachs characterizes as "the most down-trodden . . . work in the repertoire", *Il Trovatore*. This performance the critic Carlo D'Ormeville, earlier not a Toscanini supporter, described as "a brilliant reconstruction of an opera . . . abused in the most infamous circus tents that call themselves theatres"—one which "[brought] into relief every smallest detail, . . . [animated] every scene, . . . [obtained] an admirable orchestral ensemble and exquisite refinements from the chorus, . . . [suggested] to the scenographers a real artistic revolution, . . . almost guiding their pencils and brushes." And the critic Gustavo Macchi wrote: "Faced with this interpretation of *Trovatore*, no one will again dare to doubt Toscanini's worth, impartiality or artistic honesty." But one person did dare: Giulio Ricordi.

As head of his family's publishing house he had power which he didn't hesitate to misuse. "He was accustomed to being listened to and obeyed by . . . everyone in the operatic world"—not only composers but impresarios and performers—one result of which was that he could be sure the pieces he wrote as an amateur composer under the pseudonym "J. Burgmein" would be performed. But his disapproval of Toscanini's corrective innovations in the opera house was ignored; and he didn't receive from Toscanini a reply to his letter suggesting the inclusion of "Burgmein's" *Pulcinella in Love* in one of Toscanini's concerts. These were the reasons not only for his attacks on Toscanini in the *Gazzetta Musicale di Milano* that he published and wrote in, but for his attempts to turn Verdi against Toscanini. Boito's enthusiastic report about Toscanini's Scala *Falstaff* in March 1899 caused Verdi to wire Toscanini "Thanks, thanks, thanks"; but then Ricordi sent Verdi his review reporting that Toscanini's rigidity had cost the work much of the effect it had had in pre-Toscanini Scala performances, which elicited from Verdi his previously quoted statement about the "tryanny of conductors", and the statement "If things are as you say, it is better to return to the modest conductors of earlier times." (However in December 1899, as I mentioned earlier, Verdi congratulated Toscanini for his tempos in *Otello*.) To quote this publisher as if he was a qualified and disinterested person who merited *New Yorker* readers' attention and belief was fatuous; and to quote his words out of their factual context—the context without which they would be accepted, as they appeared to be offered, as representing objective, honest judgment, when in fact they represented falsifying vengeful malice born of thwarted arrogance—was an act of what is regarded as intellectual impropriety.

(A noteworthy example of Porter's treating the factual context of a statement of his as non-existent was his report, in a review of a Metropolitan Opera performance of Wagner's *Parsifal*, of having read "with admiration and excitement" a handbook about this opera—"a long, thoughtful, . . . essay that follows the drama from its sources in Wolfram von Eschenbach, through the rich fields of Wagner's thought over decades . . . to the finished work, which is traversed in an eloquent chapter. On again, through the stage history of the piece and a century of what it has meant to philosophers, poets, and sensitive critics"—to which he added the author's summary statement elsewhere: "The single word that defines the region of 'Parsifal' is 'Christian'." What Porter, like the author of the handbook, treated as non-existent was the actual nature of those "rich fields of Wagner's thought over decades" that produced in the end the libretto of *Parsifal,* and the demonstration of that nature by quotation from Wagner's published writings and his letters in Robert W. Gutman's *Richard Wagner: The Man, His Mind, and His Music.* Many years earlier I had found repellent in *Parsifal* "this sensualist's exaltation of chastity decked out in religious mumbo-jumbo"—which Gutman referred to as "sham-Christian piety". What I learned from Gutman's book was that *Parsifal* was the last of the stage works that were for Wagner "projections into the realm of art of what he wanted to accomplish as a social and political reformer"; and that what he wanted to accomplish was the elimination from German life of the Jew who—in Gutman's words about the 1850 tract *Jewry in Music* (which he characterized as "a complicated, historically inaccurate, and speciously reasoned dialectic of dramatic and musical art")—was "hindering the pure instincts of the German Folk from realizing the art-work of the future." Gutman's statement that "toward the end of his days [Wagner] seemed unable to think, write, or talk on any subject other than the Jews" summarized what he quoted from Wagner's writing—e.g., in 1881, his reference in *Know Thyself* to a Germany "exposed defenseless to the incursions of the Jews"; his statement in a letter to King Ludwig of Bavaria that "I regard the Jewish race as the born enemy of pure mankind and of everything noble in it"—this in reply to the King's view that "nothing is more repugnant" than racism. And Gutman's traversal of the libretto of *Parsifal* is an appalling detailing of its "symbolic dramatization of the atrocious racial theorizing of Wagner's last articles.")

Some years ago I stated what experience had led me to think of as Haggin's First Law of Esthetic Dynamics—that artistic gifts do not always, necessarily, inevitably produce valuable art. Gifts must be used; and value in the result depends on how they are used—specifically, whether the use is governed by the discipline that is the rarest of the gifts and the crucial one. This is true not only of the gifts for composition and performance of music, but of the specific gifts for criticism: they too must be governed by discipline—the intellectual discipline that would have kept Porter from quoting Giulio Ricordi's statement about Toscanini without mention of its factual context—the vengeful malice that motivated Ricordi. Lack of discipline has been evident in his self-indulgent operation as reporter of musical events for the readers of *The New Yorker*—in what he has chosen to write and not to write about. What most music-lovers, including those who read *The New Yorker*, are interested in, and are entitled to reports of—the accumulated instrumental and vocal music and its performances at concerts—he has chosen not to write about, because (he told an interviewer) writing about concerts bores him. His major, obsessive interests in writing are the music of this century, newly or recently composed, and opera of all centuries (with numerous minor obsessions like opera in English translation and performance of earlier music on the instruments of its period); and he has written in *The New Yorker*, apparently with the magazine's acquiescence, as if it were a specialized publication read by members of a society for contemporary music and those of a society for musicology. Thus, his readers were told nothing about the performance of Schubert's *Die Winterreise* by Christa Ludwig and James Levine in March 1983 that was one of the great events of the musical season; instead, in the weeks that followed, they were given lengthy detailed reports on innumerable new works—reports that were as meaningless to most music-loving *New Yorker* readers as the works themselves would have been. As for opera, which does interest them, their interest is not in what interests him to write about it. They are interested in an opera for itself—for the life they perceive in what they hear; he is interested in it as an occasion for his pages of musicological details of the history and the performance, past and present, of operas old and new, worth writing and reading about and not. They could be presumed to be interested in reading at length about a first performance of Verdi's *Don Carlo* in its newly restored entirety at La Scala in Milan, but not about a first performance of *La Traviata* by a

newly founded group in Norfolk, Virginia; nor a new opera, Alva
Henderson's *The Last of the Mohicans* (though "its music is not memorable"), in Wilmington, Delaware; nor a *Barber of Seville* (though "disappointing . . . routine modern") in Houston; a *Thais* in Baltimore ("sung
in French, which is surely not a tongue of common converse in Mary-
land"); an *Elisir d'Amore* (in English) by a group in the Bronx; Massenet's
Cendrillon in Ottawa, a Krenek opera in Portland, Oregon, Busoni's
Doktor Faustus in Bloomington, Indiana. All these interested Porter, but
not most *New Yorker* readers; and his self-indulgent operation has produced most of the time not the valuable critical writing his gifts promised
but a flood of historical and musical fussbudgetry that was a waste of his
attention and time and theirs.

(Hathaway wrote me from Toronto that "Porter chattered about
Massenet's touching, warm, mellow *Cendrillon* over the CBC;" but "at
the end of Act Two one was still waiting for the music to begin. It's all
introduction;" and, in another letter, that two singers he had heard had
not confirmed Porter's glowing reports, leading him to conclude that in
his determination to find opera companies of merit everywhere in the
New World Porter was hearing young singers whose wonderful voices
were as much a mirage as the little companies' worthwhile opera productions. And the perceptive young Bryn Mawr graduate whom I quoted on
p. 196 wrote that a few weeks after "one of Porter's long performing-
history opera introductions which I found, as usual, devoid of interest,"
he referred to the same work as "trash unworthy of a place in the
repertory", which left her unable to understand "why he had thought its
background deserved several pages in *The New Yorker*, or even half an hour
of his attention, not to mention ours." Equally undeserving of his
readers' attention, I add, was a single-sentence pronouncement that
"Rossini is needed to explain late Schubert," which was as mistaken as
Bernard Shaw's statement about Schubert's laying out "crescendo after
crescendo . . . gallopade after gallopade" in the "exasperatingly brain-
less" finale of his Symphony No. 9, "as Rossini does in his overtures."
What Schubert intended the finale of that symphony to communicate
does *not* need—for the listener to apprehend it—anything outside it, but
requires, on the contrary, that he concentrate his mind on it alone, in and
for itself; and a listener who does this will hear nothing reminiscent of
Rossini. It is in the first movement of Schubert's *early* Symphony No. 2
that one hears evidence of his having heard, and retained in mind,

Rossini's music—evidence one does *not* hear in the finale of the much later Ninth. And the *perpetuum mobile* rush of that finale has no resemblance to the mere reiteration of a single phrase in a *crescendo* from *ppp* to *fff* in a Rossini overture: the *crescendos* to climaxes in Schubert's finale are occurrences in a progression of developing musical thought organized in a tremendous sonata-form structure—a progression achieved by *transformation* (as against mere reiteration) of its several thematic ideas, each of which, after being stated, is elaborated, developed, and eventually involved with the similarly elaborated others. In short, the finale of the Ninth presents an operation of the brains Shaw said Schubert lacked.)

The season's final major operatic event for me was the concert performance of Berlioz's *Benvenuto Cellini*, in Carnegie Hall, by Eve Queler with her Opera Orchestra of New York, the chorus of the Mendelssohn Club of Philadelphia, and a cast headed by Nicolai Gedda. As in the case of Verdi's *Macbeth*, I heard Berlioz's opera after an interval long enough for me to marvel anew at the riveting operation of his distinctive mind— as in the incandescent comic trio in the first act, and the orchestral introductions that prepared one's mind for each scene. That first-act trio required an orchestra, singers and conductor of high competence, all of whom Queler provided. This was my first encounter with her work; and her assured, expert and effective dealing with her complex task was most impressive. Notable in the excellent cast were Mariella Devis, the Teresa, whose clear, bright, steady light soprano voice produced the role's occasional florid passages with ease, and Jean-Phillipe Lafont, a superb comic, in the role of Fieramosca. But Gedda was, from his very first phrase, the occasion's commanding presence, with the sound of his still remarkable voice and the style and expressiveness with which he used it. Ten years or so after the performance he recorded with Colin Davis one could be apprehensive about the high C of his aria in the fourth tableau; but he managed it securely by attacking it *fortissimo;* and having managed it he held onto it triumphantly, earning fully the prolonged applause at the end of the aria.

Of the single long paragraph—the forty narrow lines of a little more than half a *New Yorker* column—that Porter wrote about this event, the first five lines were devoted to the opera's performance history; nine to the history of the successive versions made by Berlioz in the attempts to get it performed, and by Liszt and Bülow for their performances; five to

"Wagner's famous remarks", which made no valuable point about the work that justified their being quoted, but were merely that infamous character's sneer about "this artificial remodelling of old ideas" not being "real artistic creativeness", and as such made Porter's obsessive quoting of them grotesque; and nineteen to details of the performance. All he found to say about the music was that the first-performed 1838 version presented by Queler "is more exuberant and shapely than the reworkings," and—in reference to the high notes of Cellini's part—that "there is nothing absurd about the high notes of a Berlioz hero."

The New York City Ballet's pre-*Nutcracker* offerings in the fall-winter season of 1977-78 included a *Square Dance* notably enhanced by Merrill Ashley's sharp clarity and flashing speed, and by the grandeur that Bart Cook's powerfully sustained flow of largely sculptured movement imparted to the *Sarabande* Balanchine had inserted for the previous year's revival. Notable too were Ashley's later performances in additional new roles—in *Allegro Brillante*, *Tchaikovsky Piano Concerto No. 2*, *Tchaikovsky Pas de Deux*, the *Theme and Variations* of *Tchaikovsky Suite No. 3*, the solo originally danced by Marnee Morris in *Who Cares?*. And Cook not only achieved impressively the powerful tensions of the *Aria I* of *Stravinsky Violin Concerto*, but revealed a gift for comedy in the *Costermonger Pas de Deux* of *Union Jack*.

Devised for dazzlingly effective use of Ashley's special gifts, Balanchine's new *Ballo della Regina*—to Verdi's ballet music for the Paris production of *Don Carlo*—made use also of Robert Weiss's soaring elevation and his speed in turns. A striking contrast to this sunny piece was the strange progression Balanchine contrived for Hindemith's arid and ugly *Kammermusik No. 2* —e.g. the opening relentlessly driving canonic *perpetuum mobile* of the two couples of principals, Karin von Aroldingen and Sean Lavery, Colleen Neary and Adam Lüders; the context of intricate prowling and menacing movement by the group of eight boys in the background. With the technique Lavery exhibited in this work, and the gift of presence he had revealed in *Vienna Waltzes*, he performed impressively in *Allegro Brillante* and *Tchaikovsky Pas de Deux* with Ashley. Lüders, on the other hand, presented an image of virtuosity as yet unharnessed in *Theme and Variations* with her, but achieved the most effective *Phlegmatic Variation* in *The Four Temperaments* since Todd Bolender's.

An important event was Peter Martin's first choreography, *Calcium Light Night*, his setting, improvisatory in style, of pieces by Ives: a succession of solos by Daniel Duell, then solos by Heather Watts, then duets by the two, which offered the interesting and at times amusing play of an individual mind with whatever movements occurred to it at the moment. In their matter-of-fact manner they made demands that Duell's technique enabled him to meet in matter-of-fact fashion; and they provided Watts with exactly the right role for her. Duell, in addition, brought his unstraining large and clear movement to the brief solo of the first *Pas de Trois* of *Agon* and the opening *Ballabille* and concluding *Tarantella* of *Bournonville Divertissements*.

Concerning the collaboration of Baryshnikov and Balanchine that began in the fall of 1978 Baryshnikov was quoted as saying, "I would love to be an instrument in his wonderful hands," and "The repertory of the New York City Ballet is enormous. I have so many opportunities to try myself out." Unfortunately illness kept Balanchine from creating anything new in the seasons of 1978-79; and it was therefore in the hands of Robbins that Baryshnikov was an instrument appallingly misused in *Opus 19/The Dreamer*. But he did have the opportunities to try himself in a number of Balanchine's ballets in the company's repertory; and whereas he fitted easily into the Balanchine versions of *Coppélia* and *Harlequinade* that related to what he had done previously, the idiosyncratic technique and style of Balanchine's own ballets required time to adapt to and become comfortable in. As a result his performances in *Rubies*, *The Prodigal Son*, *The Four Temperaments*, *Apollo*, *Donizetti Variations*, *La Sonnambula* and the rest gained in effectiveness in the course of the year; but from first to last they were fascinating, exciting, moving. His brand of buffoonery in the *Costermonger Pas de Deux* of *Union Jack* revealed a marvelous gift for comedy; and the subtlety this gift was capable of made the succession of quiet, small-scale details of movement and facial expression in *The Steadfast Tin Soldier* one of the memorably great achievements in the theater in my experience.

(The revived *Apollo* Baryshnikov performed in was Balanchine's deplorable abbreviation of his choreographic realization of the scenario embodied in Stravinsky's score that began with Apollo's birth and ended with the ascent of Apollo and the three Muses to Parnassus. Balanchine now omitted the opening scene, in which one had seen the newborn god spin himself free of his swaddling clothes, teeter and attain secure footing, and receive his lute from the two handmaidens; and omitted also was the concluding ascent to Parnassus: the ballet's conclusion now was the earlier pose with the fan-like spread of the extended legs of the Muses in arabesque behind Apollo's supporting body. Moreover, not only the music of the opening scene was omitted, but also Stravinsky's impressive orchestral introduction—which is to say that Balanchine damaged not only his ballet but Stravinsky's musical work. The progression of music and movement after these amputations of its original beginning and conclusion was still overwhelming; but there were some who had experienced its even greater impact when it had included the beginning and end that now were omitted.)

Memorable experiences were provided by Martins's elegant performance in *La Source* and comical performance in *Stars and Stripes*, both with Ashley; *Divertimento No. 15* with Farrell, Nichols, Saland and Martins; *La Valse* with Farrell, Lüders (impressive again in a role with dramatic implications) and Francisco Moncion, who was seen also in his other uniquely arresting performance as the Dark Angel in *Orpheus*; Ashley in *Theme and Variations, La Source, Divertimento No. 15*, the *Pas de Deux* from *Flower Festival in Genzano*, all with Martins, and *Tchaikovsky Piano Concerto No. 2* with Lavery and Nichols; Nichols in the Verdy role in *Emeralds*, and in the *Sanguinic* Variation of *The Four Temperaments* with Daniel Duell.

Also notable for me were the performances of *Who Cares?* with d'Amboise, in which his diminished powers now necessitated the omission of *Clap Yo' Hands* and details of other numbers, but in which it was moving to see how much he still managed to achieve, in the style that not even a Martins could approximate. (But what it impelled Arlene Croce to was the comment that " d'Amboise has become the Cheshire Cat; he's down to nothing but his famous grin"—which was, among other things, not true.)

Martins's next ballet, in the fall of 1979, was *Sonate di Scarlatti*, a skillful use of a dance idiom that was largely Balanchine standard, but with the impress of an individual mind, which however could produce nothing of interest for Stravinsky's uninteresting *Eight Easy Pieces*. And an event of greater magnitude than these ballets was Martins's reappearance, after eight years, in *Apollo*—a performance which now had the grandeur his dancing had been exhibiting in other roles. Though

Heather Watts was an unsuitable Terpsichore, Nichols provided a striking Polyhymnia and von Aroldingen an acceptable Calliope. And *Orpheus* offered not only Martins's dramatically eloquent performance in the title role but von Aroldingen's powerful contribution to the *pas de deux* representing Orpheus's resistance and final yielding to Eurydice's attempts to get him to look at her, an achievement in imaginative invention on the level of the seduction *pas de deux* in *The Prodigal Son*. Lüders's Dark Angel was not satisfying to someone who had seen Moncion in the role. But he was now increasingly impressive in classical roles, with the controlled technical powers and assured style he had begun to exhibit in *Chaconne* and the *Pas de Deux* from *Flower Festival in Genzano*.

Beautiful performances in new roles were Ashley's second movement of *Symphony in C* and Nichols's Sugar Plum Fairy in *The Nutcracker*. On the other hand I found Jean-Pierre Frohlich's sharply thrusting exuberance less effective in the *Ballabille* and *Tarantella* of *Bournonville Divertissements* than Daniel Duell's poised large movements.

Concerning the company's spring season I wrote (in *Ballet News*, September 1980) that one point of interest in Balanchine's presenting *Le Bourgeois Gentilhomme* was the mere fact of his reviving this ballet after almost fifty years. He was quoted once as contending that the ballets which exist for us today cannot be the ones made with dancers who are not alive today, but can be only the ones made with dancers of today: "It is like a butterfly. I always say butterflies of yesterday don't exist." But actually his company's repertory was made up mostly of butterflies of yesterdays, ranging from *Stravinsky Violin Concerto* to *Orpheus* and all the way back to *Apollo*, performed necessarily by dancers other than the ones he made them with, who in some instances were less effective, but in other instances more effective, than the original ones. Thus the major occasions of the spring season included the performances of *Apollo*, whose extraordinary impact was not merely that of the unique choreographic invention of the work itself, but that of the execution of this invention by the dancers. There have been beautiful and moving embodiments of the title role—Lew Christensen's in 1937, André Eglevsky's in the 40s. Conrad Ludlow's, Edward Villella's and the young Peter Martins's in the 60s; but they did not attain—in beauty of movement and its sustained continuity, tension and grandeur—what was attained by the Peter Martins of today. Moreover, whereas the

Terpsichore in the earlier performances of the winter season had been Heather Watts, whom I found ineffective in the role, in the spring Suzanne Farrell brought to it her distinctive style and beauty of movement and *its* sustained continuity, tension and grandeur.

So with *Le Bourgeois Gentilhomme:* At its conclusion the actor-director sitting next to me was silent for a few moments, then commented, "That theater sense of his!"—a feature of the Balanchine operation which hasn't received the attention it has merited. This ballet was one of the impressively original and effective early dramatic ballets—some serious, like *The Prodigal Son, Cotillon* and *Le Baiser de la Fée,* some comic, like *Pastorale, Le Bal, Concurrence* and *Jeu de Cartes*—in which he employed "that theater sense of his", and specifically his gift for comedy that generates the fun in *Le Bourgeois Gentilhomme.* And the somewhat changed version he presented now was more effective than the one he staged for the Ballet Russe de Monte Carlo in 1944, because Martins and Farrell provided him with far greater capacities for the roles of Cléonte and Lucille than Nicholas Magallanes and Nathalie Krassovska did in 1944. Those greater capacities made possible, in a fleeting encounter before the inner curtain, the few exquisite adagio movements that established the touching relation of the two young lovers. Then Martins's comic gift cut loose in the successive incidents in which—in the disguises of a crotchety old tailor, a young dancing master and a bearded Turkish aristocrat—he made sport of the *nouveau riche* father determined to advance himself socially by marrying Lucille to this ostensibly aristocratic suitor. And Farrell's dramatic gift was brought into play first—after Lucille repelled the man her father intended her to marry—in the solo expressing her despair, and later, comically, in the *pas de deux* in which, at each attempt by the disguised Léonte to win her, she lowered the hand interposed between her face and his to take another look at him, and her face registered first incredulity at what she saw, then distaste, then the horror that impelled her to another lunge for freedom—until the ostensible Turk revealed for a moment the face of Léonte behind his beard, causing her to begin to dance joyfully with him. In these scenes Frank Ohman provided a suitably fatuous and grotesque embodiment of the *nouveau riche* butt of Léonte's ridicule and dupe of his trickery.

Given Balanchine's theater sense, one is at a loss to understand his not continuing to use the talents that provided the distinguished *Danses Concertantes* designed by Eugene Berman and *Don Quixote* designed by

Esteban Francés, and his continuing use of scenery so misconceived and ineffective for its theatrical purpose as Rouben Ter-Arutunian's—this time a room in the palace of a seventeenth-century French *nouveau riche* that looked instead like a huge lobby of an American skyscraper.

Balanchine's major new work for the season was *Davidsbündlertänze*, to Schumann's set of imaginative piano pieces with that title. As he did with the waltzes of Brahms's *Liebesliederwalzer*, Balanchine used the substance of the Schumann pieces for the purposes of his own dance imagination in the sequences he devised for his four pairs of dancers—sequences conveying the momentary states of mind and feeling of four pairs of lovers. And as with *Liebesliederwalzer* he provided in the theater program only the title of Schumann's musical work and the names of the dancers in his ballet—Farrell and Jacques d'Amboise, Martins and Watts, Ib Andersen and Kay Mazzo, Adam Lüders and Karin von Aroldingen. From this the spectator might infer that the absorbing dance invention he was seeing—from beginning to end, from the delightfully capricious first dance by Farrell with the for once baffled d'Amboise to the affecting conclusion performed by Lüders and von Aroldingen—was that of one of Balanchine's plotless pure dance ballets derived solely from the music, and that Lüders's agitated last solo and his final duo with von Aroldingen were Balanchine's use of Schumann's music for the affecting end of the relation of this imaginary pair of lovers. But some spectators saw in these sequences an unexpected interjection by Balanchine's theater sense of a stunning *coup de théâtre* in which it was Robert Schumann who performed what was a hallucinatory solo (during which five spectral Philistines in black, carrying enormous black quill pens, appeared briefly), and who, in the final duo, withdrew from a grieving Clara Schumann into the darkness of his insanity. And a couple of weeks later, in an interview, Balanchine not only confirmed that Lüders and von Aroldingen, in their dance sequences, represented Schumann and his wife, but added that the sequences performed by the three other couples conveyed attributes and moods of the two imaginary characters Florestan and Eusebius, embodying Schumann's opposing high-spirited and reflective selves, in his pieces of music. (One further comment to make on the final sequences is that they revealed impressive dramatic powers in Lüders in addition to the control and assurance of technique and style in classical dancing he had begun to exhibit.)

The filmy white draperies with which Ter-Arutunian covered the sides of the stage and the metallic-looking ornaments he suspended over it formed an abstract setting that was incongruous with the Christmas-card-like backdrop of a lake and a radiance-emitting church surrounded by pink and blue clouds.

The not only lovely but clearly structured, concentrated, and in the end impassioned Fauré Nocturne for which Balanchine made his extraordinary walking *pas de deux* in *Emeralds* is uncharacteristic of Fauré's instrumental music. What is characteristic is the amorphous spinning out of sounds without clearly defined statement—a sort of doodling—which I hear in the Ballade Op. 19, and which elicited from Balanchine, in *Ballade*, a succession of expertly contrived movements that were made interesting and effective by the grace and brilliance with which Merrill Ashley and Ib Andersen executed them. The Ter-Arutunian scenery was dreary this time.

Recalling the *Walpurgisnacht* scene in *Faust* as one of orgiastic revelry, I was puzzled by the mostly bland Gounod music for which Balanchine devised the mostly bland choreography of his ballet with that title. Contrast was provided by a couple of pieces in fast tempo; greatness by what Farrell's powers stimulated him to produce—a solo, and later an adagio in which she was partnered by Lüders—and what those powers made of it.

In addition Stanley Williams contributed to the season two new pieces for his endlessly delightful *Bournonville Divertissements*: a *pas de deux* from Rossini's *William Tell* with Kyra Nichols and Lüders, and the *Jockey Dance* from *From Siberia to Moscow* with Martins and Andersen. One had admired the seemingly effortless precision and elegance of Nichols's classical dancing in the first and last movements of *Symphony in C*, the *Sanguinic* variation of *The Four Temperaments*, *Divertimento No. 15* and *Square Dance*; now she enlivened it with the amusing style of the peasant *pas de deux*. And in the *Jockey Dance* that had Martins and Andersen in jockey costumes galloping side by side around the stage, then competing in tests of skill with much cracking of whips and other manifestations of mutual defiance, Andersen, despite his slighter body, astonished one with the power and humor that matched Martins's.

Even more astonishing was the way Andersen's greater energy transformed the roles in *Symphony in Three Movements* and *Stravinsky Violin Concerto* in which he substituted for Bart Cook. In *Symphony in Three Movements* his partner was Watts, with whom he danced also in Martins's

Calcium Light Night, and on the other hand in the first movement of *Symphony in C, Divertimento No. 15* and the *Pas de Trois* from Bournon-ville's *La Ventana*. And whereas he was impressively effective in all of these, I found Watts effective in *Symphony in Three Movements* and *Calcium Light Night* (as also in the role of the flaming-haired *femme fatale* who attracts Martins in *Vienna Waltzes*), but not in *Symphony in C, Divertimento No. 15* and *La Ventana*. I have with her dancing in classical roles the difficulty I had with Lupe Serrano's: to my eye Serrano appeared to produce the fluid movements of a classical *pas de deux* with arms and legs of steel; and Watts, in such movements, looks as if she is bending stiff wire.

Postscript 1983 Balanchine's statements didn't lessen my difficulty with the rationale of his combining invention about the real Robert and Clara Schumann and invention about the imagined Florestan and Eusebius in *Davidsbündlertänze*. And I came to see the work, at later performances, as an alternation of the invention for Lüders and von Aroldingen about stages in the Schumanns' lives, and the invention for the other dancers that presented to my eyes fascinating movements in and for themselves: what Balanchine had devised, with the particular capacities of the dancers, in response to the particular pieces of music, and its effect in combination with the music—that effect, in particular, of the progressions of movement in strikingly different styles for Farrell's several appearances, and of the varied invention for the special sensitive style of Andersen. It was these later performances, moreover, that brought recognition of all this invention as an astounding achievement of Balanchine's undiminished powers.

I missed the fall 1980 season and its small new pieces by Martins; but concerning the Tchaikovsky Festival in June 1981 I wrote (in *Ballet News*, September 1981) that the homage was not only understandable but inevitable in the light of Balanchine's long creative involvement with Tchaikovsky. One wondered only why he hadn't done it sooner—why, after the Stravinsky Festival in 1972, his choice for such homage with 1975's festival hadn't been Tchaikovsky, whom he associated with Stra-vinsky as another master musician and major contributor to the deve-lopment of ballet with his ballet scores. Moreover, the "compelling descriptions of dance movement" that Balanchine once said he found

even in Stravinsky's non-balletic works were to be found also in Tchaikovsky's instrumental works: the impassioned *pas de deux* in the first
movement of Balanchine's *Piano Concerto No. 2* was "described" to him
by the phrases of Tchaikovsky's extensive melodic episode for solo piano
at that point in his score; the delightfully capricious *pas de deux* in waltz
time in Balanchine's *Theme and Variations* (in his *Suite No. 3*), and the
grand supported adagio that follows, were described to him by Tchaikovsky's writing in those two variations. And the 1981 Festival was the
homage to Tchaikovsky the composer not only of uniquely beautiful and
effective ballet scores but of instrumental works that described ballet
movements to Balanchine.

What the homage to the composer of ballet scores clearly called for was
a production of the one ballet not already in the company's repertory,
The Sleeping Beauty, in which Tchaikovsky's invention attains its greatest
heights of imaginative power and musical beauty, and of which Balanchine retained memories of the dazzling Maryinsky Theater staging he
participated in. But the enormous cost of such a production today was
prohibitive; and so this great work was represented in the Festival only by
the waltz at the beginning of Act I, for which Balanchine contrived a
Garland Dance that was a masterly orchestration of movement first by the
company's corps, and later by an additional group of little girls from the
School of American Ballet, who astonished and charmed one with the
fluidity and grace of their execution of the waltz steps and the assurance
with which they steered their way through the ensemble involvements.

For the most part, then, the homage was paid to the composer of
instrumental works that invited use for ballet. The first of the new ones,
presented at the Festival's opening gala, was *Mozartiana*, Balanchine's
setting of the Suite No. 4, an orchestration of four of the piano pieces by
Mozart that Tchaikovsky described as "miniature masterpieces . . . little
known, not only by the public, but also by the majority of musicians." In
his first setting of this work for Les Ballets 1933 Balanchine tailored the
principal girl's role to the gifts of the young Tamara Toumanova; in his
staging for the Ballet Russe de Monte Carlo in 1945 he tailored the role
to the different gifts of Alexandra Danilova; and his tailoring of it to those
of Suzanne Farrell last spring entailed changes in the character and
structure of the entire ballet. Gaiety predominated in the 1945 *Mozartiana*, right from the start in smiling Lazovsky's pointing up of the
rhythmic eccentricity of his dance to the opening Gigue; again, in the

theme and variations, in smiling Danilova's vivacious performances, with and without Franklin, of the lively variations; and again—after her supported adagio in a style of overwhelming grandeur—in the lively concluding coda. In marked contrast, last spring's *Mozartiana* began with the solemnity of the *Preghiera*, in which Farrell and four little girls from the School of American Ballet, in black costumes, performed movements expressive of grief. This affected the character of the Gigue and Minuet that followed, which, also performed in black costumes, were animated but not gay. And not only the variation in slow tempo but the first lively ones were, as performed by an unsmiling Farrell, breathtakingly beautiful but not gay. Only in the coda did one see smiling high spirits at last.

The work gained not only by Farrell's participation but by Ib Andersen's—his accomplished partnering of Farrell, and his elegant and finished solo dancing. The costumes that Rouben Ter-Arutunian designed for the girls were made of a material which caused them to look unattractively stiff and bulky; but the "ice palace" of glistening plastic tubing contrived as the festival's permanent set by Philip Johnson and John Burgee, and lighted by Ronald Bates, was remarkably effective. Altogether, then, *Mozartiana* was a major contribution to the festival; and it was unfortunate that because of an injury to Farrell and Andersen's illness all its remaining performances had to be canceled. Balanchine's two additional contributions were *Hungarian Gypsy Songs*, of which the performance I expected to see was canceled; and, for the festival's concluding performance, a setting of the *Adagio lamentoso* finale of Tchaikovsky's Sixth Symphony, the *Pathétique*, which described for Balanchine the movements of grief, terror and despair that were in effect an impressive memorial service for the composer.

The *Pathétique's* finale was preceded by its *Allegro con grazia* second movement, for which Jerome Robbins contrived graceful turns and lifts by Patricia McBride and Helgi Tomasson in the opening *grazioso* that continued without the change one expected to see with the music's change to the lamenting phrases of the middle section. Robbins also contributed to the opening gala *Pas de Deux*, to the second movement of the Piano Concerto No. 1, which was made enjoyable by the extraordinary gifts exhibited by young Darci Kistler with Andersen.

But Robbins's major contribution, in length and audience response, was *Piano Pieces*, in which he used a number of mostly unfamiliar and attractive pieces for a work similar to his *Dances at a Gathering*. The many admirers of *Dances at a Gathering* responded to *Piano Pieces* with a roar of approval at its conclusion and a standing ovation for Robbins; and if, as honesty requires, I say I don't admire *Dances* and didn't care much for *Piano Pieces*, I should add that this is not a result of perversity or prejudice—i.e., of judgment before or without experience—or failure to perceive Robbins's talents. I do perceive the talents and do admire some of their achievements; but I have learned from experience that possession of talent for an art doesn't inevitably produce valuable achievement in that art. Thus I have admired Robbins's *Fancy Free, Afternoon of a Fawn*, the Mack Sennett ballet in *High Button Shoes* and ballets in a couple of other musical shows—which is to say his early achievements in comedy; but not the early embodiments of his Serious Thoughts on the Human Condition, like *Facsimile* and *The Age of Anxiety*, and not, in his recent years with the New York City Ballet, the results of his being, in Arlene Croce's words, "fatally attracted to pretentious undertakings." What can be said for *Piano Pieces* is that being half as long as *Dances*, it had half as many sentimentalities, cutenesses and pretentious solemnities. And it was danced beautifully by Kyra Nichols, Maria Calegari, Andersen, Daniel and Joseph Duell and Bart Cook.

The third new ballet at the opening gala was Peter Martins's *Capriccio Italien*, which he had made for the spring workshop of the School of American Ballet, and which was performed at the Festival by the talented students who had performed it at the workshop. This was Martins's first try at orchestrating the movements of large groups; and the series of pieces he made for Tchaikovsky's sectional work revealed that he had learned from Balanchine's ballets to do it skillfully and effectively. In the slow declamatory opening section he had rows of dancers in splendid white-and-gold classical ballet costumes, led by a ballerina and her partner, execute grand supported-adagio arabesques, lifts and turns in changing formations; in the lively section that followed he had three boys and six girls in peasant costumes execute various folk-dance steps and formations; a second section with the classical ballet group's adagio movements was followed by a second lively section in which the three boys and six girls performed a delightful tarantella in Bournonville style that Martins had devised; and he combined the two groups of dancers for a brilliant finale. Lisa Jackson was an impressive ballerina, partnered well by Afshin Mofid, with Gen Horiuchi a brilliantly acrobatic leader, and Michael Byars and James Sewell his capable associates, in the trio in peasant costume.

Good as this was, it was surpassed by what Martins invented for the second, third and final movements of the Symphony No. 1: in the second movement the striking entrance of Kistler and Sean Lavery on the empty stage and their arresting supported-adagio movements until the entrance of corps dancers in white costumes; then the interaction of the two principals with the corps during the remainder of the movement; the invention for corps dancers in blue costumes in the third movement's Scherzo, with Kistler entering in the Trio and weaving in and out of a formation of girls, drawing them after her one by one in what became a line which she led gaily about the stage. The finale was made unusual and puzzling by the fact that the two principals, who had been central in the preceding movements, didn't participate with the corps in this one, but entered only at its conclusion, with the return of the *Andante lugubre* introduction in the music, and only to join the final line-up of the entire cast and participate in its gradual withdrawal that left the stage empty for the orchestra's acceleration and crescendo to its concluding flourishes. Whatever Martins may have intended with this, the principals' nonparticipation in the movement and their entrance only for the solemn conclusion to what they hadn't participated in was not for me a logical and satisfying completion of the movement's structure.

One of Balanchine's objectives in the Festival was to acquaint the public with unfamiliar works by Tchaikovsky; but the sextet for strings, *Souvenir de Florence*, is not unfamiliar; also it is not very interesting; and John Taras didn't succeed in making it interesting with his choreography. The *Concert Fantasy* that *is* unfamiliar turned out to be a very inferior work which deserves its obscurity, and which Jacques d'Amboise's incoherent choreography made even worse. He did better with the brief Scherzo Op. 42, for which he produced a grotesquerie in which Patricia McBride danced effectively. The infrequently heard Suite No. 1 begins with a strangely somber Introduction which is followed by a Fugue that is more interesting than most of Tchaikovsky's fugues; and in his settings of the two pieces Joseph Duell moved the dancers—with one exception—understandingly and effectively. The exception was Adam Lüders, the work's protagonist, who, after successfully repelling the attacks by a group of the corps in the Introduction, didn't participate in the Fugue, but nevertheless appeared briefly with upraised arms at the conclusion of what he hadn't participated in—the balletic intention of which wasn't clear to me.

Balanchine's *Garland Dance* was the first piece in *Tempo di Valse*, a group of waltzes that included also his *Waltz of the Flowers* from *The Nutcracker*, in which the Dewdrop of Kistler in a later performance was much more beautiful than that of Watts in the first performance. D'Amboise contributed a satisfying *Valse-Scherzo* which Nichols and Daniel Duell performed delightfully; Taras a skillful Variation VI from the Piano Trio in A minor, which provided one of the rare opportunities to see the lovely dancing of Allegra Kent, partnered by Andersen. Taras also produced an excellent setting of the waltz from *Eugene Onegin* for students of the School.

Additional offerings at the opening gala were Lisa's final aria from *The Queen of Spades*, sung well by Karen Hunt in what my neighbor said was English, Lensky's final aria from *Eugene Onegin*, sung superbly by Howard Hensel in recognizable Russian, a duet from the unfinished opera *Undine* that turned out to be Odette's supported adagio in Act II of *Swan Lake*, sung by Hunt and Hensel in English, and the Overture-Fantasy *Romeo and Juliet*, shaped admirably by Robert Irving, who could not, however, improve the less than admirable sound of the orchestra. A later program included three songs, sung by Hunt in German with excellent piano accompaniment by Gordon Boelzner. And between the Robbins and Balanchine settings of the second and fourth movements of the *Pathétique* the orchestra performed the third movement.

A regrettable consequence of the festival was the omission from the spring repertory of the delightful *Bournonville Divertissements* as well as *Union Jack* and *Jewels*. With Ashley still recovering from her injury, her solo in *Who Cares?*, in which she had produced the excitingly fast spins and the elegantly flowing arm movements it required, was assigned on opening night to Heather Watts, whose fast turns were slower and arm movements angular. Watts also was the unsatisfying replacement for Ashley in *Square Dance* and the Terpsichore in all the performances of *Apollo* with Andersen. The performance of *Le Bourgeois Gentilhomme* that I saw was made notable by Kent's dancing in the role of Lucille; but I must add that Martins was overdoing his strokes of comedy. Lourdes Lopez projected a stronger image than Kay Mazzo's in the opening movement of *Stravinsky Violin Concerto* that made her a more effective partner for Martins in Aria II. Lavery performed in *Ballo della Regina* with technical brilliance that was not entirely satisfying only to someone who retained the image of Robert Weiss's lightness, elegance, elevation and speed, especially in his spins. The season's greatest excitement was created by Kistler, who during the winter season had stepped from the classroom to the stage in full possession at sixteen of the technical brilliance, the security, the stamina and, most extraordinary, the matured style that a dancer usually acquires only with years of experience. Observing the maturing effect of such experience in the dancing of Nichols had also been exciting; and the style in which the movements seem merely to come into existence without human effort attained a new high point in a post-Festival performance of *Theme and Variations* (in *Suite No. 3*). One of the season's memorable performances was the *Divertimento No. 15* in which the marvelous solos of the variation movement were performed by Elyse Borne, Calegari, Stephanie Saland, Kistler and Nichols.

Postscript 1983 As in the case of *Davidsbündlertänze*, it was at the additional performances of *Mozartiana* in January 1982 that I came to perceive in the work yet another amazing achievement of Balanchine's undiminished powers of innovative invention, manifested this time in the quirky movements in perverse rhythms of the Gigue, the profusion of novel movement in the solos and duets of the series of variations. As it happened, the movements devised for Andersen were, at these later performances, executed by Martins with *his* elegance and finish; and Castelli's clarity gave the movements of the Gigue the effect they hadn't had when Christopher d'Amboise had substituted for him at the première.

Arlene Croce provided accurate perceptions of detail in *Mozartiana*: the "twists and leaps close to the ground" and the "swift jokes" in the Gigue; the "rapid small needlework in Farrell's variations". But she saw also that the four girls who danced the Minuet "are all projections of Farrell," and that it is "in air perfumed by [these] by now permutations of herself" that Farrell later "dances four variations, one for each member of the shadow quartet;" whereas I could see nothing in the flow of large movements by the four girls to the music of the Minuet that brought Farrell to mind, or that related to the "rapid small needlework" of her four variations, or that was recalled by this small needlework. In a later report Croce saw Farrell and Andersen in the *pas de deux* as "queen and consort", and Castelli as the "artist figure who takes his inspiration" from the four little girls in the *Preghiera* and the four grown girls in the Minuet (which was not visible to me in what Castelli did); and she went on to say that "while the queen collects in her four variations all the attributes" of those girls "that could possibly interest her consort-lover, Castelli is off in another part of the palace painting those attributes into murals (which he signs 'Titian')"—this off-stage activity of his being made visible in "the interaction of Farrell and Andersen" in the *pas de deux*. On this my comment has to be what a friend told me Farrell had said to him about the violent distortions Croce had seen in her dancing before her departure from the company in 1969: "I don't know what she's talking about." One could make the same comment about the statement at the end of Croce's report on Balanchine's *Davidsbündlertänze*—that "like [Schumann's] music, it wears its heart on its sleeve even when there is no arm inside." These occasional flights of the Croce imagination call for the mention they haven't received in reviews of the collections of her writing in *Afterimages* and *Going to the Dance*.

At a later performance of Jacques d'Amboise's *Valse-Scherzo* I discovered that what I had found "satisfying" at the first performance was merely the gifts Kyra Nichols and Daniel Duell managed to reveal in details of choreography that looked as if devised in sheer desperation by someone incapable of using those gifts effectively.

For the spring 1981 workshop of the School of American Ballet Martins had made not only *Capriccio Italien* but another orchestration of the movements of large groups—this one for the music by Drigo and the scenario of a 19th-century story ballet, *The Magic Flute*, choreographed by Lev Ivanov in 1893. It was a task set by Balanchine, which Martins executed with skill, producing an effective version of an old-fashioned ballet that was suitable for a school workshop, but not for the New York City Ballet's repertory to which Balanchine added it in January 1982. It was followed by a Robbins orchestration of movements of large groups, *Gershwin Concerto*, mechanical and uninteresting except for what Robbins made in jive style for the middle movement's blues.

In this fall-winter season it was dancers' new roles in the repertory that commanded interest: Nichols's performances in *Scotch Symphony* and the *Pas de Deux* from *Flower Festival in Genzano;*

Kistler's in the second movement of *Symphony in C* and the two principal roles of *The Nutcracker;* Lopez's in the von Aroldingen role in *Who Cares?* and with a soaring Daniel Duell in the third movement of *Symphony in C;* Calegari's in the fourth movement of *Symphony in C* and the two roles of *The Nutcracker;* and—most extraordinary—Farrell's in *La Source,* which she had danced once before in her own style, but in which this time she surprised and delighted one by giving her large movements the subtle inflections of the style of the original Verdy performance.

The spring season's Stravinsky Centennial Celebration could have had a notable point. When Stravinsky, in one of his published conversations with Robert Craft years earlier, had said Nijinsky's choreography for *Le Sacre du Printemps* had revealed his ignorance of music and of its proper relation to dance movement, I had written that this was contradicted by what major critics had said after the première—that where Stravinsky had seen only "rhythmic chaos" André Levinson had reported seeing that "in their simplified gymnastics the dancers bend their knees and straighten them again, they raise their heels and fall back on them, they stamp in place, insistently marking the accented notes. . . . An all-powerful constraint dominates them, disjoints their limbs, lies heavy on the necks of their heads," which convinced me that what Nijinsky had produced *had* had the relation to the music that Stravinsky had said it didn't have. At that time I had to say there was no way of discovering whether Stravinsky or Levinson had been right. But in 1974 an article by Robert Craft included an amazing letter from Stravinsky to Maximilian Steinberg a month after the première of *Le Sacre* in which Stravinsky wrote: "Nijinsky's choreography is incomparable. Everything is as I wanted it, with very few exceptions." And in a review of Lincoln Kirstein's *Nijinsky Dancing* in 1976 Craft wrote: "Only in 1967, with the recovery of the score that he had marked for Nijinsky and used in rehearsals with him, did Stravinsky recall the original conception and reaffirm his former approval of Nijinsky's realization of it." Moreover Craft reported in a footnote Marie Rambert's discovery of the score in which she had written down everything Nijinsky had said during the rehearsals, which led him to write: "Surely the New York City Ballet, which can hardly avoid the *Sacre* during the approaching Stravinsky centenary, should recognize an obligation to present the Nijinsky version, as preserved in Stravinsky's and Dame Marie Rambert's promptbook scores. Thus, at last, justice might be done to Nijinsky's, as well as Stravinsky's, masterpiece." Craft called on Kirstein to bring this about; and the September 1981 issue of *Ballet News* that published Bronislawa Nijinska's account of her brother's making of his ballet in her *Early Memoirs* included an editorial in which Karl F. Reuling, citing Kirstein's long-time championship of Nijinsky as a choreographer, endorsed Craft's proposal. But it was addressed to the man without the power of decision in the matter; and the possessor of this power held fast to his characteristic ad hoc and perverse dictum—ad hoc to justify his rejection of the idea, perverse in denying the fact of Nijinsky's choreography— that *Le Sacre* was unchoreographable. Thus the historic ballet score that would have provided a major point for the 1982 Celebration honoring Stravinsky as a composer for dance was conspicuously absent from it, as it had been from the festival in 1972. And so were again his other major ballet scores—the historic *Petrushka*, the great *Le Baiser de la Fée* (the entire score for Stravinsky's scenario that Balanchine choreographed in 1937), the *Jeu de Cartes* (also choreographed by Balanchine in 1937). Moreover, of the Stravinsky music other than the ballet scores, what remained for the 1982 festival, after all that had previously been choreographed, ranged from minor to trivial and worse, and elicited little of consequence in the choreographies. Whereas in 1972 Balanchine had contributed the overwhelmingly innovative *Stravinsky Violin Concerto* and *Symphony in Three Movements*, his major contributions in 1982 were not choreographies of instrumental works but endlessly uninteresting realizations in stage spectacle, with very little dance, of vocal dramatic works, *The Flood* and *Perséphone*, each in its different way not worth the efforts originally of Stravinsky and now of Balanchine and the performers. To these he added a few small choreographies—an amusing burlesque for Stravinsky's *Tango;* some lovely Farrell arm-weaving for his *Elégie;* a breathtaking new Farrell *perpetuum mobile* rush for his *Variations,* which was delayed and not performed until after the festival period.

Other ballets worth mentioning were Lew Christensen's attractive setting of *Norwegian Moods;* and Peter Martins's clever number for *Piano Rag,* which had Kistler flirting strenuously with four young men and— deserted by them—ending with a Martins stroke of comedy: her lunge forward with arms extended, hands clasped in reverse, and face expressing the giggling appeal "Aren't I the fool?" Martins produced in addition for the ugly Concerto for Two Solo Pianos another large-scale orchestration—this one of the unattractive movements by Heather Watts, the attractive ones by Ib Andersen and the dynamic Jock Soto, and the contextual ones by a number of girls of the corps. (It elicited from Croce a transcendant specimen of her invention-spinning—about Martins's having made "a ballet that was not about its music" but instead "has a dramatic subject, which it projects through the music," beginning with Watts's entrance. "Martins's ballet is in part about a destructive kind of honesty in the heroine . . . and the ballerina's role, as Martins has understood it through Watts, is to illuminate a general condition through a process of self-exposure. . . . Watts projects the kind of tension that is felt today by many women. She transcends herself and becomes part of the spectacle of the world. The role makes her a star.")

In sum a mostly unfestive series, in which the spirit-lifting events were the performances of earlier Balanchine ballets, including an *Apollo*—made riveting by Martins, with beautiful contributions by Farrell, Nichols and Calegari—that was the Celebration's high point.

As it happened, excitingly festive occasions were being provided in this period in the Metropolitan Opera House by the Royal Danish Ballet. Though this company, when I had last seen it in 1966, had included major figures like Erik Bruhn and Nils Kehlet, it had presented mostly bland performances of boring ballets by Ashton, Cullberg, Robbins and Fleming Flindt that had left me with no interest in its subsequent visits. But the reports of the rejuvenated company's performances in its Bournonville Festival in Copenhagen a few years ago—added to what I had learned to perceive and enjoy enormously in the New York City Ballet's *Bournonville Divertissements*—led me this time to the Royal Danish performances of Bournonville's *Kermesse in Bruges*, Act 3 of his *Napoli*, with its endlessly delightful concluding *Tarantella*, and *A Folk Tale*, and also the version of *Coppélia* that differs in part, especially in the third act, from the Russian version familiar to American audiences. They provided experiences, new and special in style and tone, that were made enthralling, most immediately, by the flow of exquisitely delicate bodily configuration that seemed merely to come into existence without any effort of the amazing young ballerina Lis Jeppesen, the superb dancing by Kehlet again and the young Arne Villumsen and Frank Andersen, among other principals, but then also by the context for these solo achievements—the company's ensemble operation that was unlike any I could recall, by dancers disciplined to exhibit not just unfailing precision but an appearance of intimacy, harmony and happiness in their working together.

Though Balanchine had managed to complete *Variations* by the end of June, the illnesses that developed in the summer and fall prevented further activity with his company; and it was Martins who provided the new works for its fall-winter season of 1982-83. *Delibes Divertissement* revealed the skill Martins had acquired in using what he had learned from his study of the Balanchine operation: it was a convincing and interesting facsimile of what Balanchine might have produced for the Delibes music. But *Rossini Quartets* exhibited, surprisingly, a lack of this skill not only in the orchestration of the movements of the group but in the invention for Farrell. Preoccupation with these choreographies, administrative supervision of the company in Balanchine's absence, and personal decision combined to reduce his dancing to two performances with Farrell in *Tzigane*. Ib Andersen's increased power of presence and movement made him effective in place of Martins in *Apollo*; but Joseph Duell, as I mentioned earlier, was not an adequate replacement for him in *Stravinsky Violin Concerto, Union Jack* and *Davidsbündlertänze*.

Lavery proved to be not an adequate replacement for Jacques d'Amboise in *Who Cares?*; and his shiny black costume in place of d'Amboise's polo shirt and slacks was one of the garish new costumes that were damaging to the work. Gen Horiuchi as the Oberon in a performance of *A Midsummer Night's Dream* was miscast: in his confrontations with Titania he exhibited not regal anger but boyish petulance. This performance had Daniel Duell's effective Lysander; and another performance with Andersen's Oberon had the impressive Helena of Lourdes Lopez and Hermia of Judith Fugate. Calegari, after exhibiting her distinctive elegance in her first *Swan Lake*, attained complete achievement in the role in her second one—these in addition to her beautiful Sugar Plum Fairy in a *Nutcracker* with Nichols's Dewdrop, and her participation in an outstanding *Serenade* with Farrell and Nichols. And memorable in the pre-*Nutcracker* two weeks were Nichols's performances in *Theme and Variations* and *Divertimento No. 15*.

At the end of a performance of *Davidsbündlertänze* in the spring I leaned forward and startled Edwin Denby, who was sitting motionless and silent in front of me, with the question "Do you believe you really saw what you saw?", which it was hard to believe *I* had really seen. I mentioned earlier the increasing magnitude and impact for me of this ballet and *Mozartiana* in the seasons following their premières—the result not only of increased perception on my part but of the increased effectiveness of the dancers' operation in their roles: the heightened definition, tension, projective force of their movements. And in the spring of 1983 what I saw being done by Farrell, by von Aroldingen and Lüders, by Andersen and Saland, by Martins and Watts in *Davidsbündlertänze*, and by Farrell, Andersen and Castelli in *Mozartiana* exceeded even what I had seen previously. This happened also in the performances of other Balanchine works: the *Symphony in Three Movements* with Calegari, Lopez, Lisa Hess, Castelli, Joseph Duell and Soto; the Symphony Op. 21 of *Episodes* with Saland and Daniel Duell; the *Monumentum pro Gesualdo* with Farrell and Lavery; and, most astonishingly for me, the *Kammermusik II* with von Aroldingen, Lopez, Joseph Duell and Tomlinson. And it was not only the principals but the corps that made the performances extraordinary in this way.

Nor was it only Saland, with her sharper definition of the Mazzo/Leland role, and Andersen, with the somewhat more robust body that made his sensitive movements count for more, who, in *Davidsbündlertänze*, revealed new strengths. Expansion of bodily frame contributed to Lavery's grand style in *Tchaikovsky Piano Concerto;* and Nichols attained new heights not only in this ballet but in *Ballo della Regina* and *Donizetti Variations*. But it was Calegari, above all, who commanded marveling attention in performance after performance, role after role, most notably in *Swan Lake*, in which she demonstrated that, in Croce's words, in a company with "many brilliant executants of steps, Calegari is also a brilliant executant of shapes"—that "when she strikes an arabesque you see her simultaneously stretching and holding the shape." This shaping was central in the varying other roles—in the exquisite flow, produced with dazzling speed, of the spins of the Marnee Morris solo of *Who Cares?*, the *Choleric* Variation of *The Four Temperaments*, the first and and last movements of *Symphony in C*, the second *Pas de Trois* of *Agon*, the slow middle movement of *Symphony in Three Movements*.

Lopez too was impressive in the von Aroldingen role of *Who Cares?*, *Symphony in Three Movements*, the second principal role of *Tchaikovsky Piano Concerto*, the third movement of *Symphony in C*—this with a soaring

Daniel Duell, who in Martins's *Calcium Light Night* revealed in full measure the accomplished dancer he is. And though Lavery in *Who Cares?* was more relaxed, engaging and effective than in the preceding season, it was Joseph Duell who presented the more convincing musical-show hoofer in appearance and style.

Some experiments with dancers in new roles were successful, some not. Andersen was excellent in *Donizetti Variations* and the first *Pas de Trois* of *Agon;* but in *Orpheus* he lacked the powers of presence and projection Martins had exhibited in the opening scene, and was disadvantaged by von Aroldingen's disproportionate size in the great *pas de deux*. Tomlinson's Dark Angel, in this ballet, was impressive; but like Lüders's it lacked Moncion's arresting presence in the role he created and could still do. Daniel Duell's second performance in *Coppélia* was made outstanding by his superb dancing and partnering of McBride in the final classical *pas de deux*. And McNaughton achieved in make-up as well as movement a remarkable approximation of Baryshnikov's Tin Soldier. But Puleo was not an adequate replacement for Bart Cook in the *Melancholic* Variation of *The Four Temperaments;* and Horiuchi's crudely acrobatic performance in the role in *Tarantella* that one had seen danced with elegant assurance was unacceptable.

The two new ballets provided for the spring season by Robbins were the appalling *Glass Pieces* that I saw and the *I'm Old-Fashioned* that—after the reservations that modified the initial warm approval expressed in the *Times* review—I felt I could miss. What saved this situation was *Ballet d'Isoline* (to music by Messager), which Helgi Tomasson had made for the annual workshop performances of the School of American Ballet—a beautifully contrived large-scale classical ballet whose success at those performances led to its being presented by the company, its première made exciting and moving—seemingly an *hommage* to Tomasson—by Farrell and Martins in the principal roles, and the dancers' joining in the audience's applause when Tomasson came on stage for his bow.

What the New York City Ballet had for many years that no other company had—a choreographer of unique genius to provide new ballets for its every season—it lost when he died in April. True, the company was left with its enormous accumulated repertory of his ballets, concerning which Peter Martins, its new co-director, said: "Of course, the most important function of this company is to keep the repertory alive, and to keep the Balanchine ballets intact." But this was made less reassuring by Martins's further statement: "Still, we must think ahead, because this is not a museum, it's a creative institution. We will have to look for new choreographers . . ." I dispute the pejorative implication of Martins's word "museum": if it is right for the paintings by the great masters to be kept permanently on view in the museums of Europe and this country, it would be right for the New York City Ballet to devote itself to doing this with the ballets of Balanchine. And I find it preferable to what I see, when I think ahead, as the realities of the company's operation as the creative institution Martins said it was: possibly an occasional new ballet of Tomassons's, but certainly the constant addition of new works by the creator of *Glass Pieces* that will leave less and less room in the company's programs for the works of Balanchine. These realities lead me to believe that the preservation of the Balanchine repertory requires not just the one Balanchine festival that has been mentioned but an annual festival— which would be appropriate, it seems to me, for a company created originally to perform the works that now constitute the major reason for its continued existence.

The Vienna Philharmonic's Conductors 1918-37

Hugo Burghauser, the Vienna Philharmonic bassoonist who was the orchestra's chairman from 1933 to 1938, and who in 1966 gave me his recollections of its experiences with Toscanini for the book *The Toscanini Musicians Knew*, continued, in subsequent conversations, with other recollections which had the value of coming from someone who had himself witnessed what he spoke of. When, on one occasion, he described how Toscanini, in the greenroom after George Szell's first rehearsal with the NBC Symphony, berated Szell for a method of rehearsal that Toscanini regarded as mistreatment of the orchestra, and how Szell apologized abjectly, I asked in amazement how he knew this; and he answered with a spreading of upturned hands; "I was there." He had known Szell in Europe, had been at the rehearsal, and was in the greenroom with Szell when Toscanini stormed in. And one of the especially notable occasions when he "was there" was Arnold Schönberg's rehearsal with a small Vienna Philharmonic group, in the 20s, for a performance of his *Kammersymphonie*. At one point the clarinettist Polatschek leaned over to whisper to Burghauser that he had just discovered he had by mistake been playing a clarinet in B-flat instead of the one in A specified in the score, and Schönberg hadn't noticed it—which led to Burghauser's suggestion that the musicians play wrong notes to see if Schönberg would hear them, and their discovery that he did not hear them.

Part of Burghauser's interest in relating such incidents to me arose from the fact that I was someone who also could say "I was there." Thus, he told me once how Toscanini, at his first orchestral rehearsal of *Tristan und Isolde* in Bayreuth in 1930, had corrected mistake after mistake in the

226

parts that had gone uncorrected by all who had conducted *Tristan* in Germany until then—"which," Burghauser remarked, "was for Furtwängler, a man of great vanity, an unbearable humiliation, and the reason for his antagonism to Toscanini." And as it happened I could describe an earlier "unbearable humiliation" that could have been the initial cause of Furtwängler's antagonism to Toscanini. That is, "I was there" in Carnegie Hall in January 1925 at Furtwängler's first guest appearances with the New York Philharmonic, and witnessed his triumphs with orchestra, public and press that led to his being re-engaged for two months of each of the subsequent two seasons. And I was there again in February 1926 when Furtwängler, arriving after Toscanini's first guest engagement with the Philharmonic, and expecting to repeat his triumphs of the preceding year, encountered instead the lessened responses of an orchestra, a public and a press still overwhelmed by the performances they had just heard conducted by Toscanini. For Furtwängler, accustomed to triumph after triumph, this was not merely a disappointment but an "unbearable humiliation", which—since he could think of others only as being motivated by the same vanity and jealousy as his own—he regarded as having been contrived by Toscanini. But an incident described by Rudolf Serkin indicates that Furtwängler's antagonism had begun even earlier. In 1924 a performance of Brahms's Symphony No. 2 by Toscanini with his La Scala Orchestra in Zürich was for Serkin an "incredible revelation"; but Furtwängler, at a private reception after the concert, "embarrassingly and painfully told Toscanini in violent terms what he thought" about some things in the performance. Toscanini listened, in Serkin's words, "like a little boy"; then he answered: "When Steinbach [the conductor contemporary with Brahms whose performances of Brahms's symphonies were considered authoritative] came to Turin and conducted the Brahms Second Symphony, after the first rehearsal he turned to the orchestra and said: 'I have nothing to do. Who is your conductor?' And the answer was 'Toscanini'."

Moreover, Burghauser and I could talk about occasions when both of us had been there. Thus, I told him of having been charmed, in Salzburg in the summer of 1928, by the *Così Fan Tutte* conducted by Bruno Walter, and how, in Vienna the following winter, I had been overwhelmed by the more spirited, sharper-witted *Così* conducted by Richard Strauss, of which I recalled in particular Strauss's witty piano accompaniments for the recitatives. Burghauser had of course played in both performances; and as one who placed Strauss above all the German conductors he had worked with, he nodded and smiled as I spoke, then told me of his visit to Strauss in Montreux in 1949, the year of his death. The royalties from Strauss's works were still being withheld from him; and though Boosey & Hawkes were providing him with room and meals at the Montreux Palace Hotel in return for the new works they were to receive from him, he didn't have money for tips, or for the repair of the frayed cuffs of his shabby coat. At one point, said Burghauser, "I begged him to write out those enchanting accompaniments for the recitatives of *Così Fan Tutte*. But he pointed to the *Vier letzte Gesänge* and the Duettino for clarinet and bassoon, which he had to finish. So the accompaniments for *Così* were lost."

On another occasion Burhauser's indignant and scornful comment on some nonsense of Daniel Barenboim's about Furtwängler's superiority to Toscanini, in a *New York Times* interview, led me to recall Furt-wängler's Beethoven Ninth in Salzburg in 1937, in which his preoccupa-tion with now this, now that effect of the moment had destroyed continuity and shape. Burghauser gave me a sharp look and said: "Tos-canini was there. He felt that this courtesy was required of him. This made Furtwängler more nervous than usual, and his first downbeat even more indecisive than usual; so the horns did not play the two notes of their opening fifth exactly together—which was for Toscanini only the beginning of his torture from the performance, especially from Furt-wängler's exaggerations of expressiveness in the slow movement." And from this Burghauser went on to tell me what had happened between Furtwängler and Toscanini the day before the Ninth, and what happened after the Ninth—which is to say that he gave me the true account of the historic confrontation, as against the myths about it in articles and books since then.

My own thought after this was merely to publish the truth about the confrontation. But a friend who had been fascinated by the reports of my conversations with Burghauser persuaded me to combine all the recollec-tions of the conductors Burghauser had played under and I had heard into the narrative that follows.

It was in the winter of 1918-19, Burghauser told me, that he became a member of the orchestra of the Vienna State Opera, which outside the opera house carried on, as an autonomous corporate entity, its activity as Vienna's principal concert orchestra, the Vienna Philharmonic. The conductor of its annual series of concerts at that time was Felix Weingartner, whose performances I didn't know until I began to hear them on records in the early 30s. Part of what Burghauser said about him confirmed what I had heard on those records: that his style of performance was not romantic, with big rubatos, but straightforward, with only the subtlest modifications of tempo, and achieving the utmost clarity of rhythm. This spare musical style, produced by the spare gestures of his conducting style, was at times thought to be rigid by what Burghauser called "the average listener"; but the musically experienced listener appreciated the subtlety of which Weingartner was a master. His performance of Schubert's *Unfinished* Symphony, for example, though completely controlled and contained, had the lilt of Schubert, and an intensity of expression which Burghauser didn't encounter in any other performance until, much later, he heard it surpassed in Toscanini's. Burghauser spoke also of the dramatic power of Weingartner's performances at the Vienna Opera—in particular his *Tristan und Isolde:* when he first heard it, he couldn't imagine anything more passionate in dramatic expression.

Almost sixty, Weingartner was astonishingly youthful in appearance and in his singular behavior when he conducted. He was married (when Burghauser joined the orchestra) to his third wife, an American singer named Lucille Marcel, who was extremely beautiful and also sang beautifully. At the Philharmonic concerts in the Musikvereinsaal she sat in the first box; and Weingartner, at some point in the work or performance, would turn and smile to her, as if he were performing in private, not for an audience of eighteen hundred. This sometimes gave the performance an unintended effect—one example Burghauser recalled being the *Gretchen* movement of Liszt's *Faust* Symphony, in which the effect was that of a movie love scene. As concert behavior it was unprecedented and embarrassingly ridiculous.

Lucille Marcel died very suddenly, leaving Weingartner heartbroken; but he recovered very soon, said Burghauser; and the orchestra's first South American tour of several months with him was also his honeymoon trip with his fourth wife. She was another young American. Betty Calisch, a highly gifted actress, who appeared in the title role of Auber's opera *La Muette de Portici,* with Weingartner conducting, and made the performance a great success. And the new marriage caused Weingartner to look and act again like a youngster, and to conduct with renewed vitality, expressiveness and fire.

It was Weingartner's absence immediately after Lucille Marcel's death that was responsible for the guest appearance with the Vienna Philharmonic, in the spring of 1921, of the legendary Artur Nikisch. Half a century earlier he had been a violinist in the orchestra; now, at seventy, he returned to provide most of its members at this time with their greatest experience. He was called *"der Magier"*—someone with magical, hypnotic power; and the legend was that if he stood on the podium and conducted without an orchestra, the audience would hear an orchestra playing in response to his conducting. The reality that one heard, said Burghauser, was "a dream-like romanticism" under a control which kept it from becoming "an indulgence in some private violent feeling". And what one saw—the movements of extraordinarily beautiful marble-white hands and three-inch white cuffs between the hands and the black sleeve of the tailcoat—was like the waving of a magician's wand, which probably hypnotized impressionable listeners in the audience.* Even for the orchestra the experience of those movements that were as though made in a dream was like magic.

When, after Nikisch's death a year later, Weingartner conducted a performance of Beethoven's *Eroica* in his memory, the unanimous judgment of those present was that Weingartner was Nikisch's successor—concerning which Burghauser remarked that they would not have thought this if they had heard Toscanini, but not even Toscanini's name was known there at that time. To demonstrate this Burghauser cited the incident related to him by a New York Philharmonic musician, which that musician, the cellist (later a conductor) Alfred Wallenstein, had related also to me in *The Toscanini Musicians Knew*, and which I prefer to report in his own words:

> The first time I heard about Toscanini was in 1921, at a rehearsal of the Leipzig Gewandhaus Orchestra, where Nikisch said: 'Gentlemen, I have just come from Milan, where I heard a performance of *Siegfried* conducted by a man named Toscanini that was the greatest performance of opera I

---

*It was interesting to have this confirmation of what the conductor Stiedry, years earlier, had told me—of Nikisch's counseling him on the importance for a conductor of having beautiful white hands and three-inch white cuffs.

have ever heard. Remember this name; because you will hear much of it.' . . .

This reminded Burghauser of Toscanini's judgment of Nikisch years later: though he rarely spoke of his colleagues without some reservation, Toscanini had said without *any* reservation that *the* great conductor had been Nikisch. I refrained from saying that when I had asked Toscanini his opinion of Nikisch, his answer had been different: "Is good conductor—but make performance for public [Toscanini made gestures of Nikisch putting on an act]. And sometimes he do not look at [i.e. study] score." Then with increasing intensity: "When I conduct I am always prepared! I do not stand before public to show I am Toscanini—never!"*

The conductors at the Vienna Opera, in those first years, included its co-directors, Richard Strauss and Franz Schalk. By 1928-29, when I was in Vienna, Schalk was Director and principal conductor, and Strauss only appeared occasionally as guest conductor. And whereas I was delighted by Strauss's superb performances of *Così Fan Tutte* and *The Magic Flute,* and amazed by the first-rate playing he got from the third-rate Vienna Symphony of that time in Mozart's Symphony K. 201, Schalk's performances seemed to me products of musically unenlivened technical competence. Burghauser's high estimate of Strauss was therefore not surprising to me; but I was unprepared for what he said about Schalk: that having been engaged by Gustav Mahler at the beginning of the century, he had developed very slowly into one of the greatest opera conductors. (He was not a symphonic conductor, but for many years conducted choral works of Bach and Handel at the monthly concerts of the Society of Friends of Music.)

Burghauser had become acquainted with Schalk's idiosyncratic conducting at the conservatory, where every week Schalk had conducted a student orchestra or opera rehearsal. At such a rehearsal, after beginning the piece, he would leave his music stand and walk about, peering over a

---

*It was Schuch, the great Director of the Dresden Opera, whom Toscanini spoke of warmly without any reservation on this occasion. When I asked about him Toscanini's face lighted up and he exclaimed: "Oh *yes!* Is *good!* Is *good* opera conductor! He came to La Scala—is good conductor of Italian opera. I also hear him in Dresden—I hear *Oberon*—I remember overture is very beautiful." This statement, and others like it, revealed the generous emotion with which Toscanini recognized great achievement by anyone, and the joy it gave him.

student's shoulder at the music and listening to what the instrument or voice was producing, and only now and then returning to his stand to correct dynamics or balance. And the extraordinary thing about this was that his interpretive leadership continued to be felt by the students even when he stopped conducting and was walking about and they couldn't see him.

In the opera house too, when Burghauser began to play there as a young professional, there were not only the times when Schalk appeared to the audience not to be conducting at all, though actually he was making tiny movements with his long baton which the audience couldn't see, but which conveyed their unmistakable significance to the musicians who did see them. There were also the times when Schalk beat only part of the measure; and the times when he didn't do even that: Burghauser recalled how in the scene of the apprentices and girls in the third act of *Die Meistersinger* Schalk would give the first downbeat, then stop beating, lean back, and look at the vocal ensemble and orchestra that performed with the feeling of still being led. All this was possible because the musicians were so well acquainted with him—to the point where there was the essential mental contact between them. It was this mental contact that enabled Schalk to take the orchestra, in his idiosyncratic way, through the hair-raisingly fast and difficult introduction to the third act of *Der Rosenkavalier;* or when a singer suddenly was not together with the orchestra, to get them together again in an instant. Moreover the very fact that Schalk indicated his wishes so slightly and incompletely compelled the musicians playing with him to exercise their maximum of attention and concentration.

This was true also with Strauss, because of a conducting style whose extraordinary economy represented the highest self-discipline. To the audience he appeared immobile; since he kept the movements of his baton in front of his chest, and produced them not with his shoulder or his upper arm but at most with his forearm, and usually with only his wrist. But this minimum activity created an extreme concentration in the musicians; and so his mere glance or smallest movement could elicit from them, in a volcanic work like his *Elektra*, a volcanic response. And in *Tristan und Isolde*, which Strauss himself considered the most dynamic work in the entire literature of opera, there was the contrast between the quiet of his conducting operation and the intensity of expression to which it impelled the performers. Many in the audience were deceived into saying "Strauss again slept through the whole performance"; but the musicians who saw his eyes, the expression on his face, the almost invisible movements of his baton, and who responded to their compulsive force, knew the contrary.

The most interesting and impressive of Burghauser's recollections of Strauss's operation with the Vienna Philharmonic was the one of their two-month South American tour. Strauss wanted to finish the orchestration of his opera *Intermezzo* in those two months; and this may have been the reason for what he decided about rehearsals of their twelve programs. In Rio de Janeiro, where the tour began, he held a hall rehearsal in the large opera house; and in the Colón in Buenos Aires he rehearsed a few crucial transitions; after which he said that since they had played the works together many times and were well acquainted with them, they would from now on meet in the evening at the concert. And the next two months they played the concerts without rehearsals and without a single mishap. Burghauser thought Strauss had counted on the fact that when an orchestra was on tour in a foreign country its concern for its prestige made it play with greater concentration than at home; and that even when the program had been played repeatedly, playing it again without rehearsal also increased that concentration. And actually the orchestra played on this tour with more than its normal precision and expressiveness.

In 1927 Weingartner resigned; and Furtwängler, who in 1922 had succeeded Nikisch as conductor of the Berlin Philharmonic and Leipzig Gewandhaus Orchestras, and who had made guest appearances with the Vienna Philharmonic, accepted its invitation to conduct its entire annual series. When I came to Vienna in the fall of 1928 Schalk and Strauss were still conducting at the State Opera; but whereas I was excited by Strauss's performances of *Così Fan Tutte* and *The Magic Flute*, everyone else in Vienna was excited about Furtwängler; and I discovered that what excited them in his performances first surprised and then shocked me. Most shocking was the performance of Beethoven's Ninth, which, as it happened, I heard only a few days after Karl Muck's performance of it with his Hamburg Philharmonic in Copenhagen. As against the disciplined Muck operation, and the coherently proportioned structure it produced, still fresh in my mind, Furtwängler offered excessively slowed-down *diminuendos* to barely audible *pianissimos* in alternation with frenetically whipped-up *crescendos* to huge *fortissimos*, which achieved not a coherent realization of the music's structure but a demonstration of his fluctuating emotional states. Moreover it was a demonstration to the eye as well as the ear, with his rapt stance in the *diminuendos* and violent gesticulation in the *crescendos*; and it impelled the audience to an outburst of hysteria at the end. Nor was it only Burghauser's "average listeners" whom the Furtwängler operation impressed: at a gathering of what my hostess informed me was the élite of Viennese musical society I was interrogated about my impressions of music in Vienna; and when, instead of agreeing with their admiration of Furtwängler's performances, as was expected of me, I spoke of what had seemed to me open to objection, the response, after a moment of stunned incredulity, was indignation, outrage and personal offensiveness. Asked, for example, what I *had* been impressed by, I said "Strauss's performances of *Così Fan Tutte* and *The Magic Flute*"; which elicited my hostess's disdainful "The worst, of course!"

But Burghauser, when we talked about Furtwängler, not only recognized what I referred to in the performances but gave me an extraordinarily interesting explanation of it which represented the experience of the many years in which he had played under Furtwängler and got to know him well personally. He began with what he wanted to establish first, because of the controversy about it: the fact that Furtwängler was a generous man, kind-hearted and even soft-hearted in his response to appeals to that generosity, and this at great personal risk in the dangerous period of the Third Reich. With that established, Burghauser went on to what had to be said about Furtwängler's conducting: the lack of clarity and decisiveness of the gestures that conveyed to an orchestra what he wanted it to do; the extreme expressiveness in performance that he often carried to the point where it was "over-romantic" and "rhapsodic", with damage to rhythmic structure—all of which made his conducting very different from Weingartner's and Strauss's. And then Burghauser gave his explanation of what was visible and audible in the conducting: that it was related to an important personal characteristic of Furtwängler, namely his vacillation. Whatever the situation—personal, artistic, political—he had great difficulty in making a decision, postponed it as long as possible, and sometimes did not reach it at all. The political example Burghauser cited was his inability—in spite of his moral convictions and moral statements—to reach a clear and definite position and decision concerning the Third Reich. And the same indecision produced his vague initial downbeat, and what Burghauser called his "rhythmic incongruities", by which I understood Burghauser to mean that because Furtwängler was unable to decide his modifications of tempo in advance of the performance and made them on impulse of the instant in the course of the performance, they were often excessive and created disproportion in the rhythmic structure.

Elaborating on this, Burghauser described Furtwängler's very first concert in Vienna in the season of 1913-14—a guest appearance with the Vienna Tonkünstler Orchestra by an unknown young conductor from the Baltic Sea town of Lübeck who, for the opportunity to conduct in Vienna, had agreed to repeat without any rehearsal, at a popular Sunday concert, the program the orchestra had performed under its regular conductor a few days before. Burghauser was one of several students at the conservatory who had been permitted to sit on the stage behind the orchestra, and who, facing Furtwängler, saw him give an initial downbeat (for Beethoven's *Pastoral* Symphony) so vague that none of them could tell when the orchestra was to begin to play. For this downbeat, which remained a prominent and much-discussed feature of his conducting, the orchestras, said Burghauser, developed in time a sixth sense that enabled them to begin—often even to begin correctly, but certainly not always correctly: the two notes of the horns' opening fifth of Beethoven's Ninth were rarely played precisely together. And Furtwängler had answers to the criticism of his practice. Burghauser told me one of them: that a precise and sharp downbeat was, for Furtwängler, not a way of obtaining the concentration and expressiveness he obtained with his slow movement down—down—down. And a musician whose teacher was a close friend of Furtwängler told me another: if, for a quiet entrance, he were to give the usual definite downbeat the entrance would have emphasis, almost an accent, which it should not have; but with *his* downbeat he led the orchestra into an entrance in which the sound appeared to be there out of nowhere. He had an answer also to the criticism of his "rhythmic incongruities"—one, said Burghauser, which denigrated what he was unable to achieve: that in performance of great music rhythmic correctness and precision were of secondary importance; what was of primary importance was "expressiveness, *Steigerung*, build-up, climax."

In 1919, after a few years in Mannheim that had won him fame in

Germany, Furtwängler came to Vienna again, this time as regular conductor of the Tonkünstler Orchestra. The musicians of the orchestra were aware of his technical and musical shortcomings, said Burghauser; but the public was overwhelmed by the expressiveness, build-up and climaxes. Also it was affected by what it saw: Furtwängler's tall, thin body, when he conducted a slow *cantilena*, swayed back asymmetrically; and this stance and the expressive movements of his long arms were, for the public, those of an inspired musician. And from the critics he won great praise as a young exponent of a new expressive (even expression-istic, said Burghauser) style. In the music of Beethoven, Brahms and Bruckner, which he conducted most, he was considered supreme.

Soon he made his first guest appearance with the Vienna Philhar-monic, conducting Brahms's Fourth with unusual restraint in gesture and build-up of dynamics, and achieving a very effective and powerful performance. Recalling only the shapeless first movement of the Brahms Fourth I heard him conduct in Vienna in 1929, I asked Burghauser whether Furtwängler had kept the one tempo throughout the passacaglia of the last movement. His reply was that Furtwängler's liberties in-cluded having the solo flute's two variations played in the style in which an operatic *cantilena* would be sung—something the orchestra's musi-cians simply accepted as part of his romantic style. In time they learned how completely he was dominated by this tendency to "romanticize"; and they could accept it in Beethoven's Fourth, Sixth and Eighth Sym-phonies; but in the *Eroica*, the Fifth and the Seventh they found it far removed from any classical tradition and from what Weingartner had established for them as the style of Beethoven. Of the Ninth, which was considered Furtwängler's greatest achievement, Burghauser said that whenever Furtwängler conducted a chorus he excited it to a point where the 80 or 100 people were overpowering and really did in the finale affect the public as the words "*Seid umschlungen, ihr Millionen*" said. But in the first two movements the musicians of the orchestra were disturbed by the imprecise ensemble playing that didn't disturb the public; and in the slow movement Furtwängler made the expression of feeling so romantic that it produced what for the musicians was something Schumannesque, not a movement of a classical symphony. The public, however, seeing a conductor who appeared inspired, believed it was hearing a great per-formance; and the ovations it gave him expressed its conviction that Furtwängler was not merely the greatest conductor of his time but the greatest of all time—which meant greater than Richter, von Bülow, Mottl, Mahler, Nikisch, and which the musicians felt could not be true. The public's fanatical near-worship continued until Furtwängler's death; whereas to the musicians who played under him during the last year or more of his life it was evident that illness had left him with one ear not functioning and with an inability to coordinate what was being done in the pit with what was being done on the stage. And in this connection Burghauser mentioned that while he was much loved in Vienna by the public he was much feared by the critics, who didn't dare to express the slightest disapproval of anything he did, because he could and would go over their heads to their editors with complaints that could cause them great trouble.

Eventually Burghauser came to the attempt, in the spring of 1929, to persuade Furtwängler to leave Berlin and succeed Schalk as Director of the State Opera. Here, Burghauser said with reluctance, Furtwängler revealed his character in what amounted to "shocking ethical mis-behavior". His acceptance of the directorship at the end of the spring followed the necessary negotiations about details of the contract, and the two performances that he conducted at the State Opera in June as a sort of audition, since he had until then not conducted opera in Vienna (the performance of *Das Rheingold* Burghauser described as "in the best Bayreuth style"; the one of *The Marriage of Figaro* as "not the best"). The announcement of his engagement was made some time before the date of the formal signing of the contract; and the endless interviews that followed were noteworthy for the fact that whereas usually his statements were not precise, now they didn't leave even the slightest doubt. Nevertheless the sensational event occurred which nobody—possibly not even Furtwängler, said Burghauser—could have anticipated. On the day before the expected signing of the contract Furtwängler was in Vienna, giving interviews that were published; on the day of the signing a telegram from him in Berlin informed the officials in Vienna that he could not sign the contract. There was no explanation; and the news-papers in Vienna could only publish the official announcement in the Berlin papers that Furtwängler was remaining in Berlin as General Musical Director of the city's entire musical activity—this in addition to continuing as chief conductor of the Berlin Philharmonic. In time it was learned that he had been persuaded by the offer in addition of an extraordinary salary, a residence in the city, a villa in Potsdam, a private hunting lodge, and even a car with a chauffeur.

An inevitable consequence of Furtwängler's breaking his commitment to the Vienna State Opera was his withdrawal from the Vienna Philharmonic's concerts; but in a shrewd move to preserve a link with the orchestra and with Vienna he offered to conduct the annual concert in honor of the orchestra's founder, Nicolai; and the offer was accepted. As for the Opera, his last-minute rejection created not only great embarrassment for the administration but the difficulty of filling the vacuum he had created in the little time now available.

The administration's choice was a young Viennese, Clemens Krauss, Director of the Frankfurt Opera and conductor of the Frankfurt Museum Concerts. His coming to the Vienna State Opera benefited by a good advance press and what Burghauser called "a favorable psychological climate." For in addition to his good looks he had about him the aura of the kind of legend that was a favorite preoccupation of the Viennese: he was said to be the son of the beautiful and popular ballet dancer Clementine Krauss and the popular Archduke Eugen, an art-lover and fine musician; and this was advantageous to Krauss because the Viennese, though leftist in current politics, were sentimental about the past and its Habsburgs. To the Archduke's tall figure Krauss chose to add a Spanish appearance with his sideburns, toreador's cloak and Calabrese hat.

Krauss, said Burghauser, had a smooth conducting technique which resembled that of his teacher, Schalk, but was more decisive and precise. Years earlier, in his late twenties, he had conducted the entire repertory at the Opera easily and flawlessly; now, in his middle thirties, he limited his conducting to new productions—which meant that at first he conducted very little but commanded greater attention on the rare occasions when he did conduct. And what he did on those occasions was remarkably good—an outstanding example being his Vienna première of Alban Berg's *Wozzeck*. In addition, with Weingartner and Furtwängler gone, and the popular Bruno Walter fully occupied with his Charlottenburg Opera in Berlin and Gewandhaus Orchestra in Leipzig, there was no alternative to Krauss to propose as conductor of the Philharmonic concerts; and in these too he introduced a new repertory which interested the critics but was not liked by the orchestra's conservative audience.

Unfortunately there was in 1929 the beginning of the financial crisis which within two years reduced this audience by half, so that the Philharmonic's income was insufficient for its obligations. As a way of creating interest that would increase attendance the orchestra suggested to Krauss that half of the concerts be conducted by guests; but he rejected the suggestion, saying he would conduct all the concerts or none; and though the orchestra was autonomous in its concert activity, it could not create difficulties with the man who in the opera house would continue for some years to exercise power over it as Director and chief conductor. But in the spring of 1933, with the term of his opera contract approaching its end, the orchestra informed him of its long-deliberated decision to have a number of conductors, including him, for its 1933-34 series, and to have the others without him if he so chose. His immediate angry response was to cancel his appearance at the current season's final concert, for which the orchestra engaged Karl Böhm, then a young conductor in Graz. In addition Krauss withdrew from the orchestra's post-season tour of Italy; and Burghauser, its new chairman, informed him that for this too they would engage someone else. Hitler had made a number of prominent conductors available; and one of them had actually been engaged when, at the last moment, Krauss announced his decision to conduct the tour after all.

Among the conductors whom Hitler had made available were Otto Klemperer, who earlier had directed the Kroll Opera and then had conducted at the State Opera in Berlin, and Bruno Walter. Each was invited to conduct a special post-season concert of the Vienna Philharmonic; and since Klemperer's concert would be his first in Vienna he considered carefully what to perform, and finally suggested Bruckner's biggest symphony, the Eighth, which Burghauser gladly accepted. But when Klemperer arrived at the Musikvereinsaal for the first rehearsal Burghauser told him of the difficulty that had arisen. When he had conferred with Klemperer in Berlin he hadn't known that a performance of Bruckner's Eighth had been scheduled for the same week as Klemperer's by the Konzerthaus, Vienna's other concert hall; and its management had pointed out to him that if Klemperer, making his first appearance in Vienna with the Philharmonic, conducted Bruckner's Eighth, then the Konzerthaus performance of the Eighth would have no audience. Burghauser therefore asked Klemperer if he could change the program, and was astounded when Klemperer answered that he would

conduct any one of the other eight Bruckner symphonies that Burghauser preferred, and—Burghauser having suggested the Fifth, another
big and powerful work—proceeded to rehearse it immediately without a
score.

Klemperer's initial downbeat, the orchestra's first concern, was clear,
said Burghauser; his beat thereafter, though stiff, also was clear; his
conducting style was for the most part conventional. But what produced
the impressive result that a conventional style usually didn't produce was
the unconventional movement of his left hand, which Burghauser said
was like a conjuror's in the way it conveyed and achieved his expressive
intention in this music that was prayer-like in its expression of religious
feeling. As an ardent converted Catholic Klemperer found this feeling
especially congenial, and was especially successful in conveying it: in the
finale of the Fifth Symphony the culmination of the double fugue in the
chorale of the brass had an effect it had never had in any previous
performance. Until then Furtwängler and Bruno Walter had been considered the outstanding conductors of Bruckner; but with this performance of the Fifth, his performance of the Eighth in Salzburg that
summer, and his performance of the Ninth at a special concert for the
international Eucharistic Congress in Vienna in September, Klemperer
demonstrated that he, not Furtwängler and Walter, was the greatest and
most impressive conductor of Bruckner's symphonies. And what was
noteworthy was that he achieved their greater expressive effectiveness
with performances that were kept within the limits of a classical style and
a clear, coherent rhythmic structure—in contrast with the performances
of Furtwängler and Walter, whose extreme rhythmic freedom and
irregularity romanticized and sentimentalized the works. Burghauser
was aware that these romanticized and sentimentalized performances
had great popular appeal, but maintained that professional musicians
shared his view of them as dilettantism, even if the dilettantism of
technically gifted and musically sensitive conductors. The feeling of the
professional musicians was that Klemperer had provided a replacement
of what had been lost with Weingartner and Strauss.

The entire orchestra was so impressed by Klemperer's extraordinary
first concert that he was engaged for the opening concert of the Philharmonic's series late in September. Earlier in September there was an
unsuccessful attempt by a rival conductor to wreck the special concert
for the Eucharistic Congress by informing Cardinal Innitzer of Klem-

perer's involvement in a scandalous incident in Hamburg many years before; and the Philharmonic's first regular concert provided an opportunity for Krauss to make trouble. To avoid conflict with its work at the Opera the orchestra carried on its concert activity on weekends: Saturday afternoon for the public general rehearsal, Sunday at noon for the concert. But on this occasion in September 1933 the Musikvereinsaal was not available on Saturday afternoon; therefore the general rehearsal had to be shifted to Sunday at noon, and the concert to Monday evening, when there was a performance at the Opera. Burghauser persuaded an administrative officer there to schedule for that evening Strauss's *Ariadne auf Naxos*, whose small orchestral requirements freed the players Klemperer needed for Beethoven's *Eroica*, and whose cast included none of his soloists in a Bach contata. But on the Monday of the concert the solo tenor in the cantata was notified that he would have to sing in *Ariadne* that night; and so Burghauser had to plead with Krauss, who enjoyed being able to point out that Burghauser ran the orchestra but he, Krauss, ran the Opera, and the tenor was not available for the concert. In the end Burghauser advised Krauss to consider the effect of what would have to be done: since there was no other way of informing the audience, Burghauser, at the moment when the concert was to begin, would announce there would be no concert because the tenor for the Bach cantata had been required to sing in *Ariadne* at the Opera; and since the audience would know the tenor was not needed for *Ariadne* it would perceive the nature and intent of the Opera's action. Thereupon Krauss laughed heartily at what he said was Burghauser's inability to understand a joke, and told him that of course the tenor could sing at the concert.

With this opening concert of the regular series out of the way, Burghauser's next concern was two extraordinarily important special concerts in October; but before beginning with these I will give the conclusion of his report on Klemperer, which dealt with the final concert of the Philharmonic's series that Klemperer conducted in the spring of 1934. After the Wagnerian sound one had heard in Klemperer's performances of Bruckner, said Burghauser, one wasn't prepared for the fine and subtly differentiated sound he produced in his performance of Mendelssohn's music for *A Midsummer Night's Dream*, which Burghauser characterized as "an acoustic miracle". And equally impressive in its contrasting way was his performance of Stravinsky's *Petrushka*. With the success of this concert, after the successes of the previous ones, the orchestra looked forward to a continuing collaboration with him; but this prospect was ended by his acceptance of the invitation to become conductor of the orchestra in Los Angeles.*

As for the Philharmonic's special concerts in October 1933, their extraordinary importance was the fact that they were to be conducted by Toscanini. In May 1929 he had concluded his long association with La Scala by taking the company to Berlin for nine performances of Italian opera; and on the way they had stopped in Vienna to perform *Falstaff* and *Lucia di Lammermoor*. I was still in Vienna at the time and heard the performances. But though I, like the Viennese, heard Toscanini's performances of these particular operas for the first time, I had heard other performances of his—a few in 1914-15 at the Metropolitan Opera, and in more recent years many with the New York Philharmonic—which had acquainted me with the distinctive characteristics of his performing style that made these performances of *Falstaff* and *Lucia* the marvels they were; whereas the *Falstaff* and *Lucia* gave the Viennese their first experiences of a performing style, and performances in that style, the like of which they had never heard. And since they had believed until then that what they heard in Vienna surpassed anything that was to be heard elsewhere, the

---

*This statement brought me an unpublished article from the violinist Louis Krasner, from which I learned that on 25 October 1936 Klemperer conducted the Vienna Philharmonic in the first performance in Vienna of Alban Berg's Violin Concerto, with Krasner as soloist. I learned also what had happened in the weeks before that concert. Opposition by the anti-Semitic Nazi organizations and Stahremberg fascists—to the music they attacked as *"Kultur-Bolshevist"*; to the conductor, a devout convert to Catholicism, but for them still a Jew; to the Jewish soloist—had led to pressures, from government officials and members of the orchestra, for cancelation of the Berg concerto. These pressures Klemperer had resisted, with support from the orchestra's principal concertmaster, Arnold Rosé, who had announced that contrary to custom he would be in the concertmaster's chair for the performance of the concerto. And uncertainty whether the work would be performed had continued until the day before the first scheduled rehearsal, ending only after Klemperer, on that day, had sent word to the Philharmonic that if the concerto was not retained in the program he would not conduct the concert. (He was a box-office attraction the orchestra could not afford to lose.) There had been tension at the rehearsals; there was audible excitement at the concert; and after the Berg concerto there was an unprecedented gesture by the orchestra: at the instant when the work's concluding sound faded into silence the orchestra rose as if on command and marched off the stage. To this the gesture in reply was made by the one player who remained on stage, Rosé, who stood by his chair applauding Klemperer and Krasner, and then stepped forward to clasp their hands.

experience of these performances that surpassed any they had ever heard was overwhelming. Some may have reflected that the experience had been limited to performances of Italian operas; but a year later Toscanini had come to Vienna with the New York Philharmonic and overwhelmed the Viennese with his performances of the orchestral literature—performances which, a Viennese friend wrote to W. J. Turner, "showed us things in Beethoven and Wagner that we Germans never heard before." And as a result there were again invitations to Toscanini to conduct in Vienna, which, like the previous ones, he didn't answer.

But in the spring of 1933 Burghauser, as newly elected chairman of the Vienna Philharmonic, had written another invitation to Toscanini; and in his recollections in 1966 for *The Toscanini Musicians Knew* he ascribed Toscanini's acceptance this time to the bit of "psychological diplomacy" he had put into his letter: his statement that the orchestra realized Toscanini's high standards, and therefore if its duties at the State Opera didn't leave enough rehearsal time during the day for him it was willing to rehearse with him after the evening's opera for as long as he would wish. This gave me the impression that Toscanini had accepted immediately; but in the talks a few years later it turned out that months had passed in which Burghauser too had received no answer to his letter. However, one of the visitors in Salzburg that summer was the violinist Huberman, who was spending the summer at Lago Maggiore. He talked with Burghauser about the insufficient number of qualified players, among the immigrants in Palestine, for the orchestra he was planning to form there—a matter in which Burghauser was able to offer helpful suggestions. And since Huberman was expecting to visit Toscanini, Burghauser in turn asked him to mention his letter and if possible to obtain an answer from Toscanini. The evidence of Huberman's success in this mission, said Burghauser, was the telegram that arrived soon afterwards with Toscanini's characteristically simple and brief statement that he consented to conduct two programs in Vienna on 24 and 29 October. But when Burghauser related his subsequent experiences with Toscanini I felt certain that Huberman had succeeded only because of Burghauser's "psychological diplomacy" in his letter. To Toscanini—who had left the Metropolitan Opera, he told me, because of its failure to maintain the discipline and high standard he insisted on, and had walked out of other situations for the same reason—Burghauser's statement about rehearsals had revealed an understanding of those standards and a willingness to do what they required; and this must have been what caused him to accept the invitation. And it did more than that. I had had opportunities to observe Toscanini's response to someone who he thought understood and shared his feeling about how music had to be treated in every dealing with it—that response being a trust as simple and direct, and in this as moving, as a child's. And it was clear to me that such trust in Burghauser had produced the behavior in Vienna that Burghauser told me about, in which Toscanini repeatedly had surprised him by not being the "difficult" person he could be.

Thus, when Toscanini arrived on the morning of 20 October he told Burghauser he had had a bad night in the sleeping car and therefore wished to postpone the first rehearsal to the next day; to which Burghauser replied hesitantly that if Toscanini did not appear at the Musikvereinsaal where the newspaper reporters were waiting they undoubtedly would invent sensational stories for their papers about some conjectured conflict, and that for this reason he begged Toscanini to come to the hall to rehearse just for a few minutes—which Toscanini, without demur, agreed to do. When, after two subsequent full-length rehearsals of the first program—Mozart's *Haffner* Symphony, Brahms's Haydn Variations, Beethoven's Seventh, Wagner's *Meistersinger* Prelude—Burghauser inquired about the additional rehearsals Toscanini would want, Toscanini answered that since everything was good no further rehearsals were needed. Before the rehearsal of Debussy's *La Mer* for the second concert he ascertained from Burghauser that the orchestra, as he had surmised, didn't know this work, and commented that it was *"tanto difficile"*; so there appeared to be reason to expect a stormy rehearsal; but it turned out instead that Toscanini—finding the orchestra to be, in Burghauser's words, "full of goodwill and concentration"—was extremely patient in the joint effort that achieved a performance which fully satisfied him. There were invitations to repeat the concerts in neighboring countries; and when Burghauser ventured to suggest a repetition of one of the programs in Budapest, explaining that the orchestra played there frequently, Toscanini's reply, he said, was like that of an old family friend: *"Sì, faciamolo.* Yes, we'll do it." At the reception after the concert in Budapest one of the guests was the composer Kodály, whose *Psalmus Hungaricus* had been performed by Toscanini at La Scala; and the consequence of their encounter was Toscanini's statement to Burghauser, "I am thinking of performing Kodály's *Psalmus Hungaricus*," which overwhelmed him with its revelation that Toscanini was expecting to conduct the orchestra again, and the fact that the chorus for Kodály's work made it possible to perform Beethoven's Ninth. In Vienna the next day, when Burghauser was saying goodbye to Toscanini, he asked whether they could hope the program he had mentioned would be performed the following autumn; and Toscanini's answer was *"Sì, naturalmente."* This impelled Burghauser to ask further what actually he had no authority to ask—whether, after almost a year's separation, it wouldn't be desirable for Toscanini and the orchestra first to repeat in Salzburg next summer the two programs they had just performed; and again Toscanini's reply was a mere *"Sì, va bene."* Only when the Director of the Salzburg Festival considered it necessary to ask Toscanini to confirm to him the commitment reported by Burghauser did Toscanini protest: "But I have already said yes. Why again?" And this continued to be true in the years that followed: it was the occasional intervention of others that resulted in difficulties with Toscanini, whereas Burghauser found that one thing led easily to the next—the concerts in Vienna in 1933 to the ones in Salzburg and Vienna in 1934, these to the concerts and the operas *Fidelio* and *Falstaff* in Salzburg in 1935, and these to the Salzburg *Meistersinger* in 1936 and *Magic Flute* in 1937.

For the orchestra there were the surprises of Toscanini's unfamiliar and idiosyncratic operation as conductor and musician, and what this operation achieved. Toscanini's baton, said Burghauser, did not describe the traditional geometric patterns that orchestra musicians are accustomed to rely on and look for; but its unconventional movements indicated his wishes so clearly and unmistakably that one felt oneself being led with complete assurance as if by a seer. Except in a big climax those movements involved no more than Toscanini's forearm; and it was the tip of his long baton that was most significant to the player—that told him he was to play not *piano* but *pianissimo*, not *forte* but *mezzo-forte*. Equally novel and idiosyncratic was Toscanini's use of his left hand: the horizontal movement like that of blessing, which achieved overall balance in the orchestra—a phenomenon, said Burghauser, that was a new experience for the orchestra; the forefinger raised to his lips that achieved an extraordinary delicacy; the middle finger placed on his heart with a cellist's slight vibrato that achieved the finest and most intense *espressivo.** In addition to the movements there was the powerful glance that signalled, a bar in advance, every entrance of a section or a solo player, so that one saw what Burghauser in 1966 described as a "parallel conducting of what was going on now and what was coming the next moment"—another phenomenon that was a new experience for the orchestra.** And there was Toscanini's novel practice, when he had a section of the orchestra play its part alone, of singing one of the other parts with it—which, said Burghauser, made the orchestra play with great plasticity, since Toscanini's singing, though hoarse, was tremendously expressive.

What Burghauser had spoken of in Strauss's conducting operation— the powerful effect on the orchestra of his smallest movement or mere glance—was true also of Toscanini's, and to an even more extraordinary degree. "Miraculous" was Burghauser's term for the *espressivo* that resulted from Toscanini's merely placing his middle finger on his heart with a cellist's slight vibrato; one almost held one's breath, he said, as Toscanini's mere raising his forefinger to his lips produced the utmost in delicacy and subtlety. And from this Burghauser went on to speak of the impact of such subtleties on those who experienced them—citing the powerful effect, in the musical progression characterized by what Burghauser called "rhythmic severity", of Toscanini's slight modifications of tempo; recalling how in a love scene his *crescendo* from *pianissimo* to *mezzo-forte* (as against Bruno Walter's from *piano* to *fortissimo*) achieved an expressive tenderness beyond any that Burghauser had ever experienced; recalling further the "acoustic phenomenon of eerie quiet" at the end of *Scene at the Brook* in Beethoven's *Pastoral* Symphony, which the musicians of the Vienna Philharmonic, after having played the work every year of their lives, experienced for the first time when they played it with Toscanini.

They had expected, before Toscanini's coming, some undefined greatness; but the actual powers he demonstrated, and what those

*The left hand did considerably more: in 1946 I wrote about its "constant and fascinating activity as the instrument of the watchfulness that shows itself on Toscanini's face—now exhorting, now quieting, now warning, now suppressing."
**An American horn-player told how when he had a number of bars' rest that he was counting in reverse, increasingly nervous as he counted "five—four—three", he would look up one bar before his entrance and find Toscanini's eye on him, and then simply find himself playing, as though Toscanini had reached out and drawn him in.

powers achieved, in the creation of the two concerts in October 1933 overwhelmed them. They could scarcely believe they had really participated in that creation of sound, rhythm, climax, of subtle nuances in color, rhythm, intensity. For Burghauser, who had been with the orchestra fifteen years, and for those in it who had played with Brahms, it constituted a wholly new musical life. And whereas in 1966 he had summed all this up in the statement that after its years with Weingartner, Strauss, Bruno Walter, Furtwängler, Klemperer, "the orchestra, with Toscanini, realized that this was the climax of every musician's experience. Not only because he was superior to other conductors . . . but because he made us *superior to ourselves*"—now, a few years later, he astonished me with the statement that Toscanini's achievement with them surpassed what they had heard him achieve in Vienna in opera with La Scala and in concerts with the New York Philharmonic. Nor was it only they who believed this, Burghauser added when he saw the astonishment and doubt on my face, but Toscanini: though known as one for whom perfection was an unattainable goal—for whom, that is, there were always details in a performance that did not satisfy him—he said of what they did with him that "it was simply perfect."

However, though I felt no need to try to persuade Burghauser, my doubts remained, not only because of what I remembered hearing, but because of a revealing statement by Toscanini reported to me by Alfred Wallenstein. He had, after a rehearsal at La Scala, pointed out to Toscanini that he had let the orchestra's out-of-tune playing pass without comment, whereas such playing in New York would have caused him to walk out of the rehearsal; to which Toscanini had replied: "That is because in New York I know they can do it, but here I know they cannot." Toscanini, that is, recognized and adapted himself to the different capacities of the orchestras he conducted; he knew, therefore, what he might expect of each, what was its own best, its own perfection; and he smiled as happily after his La Scala *Falstaff* and *Lucia* in Vienna in 1929 as after his Salzburg *Fidelio*, *Falstaff*, *Magic Flute* and *Meistersinger* in 1937, after the Vienna Philharmonic's performance of the Brahms-Haydn Variations in 1937 as after the New York Philharmonic's in 1935. But I am sure he knew not only that the La Scala Orchestra's best in 1929 was surpassed by the Vienna Philharmonic's in 1937, but that the Vienna Philharmonic's breathtaking perfection in the Brahms-Haydn Variations had been surpassed by the New York Philharmonic's. And he actually said once that the New York Philharmonic had been the greatest of the orchestras he had conducted.

After Toscanini's departure Burghauser and the orchestra looked forward to the two concerts with Bruno Walter. A native of Berlin, said Burghauser, Walter had, 30 years earlier, been engaged by Gustav Mahler as one of his assistant conductors at the Vienna Court Opera; and in his long association with Vienna a love had developed between him and the public that had led him to declare himself a *Wahl-Österreicher*— an Austrian by choice. This association had continued after he had left the Vienna Opera: having, contrary to general expectation, not been appointed Director when Mahler, in 1907, resigned to go to the Metropolitan in New York, Walter in 1912 accepted the post of Director of the Munich Court Opera. And whereas in Vienna he had been only a local celebrity, overshadowed by Mahler, in his prominent new post he soon acquired eminence throughout Europe. Moreoever, his musical prestige was reinforced by his connections with literary movements and his friendship with Thomas Mann, a resident of Munich, which gave him the reputation of a literary connoisseur and provided him with a spiritual soundboard. The cosmopolitan outlook of Mann and Walter and their group would later compromise them in the eyes of the Hitler régime; but in the 1920s it contributed to the fame that produced Walter's comet-like rise. His achievements in Munich led to his appointment as conductor of the Leipzig Gewandhaus Orchestra; in 1925 he became Director of the Charlottenburg Opera in Berlin, which he raised to the first rank; and as one of the founders of the Salzburg Festivals he was, in their early years, the major figure in their symphonic and operatic activities.

In this period he came as guest to conduct special concerts of the Vienna Philharmonic, which, except for an occasional work of Mozart or Schubert, he devoted to the music of Mahler. He owed his popularity in Vienna in part to his devotion to, and identification with, Mahler and his music; and it was he who, a year after Mahler's death, conducted in Vienna the world première of *Das Lied von der Erde*. Burghauser stressed the excellence of Walter's performance of this work, its superiority to all others, he said, because of Walter's shortcomings as a conductor of most symphonic music. Describing the forceful movements of Walter's left hand that suddenly, as if on the spur of the moment, called forth extreme changes and contrasts of dynamics and made the distinctive characteristic of his performances their seeming impetuousness and uncontrolled impulse, Burghauser thought all this had its roots in Walter's lifelong conducting of Mahler's music with its abundance of sudden forceful contrasts, and that Walter's transference of his manner of conducting Mahler to the music of other composers amounted to eccentricity. The other defect that Burghauser spoke of was Walter's weakness in rhythm. When in time he recognized the need of extending his repertory, he chose the symphonies of Bruckner, whose romanticism and religious feeling he felt were fully realized in performance by his extreme rhythmic freedom. The public accepted this rhapsodic style as authentic for Bruckner; whereas for a professional musician its liberties produced what Burghauser characterized as a dissolution of the work's rhythmic anatomy. It was only years later that Klemperer demonstrated the greater effectiveness of the performances of Bruckner whose build-ups to their climaxes were achieved within a strictly maintained rhythmic structure. And when this strictly maintained rhythm of Klemperer, and also of Toscanini, was accepted as correct, Walter's style was seen to be weak.

But all this, Burghauser emphasized, was true only of Walter's symphonic conducting, not of his conducting of opera: his performances of Mozart's and Verdi's operas in the 1920s and 30s were unequalled. The singers' liberties that were normal in opera worked against a strictly rhythmic performance; and Walter, with his skill and flexibility as an accompanist, fitted his liberties around theirs.

Walter's rise was ended suddenly and brutally early in 1933 by the advent of the Hitler régime. He was one of the prominent musicians who had persisted in believing they would be treated as exceptions because they would be needed for the régime's cultural prestige. But at the moment when Walter was to begin a concert of the Leipzig Gewandhaus Orchestra the police appeared in the hall and forced him to leave, alleging that they were doing this to protect him from the violent demonstrations that would otherwise occur. Within 48 hours Walter received an invitation from the Vienna Philharmonic to conduct it in a special concert—which he did a fortnight later. And the success of this concert led to his being engaged as one of the orchestra's permanent guest conductors of its regular subscription series.

Burghauser's recollection of the special concert early in 1933 included an accident that was minor in itself but had major significance. The program featured Mozart's Piano Concerto K. 466, with Walter playing the solo part and conducting from the piano. Walter was the only one who did this at that time; and it was always an extraordinary achievement and a great success with the public. But on this occasion, at one point in the finale of the concerto, his fingers took a wrong course which led them to a section that had already been played. Since this was a work it knew very well, the orchestra was able to jump back to where it rejoined the piano with only a moment of confusion in the uninterrupted performance. On another occasion the mishap would have been amusing; but at this concert Burghauser recognized it as a manifestation of the state of shock of the prominent musicians who had been cruelly uprooted by the Nazis. Someone who, like Burghauser, was familiar with their work in former years could hear the effect of their experience in their performances—in the loss of rhythmic firmness and correctness, resulting in rhythmic structure that Burghauser characterized as "out of joint". The one exception, he said, was Klemperer, who continued to exhibit neurotic eccentricities in private, but not in his musical activity in public.

Walter's two concerts in the Philharmonic's regular series in the fall of 1933 revealed something else of major importance. Conducting the orchestra a few weeks after Toscanini, Walter had the same experience as Furtwängler when, in 1926, he had returned to the New York Philharmonic after Toscanini's guest engagement: the impression of Toscanini's performances on the public caused it to respond to Walter's with much less than its usual warmth. And this turned out to be the experience of all the other conductors—Kleiber, Busch, Weingartner, even Furtwängler—accustomed to the acclaim of a public that had regarded them as unsurpassed: conducting now in Vienna, Budapest, Salzburg after Toscanini, they encountered a diminished response which bewildered them, since understanding it required them to acknowledge that the public was in effect declaring its belief in Toscanini's superiority; and which reduced them to despair, since their greatest, even frantic, efforts proved to be of no avail in the situation: whatever they did was overshadowed by Toscanini's achievements. This had not been anticipated by the Philharmonic, which recognized that it was unjust and tragic, said Burghauser, but had to accept it as the hard reality for the next four years. As such it caused the despairing conductors to fight back, each in his own manner; and Burghauser's account of the period from 1933 to 1937 included a description of the behind-the-scene counter-moves and intrigues whose defeat made possible the great artistic achievements presented to the public.

The first backstage move against Toscanini was made by Clemens Krauss, and was indirect. He was aware of how Burghauser's involvement with Toscanini's visit had—because he was someone with whom Toscanini could communicate in his own language and whose good faith Toscanini trusted—kept that visit undisturbed by misunderstandings and other difficulties; and he could expect that if Burghauser were eliminated those misunderstandings and difficulties would arise and build up to the point where, as in the past, Toscanini would put an end to his frustration and exasperation with an abrupt departure. And so Krauss directed his attack at Burghauser, who during the lull of the Christmas holiday period was summoned to the office of the General Intendant of the State Opera, where that official requested his resignation from the Opera orchestra, which would automatically remove him from the Philharmonic. But Burghauser demanded the investigative court proceeding to which he was legally entitled, and at which he would learn what he was accused of, confront the witnesses and be permitted to reply. And at this proceeding before an administrative court, a few weeks later, he discovered that the witnesses were four musical scholars and critics, including Paul Stefan and Max Graf, whose written testimony, when read, accused Burghauser of having tried to persuade them to collaborate with him in the publication of derogatory material about Krauss's operatic and concert activity, which would damage the prestige of the Opera and the Philharmonic. When this testimony had been read, however, the four protested that it misrepresented their original statements, and that they never would make those alleged accusations against Burghauser. The judges were left with what had been revealed as a machination of Krauss; and Burghauser soon received a communication from the Minister of Education and Culture, Kurt von Schuschnigg, stating that since the accusations had turned out to be unsubstantiated there was no reason to continue the investigation. The immediate consequence was Burghauser's return to his post and his activities; but the following year, when Schuschnigg, now Chancellor after Dollfuss's assassination in the summer of 1934, encountered Burghauser in the Philharmonic's guest box, he told him that, having been enlightened by the intrigue of the preceeding year, he would be accessible for any future appeal by Burghauser for assistance. And it was in fact only with this assistance from Schuschnigg that the artistic successes with Toscanini in the next few years were achieved.

As it happened, at the time Schuschnigg gave Burghauser his reassurance the sequence of events that would eventually require his intervention had already begun. As Burghauser had related it to me in 1966 for *The Toscanini Musicians Knew*, the European crisis set off by the Dollfuss assassination in the summer of 1934 caused a flight of foreigners from Salzburg that left it as desolate as if an earthquake had struck it; but Toscanini fulfilled his promise and arrived in mid-August to conduct his two programs of the preceding October. This led the Austrian government to ask him, through Burghauser, if he would conduct Verdi's *Requiem* for Dollfuss in Vienna in the fall—to which Toscanini replied that he would. And it led the directors of the Salzburg Festival to ask him if he would conduct opera the following summer—to which his reply was that he would conduct *Fidelio* if they agreed to his also conducting *Falstaff*. This would require the participation of singers from La Scala, including Mariano Stabile in the title role, who would sing in Italian, as had never before been done in Salzburg, even in the Mozart operas with Italian texts. (Burghauser saw a political gesture in Toscanini's insistence on a performance of *Falstaff* in Italian in this German town only three miles from the border of Nazi Germany; and perhaps it was that too; but I think it is important to point out the artistic reason, reinforced by strong personal feeling, that I am certain would have made him insist on *Falstaff* even if there had been a democratic Germany three miles from Salzburg. It was his determination that a great Italian composer must be accorded the same esteem as a great German; and I am certain because it was what he said to the NBC Symphony when they rehearsed music by Verdi which he suspected them of not respecting sufficiently: "Is not important only to play Wagner; is important also to play Verdi; and if you do not understand this, is worse for you!")

The Salzburg directors did accept *Falstaff*; whereupon Krauss, early in the fall of 1934, announced a production of *Falstaff* at the State Opera that season, to be conducted by him. It was entirely legitimate for him to do so; but it was customary for new productions in Vienna to be transferred to Salzburg; and so Krauss was announcing, in effect, that he, not Toscanini, would conduct *Falstaff* in Salzburg the following summer. Toscanini, asked whether he would be willing to conduct another opera in place of *Falstaff* with *Fidelio*, answered: "No *Falstaff*, no Toscanini": and the administration of the State Opera did nothing further, hoping that something would turn up and remove the difficulty before the summer.

In addition to this time bomb set for the following summer there was the trouble Krauss was literally in a position to make immediately for the Toscanini performance of Verdi's *Requiem*. It was to take place not in the Musikvereinsaal, where the Vienna Philharmonic rehearsed and gave its concerts, and where Burghauser, as its elected chairman, exercised a chief executive's powers in everything connected with the orchestra's operation; instead it was to take place in the State Opera, where Krauss, in his position of Musical Director, exercised those chief executive's powers over the Opera's personnel in its activity there, including the members of the Vienna Philharmonic when they played there as members of the orchestra of the State Opera, and including Burghauser, who was, here, only a bassoonist in that orchestra. This made it possible for Krauss to achieve his objective of depriving Toscanini of Burghauser's guidance and assistance by ordering Burghauser, when he was in the opera house in connection with the *Requiem*, to remain with the orchestra and have no contact with Toscanini. On the day of the first orchestral rehearsal, therefore, Burghauser sat with the waiting orchestra while Toscanini walked alone from the Hotel Bristol across the street to the stage entrance of the State Opera, where the man at the door asked him what he wanted and—being told *"Ho una prova"*—answered: "No stranger may enter here!" So Toscanini returned to the hotel while the orchestra waited in the opera house. After a time a search party was sent out and found Toscanini in a fury in his hotel suite, where he now refused to rehearse in the Opera. The rehearsals were therefore transferred to the Musikvereinsaal, where Burghauser could expect to be able to protect Toscanini from further machinations of Krauss.

But at the first piano rehearsal with the solo soprano the co-repetiteur from the State Opera who should have been there to play the piano failed to appear—because, he explained later, he had not been notified of the rehearsal. So Toscanini sat down at the piano, put his pince-nez on his nose, and began to play for the soprano. When at one point he stopped and asked her to sing a phrase in one breath, instead of breaking it to take breath, she answered that she was accustomed to breaking it and showed him her score in which Bruno Walter had marked the break—at which

Toscanini, still quiet, told her she would have to sing it as he asked. There were a few more such exchanges, increasing the danger of a storm; and then Toscanini's pince-nez fell off his nose to the floor. Before Burghauser could get there Toscanini was on the floor groping for the pince-nez, which he found; and sitting down again he put it back on his nose, only to discover that he couldn't see the music because the lenses had fallen out. In exasperation and fury he jumped up with a stamp of his feet; and at the terrible sound of the lenses being crushed the soprano burst into tears and fled from the room. It took more than a month to find another suitable soprano who was willing to sing as Toscanini wished; and the performance of the *Requiem* didn't take place until 1 November.

The last choral rehearsal for the *Requiem* had been held in a rehearsal room at the State Opera; and to get to it Toscanini had had to pass through the auditorium, where the stage rehearsal of the first scene of the last act of *Falstaff* was in progress. Inevitably Toscanini stopped to listen and to look through his pince-nez at the stage, where he saw not what he should have seen—Falstaff sitting outside the inn, drying and warming himself in the sun—but Falstaff in his room, in bed under a mass of bedclothes. Outraged, Toscanini warned Burghauser that if this set appeared in Salzburg he would walk out of the theater; and Burghauser, after reassuring him, impressed on the administration of the State Opera the necessity of having the correct outdoor set for Toscanini the following summer.

As time passed and the administration did nothing about the difficulty created by Krauss's intention to conduct *Falstaff* in Salzburg, Burghauser appealed to Schuschnigg, who decided that the agreement between the administration and Toscanini would be fulfilled and Toscanini would conduct *Falstaff* in Salzburg (which caused Krauss to resign from the State Opera, where he was succeeded in January 1935 by Weingartner). But there were further difficulties even after that. At the first orchestral rehearsal of *Falstaff* in Salzburg Burghauser found a young, inexperienced substitute in the chair of the first oboe, who was "ill"; and his inadequate playing caused Toscanini to walk out. Luckily the missing first oboe was located and was in his chair at the next rehearsal. But disaster threatened as late as the first stage rehearsal, when the curtain rose for the first scene of the third act to reveal the bedroom set, and Toscanini, infuriated, rushed out of the theater. Miraculously a correct outdoor set was produced overnight; and that was the last of the difficulties despite which *Falstaff*, said Burghauser, "was done—and of course done beautifully."

That was all he said about it in 1966; but in 1971 he recalled that first performance in 1935 as "an enormous event", not only because of the work itself, which had never before been heard in Salzburg, and the conductor, who was so closely associated with it, but because of the ensemble of singers from La Scala with its central member, Stabile, the great Falstaff of the Toscanini revival ever since its beginning in the 20s. The musical performance impelled the 70-year-old Weingartner, after the first act, to leap into the orchestra pit and exclaim: "Children, such perfection I have never experienced or dreamed of!" Burghauser had never witnessed such an expression of enthusiasm by anyone else "as great and as convinced of his own importance"; and what made it moving as well as surprising was the fact that it was genuine, that Weingartner really was overwhelmed.

Before *Falstaff* there had been the production of *Fidelio* conducted by Toscanini, which had required less time and effort because the soloists, chorus and orchestra had been performing the work for years under Strauss and Schalk. One orchestral rehearsal, a rehearsal of the singers with piano and the final *Generalprobe* were all Toscanini needed to be completely satisfied. This stage performance, said Burghauser, was quite different from Toscanini's later concert performance with the NBC Symphony; and he thought the reason was that Toscanini was visibly moved even by the spoken dialogue, and this response to the drama affected his tempos. In addition, pointing out how an orchestra acquired in its years of playing a kind of will power that it wasn't conscious of, Burghauser claimed to have heard, in much of the Salzburg performance, evidence of this will power having influenced Toscanini to accept from the orchestra its conviction of how to play. I couldn't dispute what Burghauser said; but I found it impossible to imagine Toscanini's will not winning out over the orchestra's in the situation; and as it happened Burghauser related an incident which demonstrated Toscanini's practice when an orchestra's will differed from his. When he began to conduct the Prisoners' Chorus in the first act in his flowing tempo, all faces, said Burghauser, turned toward him in mute protest, impelled by the conviction acquired in years of playing this music that it should be *andächtig*, prayer-like, in an *andante* tempo; whereupon Toscanini, realizing they were used to playing it slowly, said (probably pointing to the score): *"Ma signori, è Allegretto vivace e alla breve"*; "and after that, of course", said Burghauser, "we obeyed him."

In the discussion of repertory for the following summer Toscanini proposed that he conduct a production of *Die Meistersinger*. This gave Walter an opportunity to oppose Toscanini in *his* manner—with seemingly reasonable objections: the Festspielhaus stage that was too small for the movement of the opera's large choral groups; the work's enormous length; above all its heavy style that made it unsuitable for the Festival. "But my dear Walter", said Toscanini with a smile, "two years ago you conducted *Tristan und Isolde* here. Was that more suitable for the Festival than *Die Meistersinger*, which is a comedy?" There was nothing Walter could say to this; and *Die Meistersinger* was accepted.

No difficulties arose after that either in Salzburg or in Vienna, when Toscanini conducted concerts there early in the fall. But by then Weingartner had taken over as Director of the State Opera; and at a meeting with Burghauser and the Vienna Philharmonic committee he said that as he was in sole command at the Opera, so he would be sole conductor of the Philharmonic concerts, and there was no longer any need of the guest conductors who may have been necessary until then. Burghauser pointed out that they had, as always, announced the guest conductors— Walter, Weingartner himself, Knappertsbusch, Coates, Rodzinski, and (for the Nicolai concert) Furtwängler—a year in advance; and not only was it undesirable, for practical reasons, to cancel any of these eminent and popular men, but Burghauser didn't see how this could be done. Weingartner—preserving, as always, the calm affability of his manner that contrasted with what was in his mind, which could be, said Burghauser, "wildly egotistic"—replied that he left it to Burghauser's proved diplomatic skill to convince the conductors that they were not needed. And when Burghauser said again that what Weingartner demanded was, from the Philharmonic's point of view, neither desirable nor possible, and that he would not comply with it, Weingartner's affable reply was that he would give them time to think it over.

Here Burghauser mentioned that Weingartner's long career had been filled with acrimonious disputes and lawsuits which, being an extremely effective writer, he had won in his newspaper articles but lost in court. When, therefore, Weingartner was informed the next day that the Philharmonic was adamant in its stand, he called a news conference at which

he declared that his artistic objectives were being obstructed by Burghauser, and therefore Burghauser must resign or he (Weingartner) would.
The evening papers were filled with the controversy; and Weingartner was
confident of victory. In order to remove himself as a cause of dissension
Burghauser resigned; and a special meeting of the Philharmonic was held for
the election of a new chairman, at which Burghauser, to the public's
surprise, received 95% of the votes. It then turned out that Weingartner's
threatened resignation had been related only to the Philharmonic: he withdrew from its concerts, but continued as Director of the State Opera, and
tried to get the government to bring pressure on the orchestra.

Burghauser had perceived that Weingartner's demand that the Philharmonic dispense with guest conductors was his strategy for eliminat-
ing Toscanini. And when he now warned Weingartner of the danger that
he might lose his post if he persisted, it was because he could foresee
what the reaction of the administration would be when he explained that
if Weingartner's demand was granted there would be no Toscanini in
Vienna and in Salzburg—for as Director of the State Opera Weingartner
had a say about what was done there, and had already objected to the
following summer's program. But Weingartner could not believe in the
possibility of what Burghauser warned him of, which did in fact happen:
at the end of the season the administration of the state theaters paid him
the full salary of the remaining four years of his contract to obtain his
resignation. Burghauser considered this tragic; for Weingartner conducted until his departure with full command of his great powers. But no
one had been able to suggest any other solution.

Bruno Walter was appointed Weingartner's successor, with the title of
Artistic Adviser to Dr. Kerber, the Administrative Director, but actually with the duties and powers of Director: he would be chief conductor
and have the deciding voice in repertory and casting. And his first season
began, in the fall of 1936, with a gesture of good will by Toscanini, who
conducted a few performances of the Salzburg *Fidelio* at the State Opera.

In Salzburg that summer Toscanini conducted the new *Meistersinger*.
Burghauser cited his performances of this work in Turin and La Scala in
the 1890s as evidence of his love for it, and characterized his command of
it as unbelievable. After the second act Toscanini himself, in his dressing
room, was moved as Burghauser had never seen him before, muttering
"E com' un sogno. It's like a dream." (In 1966 Burghauser had said of this
second act that it "was an entirely new experience for me. In sound and

dynamics, in clarity, in expression—this was the ultimate.") At the last rehearsal before the final *Generalprobe* there had been an incident that had made a deep impression. In the course of a scene with all the *Meistersinger* and the chorus on stage Toscanini had suddenly stopped, though no one had heard anything wrong; and when there was absolute silence he had said in Italian: "People say Toscanini is a genius. No, no! I am not a genius." And pointing to the singers on the stage, "I am such a *Meister-singer.*"

For the following summer he chose to conduct *The Magic Flute.* And he also revealed a plan for a new theater to replace the Festspielhaus, whose stage was too small and whose backstage facilities were appallingly inadequate. (Two or even three principal singers had to share a small dressing room which in August was unbearably hot; and there was nothing at all for the orchestra.) Toscanini offered to head a drive in Europe and America for the necessary money; his proposal was accepted by the Salzburg authorities and, in Vienna later, by the Chancellor; and at the end of the last performance of *The Magic Flute* the following summer workmen stood waiting to begin the demolition of the old theater.

For this *Magic Flute* in the summer of 1937 Toscanini's chief concern in casting was the soprano for the Queen of Night: she had to be able to sing up to high F; and he wanted a steely power which he said required the fresh vocal chords of a young singer. And he had found exactly the singer he wanted in a girl of 20 in Budapest, Julie Osvath, who had sung more in operetta than in opera. At rehearsals in Salzburg all the other singers were amazed by the extraordinary power of her voice and her accurate intonation. But at the first performance, which was broadcast, she had finished the slow opening section of her first-act aria and was beginning the fast coloratura section, when suddenly she went haywire. As Burg-hauser told it, Toscanini panicked and stopped conducting, but the experienced orchestra went on playing, as it always did in such a situation; and after several bars order was restored. Again I refrained from telling Burghauser that "I was there" that night; and what I saw and heard happen was that when suddenly Osvath began to lag behind the orchestra in a long coloratura phrase, Toscanini (who after all was as experienced as the orchestra) kept going until the end of the phrase, where he stopped to wait for her to reach that point, and then resumed conducting in her slower tempo, amazing me with the way he stayed with her, and led the orchestra, in every change of her erratic course. At the end of the act Burghauser rushed to her dressing room to find out what had happened; and she told him that at the beginning of the coloratura section she had thought of her family in Hungary gathered around the radio listening to her—which had made her so nervous that she had lost control.

There was considerable objection that Toscanini's tempos in *The Magic Flute* were too fast. But he had said at the beginning that he had found the work as it was performed in Germany and Austria utterly boring, and was going to make it what he thought Mozart had intended it to be—entertaining and amusing; which meant faster tempos than the traditional German ones. Actually, said Burghauser, they were the same as Strauss's tempos; and in 1966 he had characterized the Toscanini performance as delightful.

At Jarmila Novotna's first piano rehearsal with Toscanini, said Burghauser, the pianist failed to appear; and before Toscanini could go to the piano himself Bruno Walter, who was present, volunteered to play. The introductory chords of "*Ach, ich fühl's*" enabled him to set his exceedingly slow tempo, in which Novotna had to continue when she began to sing. Toscanini paced back and forth impatiently, and after a few moments interrupted, exclaiming, "*Ma, caro Walter:* is *Andante*, and you play *adagio!*" Walter, embarrassed by the presence of Novotna and Burghauser, said: "My dear Maestro, you know I am always in agreement with you; but in this case I differ with you and think my tempo is correct." To which Toscanini answered heatedly: "And I, my dear Walter, am never in agreement with you!"*

It was not until he arrived in Salzburg at the beginning of the summer of 1937 that Burghauser discovered in the schedule of the Festival the listing of the performance of Beethoven's Ninth that would be conducted by Furtwängler on 27 August. Inquiring about it, he learned that Furtwängler had presented to Dr. Kerber, the Administrative Director, his claim as a German musician to participation in a festival on German soil, suggesting specifically that he conduct in 1938 a German opera, *Der*

---

*Years later Toscanini, talking once about the tempo of this aria, clasped his hands as he acted Pamina's agitation, and exclaimed: "Pamina say, 'I lose my Tamino! Where my Tamino?!' Must be *andante*, but is always *adagio!*"

Frieschütz. Kerber—taking into account, on the one hand, the need of not angering Toscanini, and on the other hand the strongly pro-Nazi native population of Salzburg—had replied that the matter of conducting opera would have to be decided by Toscanini, but that it was within the administration's power to include Furtwängler among the guests who were to conduct orchestral concerts that summer. With the matter of opera to be taken up with Toscanini later, Furtwängler had accepted the offer of 27 August for a performance of the Ninth with which he could count on overwhelming the public as always.

Burghauser knew that Furtwängler had previously declined every invitation to conduct in Salzburg—the recent ones on the ground that with his duties in Bayreuth it was impossible for him to take on additional tasks in Salzburg. And his own previous experience with Furtwängler enabled Burghauser to understand why he now not only found it possible to take on the additional task but wanted it enough to think up a claim to it as his right. He was, said Burghauser, benevolent toward lesser conductors who were not competitors, but not toward eminent colleagues whom he regarded as rivals, and above all not toward the Italian who had eclipsed him in New York in 1926, and, worse still, again in 1933 in Vienna, where he had thought himself irreplaceable when he had broken his agreement in 1929. Not only that, but Salzburg, whose invitations he had declined, had become, as a result of Toscanini's activity, a center of the international prestige and publicity that Furtwängler craved. One reason, then, for his desire now to participate in Salzburg was the fact that it was where the action was and where Toscanini was. But Burghauser perceived an additional reason. The Salzburg Festival asserted, at Nazi Germany's very border, the cultural policies of the free world which opposed those of Nazi Germany; and so participation in that Festival by Furtwängler while he retained his dominant position in the Third Reich's musical life would validate his claim that his continued activity there was not that of an adherent of Nazism, but strictly that of a musician—one who actually opposed Nazi political doctrines and cultural policies. In this Burghauser saw not merely a desire to have the benefits of both Nazi and free worlds, but the "gluttonous" hunger for all possible power that Furtwängler had revealed in the years Burghauser had known him.

I have seen a photograph of Furtwängler in the Festspielhaus with Toscanini conducting a concert; and Burghauser said he attended one of the rehearsals of Strauss's *Death and Transfiguration*.* These were occasions well in advance of Furtwängler's concert on 27 August; and he could have arranged to see Toscanini on one of his free days in that period. Instead he decided to speak to him in his dressing room in the intermission of his performance of *Fidelio* on 26 August. He first approached Herbert Graf, the stage director of the production, who pleaded duties on the stage and hurried away; whereupon Furtwängler, seeing Burghauser, requested that *he* take him to Toscanini's dressing room. Appalled, Burghauser tried to dissuade him by describing the scene in the dressing room: Toscanini on a chair, stripped to the waist, the sweat running down his body, his wife drying him and spraying him with eau de cologne while he fanned himself and perhaps refreshed himself with a few grapes. A sensitive person would have recognized that this was a time to leave Toscanini undisturbed; but Furtwängler insisted; and Burghauser finally had to give in. At his pre-arranged knock Signora Toscanini opened the door slightly, and seeing him opened it wider; whereupon Furtwängler pushed past her into the room and stood towering over Toscanini, who peered up at him, not recognizing him.

"I wish to speak to you about my future participation in Salzburg," said Furtwängler.

Toscanini, though still dazed, managed to answer: "We speak tomorrow—after Ninth Symphony;" and Furtwängler left.

What Burghauser told me about this first confrontation he had himself seen and heard. Concerning the second one, the next day at Toscanini's villa, Burghauser, who was not present, told me what Signora Toscanini, who *was* present, reported to him immediately afterward.

"I wish to ask if you have any objection to my conducting *Der Freischütz* in Salzburg next year," said Furtwängler.

"You may do whatever you want," Toscanini replied. "But I will not be here;" which ended the conversation.

This was all that Signora Toscanini reported to Burghauser as having happened; and nothing was added to it subsequently by Toscanini, who

---

*Furtwängler's comment after the rehearsal, said Burghauser with a smile, was *"Es hat nicht gekracht* [It had no impact]"; and the smile was understandable to anyone who knew Toscanini's performance of the piece. Alan Shulman of the NBC Symphony described what happened at the end of the slow introduction: "He sustained the long chord while his eyes flashed from left to right so that he had complete communication with every member of the orchestra; and when we went into the boom! of the *agitato*, half the audience jumped out of their seats from the impact."

was silent, or by his son and daughter, who hadn't been present at the meeting. One must concede the possibility that more was said which Toscanini didn't translate to his wife after Furtwängler left; but since, according to Burghauser, he customarily spoke "laconically" and to the point, one can assume he translated for her what for him was the essential point in the matter: whereas in 1936, when he had resigned from the New York Philharmonic, he had considered it his duty to recommend Furtwängler as his successor, now he did not consider himself obligated to conduct opera in Salzburg in association with the man who conducted it in Bayreuth.

Unfortunately, since Toscanini himself maintained silence, and Burghauser therefore felt unable to reveal what Signora Toscanini had told him, the public didn't receive even that little authentic information about the Furtwängler-Toscanini exchange. What it got instead was a version of it as altered in its passage through the mind of Furtwängler, who was voluble on the subject, and is the source of everything said and written about it since 1937. As Lucianna Frassati tells it in her book *Il Maestro*, it was to her that Furtwängler came immediately after the meeting and gave his much-quoted version of the exchange:

> TOSCANINI: One cannot conduct in a country where dictatorship reigns and in a free country at the same time.
> FURTWÄNGLER: There is always freedom where Beethoven's music resounds.*

And a letter to her a few days later included the following by now familiar statements:

> Neither Toscanini nor his circle . . . has any idea of my will or of my existence, whether as an artist or as a man. I feel no rancor toward Toscanini. . . . This notwithstanding that his attitude toward me is fundamentally mistaken. And I must remain apart from it! I don't want to descend like this to the bottom of the ladder, nor to be forced to fight with his weapons, let alone those of his *entourage*.

Burghauser, in the course of our talks, alluded on one occasion to Furtwängler's cloudy thinking and imprecise language, and on another

---

*Frassati writes: "Not a single less than respectful statement [concerning Toscanini] came from [Furtwängler's] mouth even in relating to me the words exchanged before the final leave-taking;" but the conductor Hans Schwieger reports Furtwängler, in Berlin in 1953, dismissing Toscanini as fit only to conduct a military band, saying, "I begin to make music where this man stops."

to his self-comforting paranoid explanations of any setback—that he was not understood, and was the object of intrigue and conspiracy. And those comments describe the Furtwängler statements I have quoted—to begin with, the ones about Toscanini and his circle not understanding him as an artist or as a man, and Toscanini and his *entourage* employing against him the kind of weapons he would not let himself be forced to use. The Salzburg confrontation didn't involve anyone in the Toscanini circle or *entourage*, but only Toscanini himself, who acted on the basis of his own objectively arrived at and accurate perception of Furtwängler as a conductor who couldn't get the horns to play the two notes of the opening fifth of Beethoven's Ninth precisely together, as a musician who distorted and falsified that work with his undisciplined extravagances of tempo and dynamics, and as a man who—to borrow the words of the *New York Times* correspondent who reported Furtwängler's de-Nazification trial—"so [overlooked] moral values and fixed principles that he was . . . willing to make maximum use of a régime which he alleged was obnoxious to him," and who made the fatuous claim that performing Beethoven's music in Hitler Germany preserved freedom there. Nor had Toscanini engaged in any tactical skirmishes against him and employed any weapons, high or low: he had done nothing at all until Furtwängler asked his question, and then he answered that question. It was an answer that referred solely to the specifics of the Salzburg situation; but Furtwängler, reporting it to Frassati, converted it into a generalization that was not what Toscanini said or meant. Toscanini did not generalize that "one" might not conduct in a country governed by a dictatorship and also in a free country: he had himself conducted in Fascist Italy and also in the free world. He said only that Furtwängler, who conducted opera in Bayreuth, might, if he wished, conduct it also in Salzburg, but not in Toscanini's company. And the reason for this was the difference he saw between his own conducting in Fascist Italy and Furtwängler's conducting in Nazi Germany.

Toscanini conducted in Italy as if the Fascist régime didn't exist—with increasing annoyance and anger in the régime, until in the end he was physically attacked by its thugs when he refused to play the Fascist Hymn at a concert in Bologna. Furtwängler claimed to have acted in the same way; but his claim was false. I have a clipping with a quotation of a passage in a letter of Alban Berg's written in May 1933, in which Berg characterizes Furtwängler's address at a Brahms festival as "a Nazi-inspired speech which made me very depressed all day." I have a photo-copy of the program of the inaugural proceedings of the *Reichskulturkammer* on 15 November 1933, at which Goebbels delivered a pronouncement on "German Culture before a New Beginning", and which opened with Furtwängler conducting the Berlin Philharmonic in a performance of Beethoven's *Egmont* Overture. His devoted secretary, Berta Geissmar, writes bitterly in her book *Two Worlds of Music* about Goebbels's lack of gratitude for the success as political-cultural propaganda of the tour by Furtwängler and the Berlin Philharmonic in Italy in April 1934, which she arranged on condition that he be received in audience by Mussolini, who gave him an Italian decoration. This was before his resignation—not an anti-Nazi protest, as he claimed, but a power play and test of strength that he expected to win, but lost. Geissmar writes also about the concert in April 1935, after his capitulation to Goebbels—an official function, a *Winterhilfe* concert attended by Hitler and the government, at which occurred the famous cordial handshake of Hitler and Furtwängler that Geissmar rightly calls a "symbolic gesture". And Robert Hupka, co-author of the book *This Was Toscanini*, has told me of having turned on the radio in 1937 for a Furtwängler performance of Beethoven's Ninth from Paris, and having turned it off when Furtwängler, after conducting *Deutschland über Alles*, began to conduct the *Horst Wessel Song*.

The fitting conclusion to all this is Burghauser's statement pointing out how Furtwängler revealed that his interest had been not in Salzburg's Festival but in Toscanini and the international public Toscanini attracted: at the Festival in 1938—with Toscanini and the international public absent—he conducted only *Die Meistersinger*, and in 1939 only one concert. (*Encounter*, July 1977)*

Encounter, incomprehensibly, granted Yehudi Menuhin "the hospitality of [its] columns" that he asked for a two-page reply, in which he wrote, among other things, that Burghauser and I had attempted "to glorify Toscanini without qualification at the expense of Furtwängler," but then himself, in what *he* recalled about them, glorified Furtwängler at the expense of Toscanini. As a musician, he said, Toscanini "was supremely single-minded, studying scores rather than reading books, and his sole distraction was to watch boxing on television;" whereas Furtwängler "was steeped in a tradition as deep and continuous as the archeological strata which he and his father studied," and "his approach to music, which he lived and breathed as Toscanini did, commanded a total fusion of all of man's conflicting elements, and . . . brought this totality of existence to his audiences." This related neither to the actualities of the connection of a musician's general culture and his performance of music, nor to such actualities as Toscanini's greeting me—when I came to listen to test pressings of his recordings with the Philadelphia Orchestra, in September

1942—with his pince-nez in one hand and the book on world government he had been reading in the other hand; his wide-ranging knowledge of the English poetry Alfred Wallenstein told me he quoted at length from memory; his life-long passionate love of painting, reported in Harvey Sachs's recent biography.

Reading the article, said Menuhin, he "felt music itself defiled" by the musical gossip of "that unholy alliance of the New York and Viennese tea and coffee shops" that Burghauser and I represented—"old gossip, unsubstantiated, uncorroborated, unexpurgated, still undigested and putrid in intestines clogged with *Strudel* and *Schlagobers*"; and, two paragraphs later, "men's-room gossip". This passage was part of what one reader characterized as "malicious and offensive in its wording, putting the much written-about sweetness of Menuhin's character in question." (Not mere sweetness but saintliness has been perceived in Menuhin's much publicized involvement with yoga, Indian music, health foods and the rest.)

What was incomprehensible, therefore, was *Encounter's* decision that this reply by Menuhin—not only without relevance to what it professed to reply to, but characteristically fatuous, and ugly in its extreme of offensiveness—had a claim to the magazine's space and its readers' attention.

Index

Index

Abbado: performances of *Don Carlo* at Metropolitan, 46-7; Mahler Second with Philadelphia Orchestra, 106; *Simon Boccanegra* with La Scala, 129-30; with New York Philharmonic, 174-5

Abraham, Gerald: *This Modern Music*, 9

Ailey, 121

Alexander, John: in New York City Opera's *Die Meistersinger*, 117

American Ballet Theatre: repertory, 119, and style, 145-7; *Coppélia* with Makarova and Baryshnikov, 109; *Push Comes to Shove* with Baryshnikov, Gelsey Kirkland's performances, *Pas de Trois* from *La Ventana*, 121; Tetley *Le Sacre du Printemps*, *Voluntaries*, 145; restored Sergeyev staging of *The Sleeping Beauty*, 146-7; *La Bayadere*, 147; Baryshnikov *Nutcracker*, 147-8; original Fokine *Firebird* and *Petrushka*, 148.

Andersen, Frank: with Royal Danish Ballet, 221

Andersen, Ib; in *Davidsbünderlertänze*, 209, 211, 223; *Ballade*, 210; distinctive enlivening style in *Symphony in Three Movements*, *Stravinsky Violin Concerto*, *Bournonville Divertissements*, *Symphony in C*, *Divertimento No. 15*, 210-1; *Mozar-*

tiana, 213, 223; *Apollo*, 216; *A Midsummer Night's Dream*, 222; *Donizetti Variations*, *Agon*, *Orpheus*, 224.

Aroldingen, von: in *Variations pur une Porte et un Soupir*, 108; *The Four Temperaments*, 144; *Kammermusik II*, 204, 223; *Apollo*, *Orpheus*, 207; *Davidsbünderlertänze*, 210, 223.

Ashkenazy: excellent performances, 45, 107, 173-4; flawed performances, 139-40, 176; on differences between earlier performances of Beethoven concertos with Solti and those with Haitink; Porter on, 174.

Ashley: in *Tchaikovsky Piano Concerto II*, *Symphony in C*, *The Four Temperaments*, *Theme and Variations*, 120-1; *Emeralds*, 143; *Divertimento No. 15*, *Bournonville Divertissements*, *Symphony in C*, 144; *Ballo della Regina*, *Square Dance*, *Allegro Brillante*, *Tchaikovsky Pas de Deux*, *Who Cares?*, 204; *La Source*, *Stars and Stripes*, *Bournonville Divertissements*, 206; Martins on, 83

Ashton, 99, 119; *Façade* and *A Wedding Bouquet*, 146

Avery Fisher Hall, 132, 156

Ax: excellent performance of Mozart's Piano Concerto K. 466, 155

ACKNOWLEDGMENTS

I am indebted to

Ben Raeburn of Horizon Press not only for adding this collection to the books of mine he has published since 1967, but for making its production another of the collaborations with him and his staff that are without precedent in my experience.

The magazines in which part of the material appeared originally, for making it available.